CW00551716

GERMAN
DESTROYERS
OF
WORLD WAR II

OTHER TITLES IN THIS SERIES

Battleships of the Bismarck Class
Battleships of the Scharnhorst Class
Pocket Battleships of the Deutschland Class
Heavy Cruisers of the Admiral Hipper Class
Light Cruisers of World War II

GERMAN DESTROYERS
OF
WORLD WAR II

Gerhard Koop
and
Klaus-Peter Schmolke

Translated from the German by Geoffrey Brooks

GREENHILL BOOKS, LONDON
NAVAL INSTITUTE PRESS, ANNAPOLIS, MARYLAND

German Destroyers of World War II
Published in 2003 by Greenhill Books, Lionel Leventhal Limited,
Park House, 1 Russell Gardens, London NW11 9NN

Published and distributed in the United States of America by the
Naval Institute Press, 291 Wood Road, Annapolis, Maryland 21402-5034

British Library Cataloguing in Publication Data available

Greenhill Books ISBN 1-85367-540-7

Library of Congress Catalog Card Number 2002114067

Naval Institute Press ISBN 1-59114-307-1

Publishing History
German Destroyers of World War II is translated
from *Die deutschen Zerstörer 1935–1945*,
first published by Bernard & Graefe Verlag, Bonn, 1995.

Edited, typeset and designed by Roger Chesneau
Originated by MRM Graphics Ltd
Printed and bound in Singapore by Kyodo Printing Company

Contents

Preface 7

Introduction **9**

Technical Data **24**

Differences, Modifications, Conversions **32**

Armament **34**
    Fire Control and Sensors 40

Machinery **41**

Flotillas, Flotilla Commanders and the *Führer der Zerstörer* **45**

The Second World War **46**
    From 1938 to Narvik 46
    From Narvik to the Capitulation 65

Individual Ships' Careers **77**

Photo Gallery: The *Zerstörer* **122**

Photo Gallery: Requisitioned Destroyers **200**

Photo Gallery: *Zerstörer* Life **202**

Camouflage Schemes **215**

Conclusions **220**

Index of Ships 223

Preface

This volume of the series introduces the destroyers of the Kriegsmarine and is a companion to five earlier volumes featuring battleships of the *Bismarck* class, battleships of the *Scharnhorst* class, the pocket battleships of the *Deutschland* class, the heavy cruisers of the *Admiral Hipper* class and the six light cruisers.

Destroyers were the workhorses of the German Fleet and were required additionally to perform duties which were really the preserve of light cruisers, which were few in number in the German Navy. Restricted by the 1919 Versailles Treaty of 1919 to sixteen 'destroyers' each of no more than 800 tonnes and sixteen torpedo boats each not exceeding 200 tonnes, Germany's new ships of the type amounted to the six *Möwe* class and six *Wolf* class pseudo-destroyers built between 1924 and 1929. The true destroyer did not make its appearance until relatively late, coinciding more or less with the signing of the Anglo-Gernman Naval Treaty of 1935, although the first designs had been drawn up some time previously. This book explains the development stage, provides a detailed review of important facts and figures and recounts the full service history of each of the ships separately, supplemented by documentary references, War Diary extracts and combat reports. The text concludes with a critical epilogue. Also provided are detailed sketches, technical tables and a comprehensive selection of photographs, most from private collections and not previously published in this compact form; many of the illustrations appear in an English-language publication for the first time.

My special thanks go to co-author Klaus-Peter Schmolke, who prepared all plans and sketches, and I also thank F. Bavendamm, who assisted with the reproduction of the photographs, and A. Diderichs, who provided valuable advice and files relating to weapons, weapons systems and ships' machinery.

Sources for photographs were: P. K. Koop Collection (149); Marine/Kriegsmarine Werft, Wilhelmshaven (1); Royal Navy (6); Royal Air Force (1); US Navy (3); private collections (41); and the MAN Archive (1).

Gerhard Koop

Introduction

The post-World War I Reichsmarine continued to use the term 'torpedo boat' for surface warships displacing less than 800 tonnes and carrying torpedoes as their primary armament, and it was not until the first true destroyers were under construction, from 1934 onwards, that the term *Zerstörer* (destroyer) came into vogue in Germany. The lost war brought the dissolution of the Imperial Navy, and Germany was obliged to surrender as reparations large parts of her Fleet—generally the most modern units. Most of these found a watery grave as a result of the mass scuttling at Scapa Flow in 1919, and this bravado had to be paid for by handing over or scrapping further ships.

On 16 April 1919 the Germans were instructed to set up a 'Provisional Reichsmarine', a measure legitimised by the elected Reichstag on 30 July 1920, and the Wehrgesetz (Armed Forces Law) was passed on 23 March 1921. The scuttling of the High Seas Fleet at Scapa Flow on 21 June 1919 was a direct consequence of the dictated terms of the Versailles Treaty. As regards torpedo boats and destroyers, Article 181 stipulated that a future German Navy might have no more than sixteen destroyers and sixteen torpedo boats, four of each being in reserve. Article 190 laid down that when any of these boats* was fifteen years old—calculated from the launch date—it could be replaced by a new vessel, but a new German destroyer was not to exceed 800 tonnes, nor a torpedo boat 200 tonnes. This latter requisite was a step back into the nineteenth century, for it had been the tonnage of the very first torpedo carriers. The size and type of armament, including mines and torpedoes, ammunition and equipment, were subject to the inspection and approval of the victorious powers.

The Treaty of Versailles made it impossible for Germany to keep abreast of modern destroyer construction. Whichever way one looked at it, an 800-tonne 'destroyer' was a torpedo boat. Nevertheless, the Reichsmarine was obliged to respect the limit with its first new boats, and thus there came into being, in compliance with Versailles, twelve 'destroyers', the six

vessels of the *Möwe* class ordered in 1923 (*Möwe, Seeadler, Greif, Albatros, Kondor* and *Falke*) and the six *Wolf* class ships ordered in 1924 (*Wolf, Iltis, Luchs, Tiger, Jaguar* and *Leopard*) carrying three 10.5cm (4.1in) guns—the originally intended 12.7cm (5in) armament having been disallowed—and two triple sets of torpedo tubes. Speed was about 33 knots.

Personnel
Article 194 restricted the future German Navy to a personnel strength of 15,000 men, of which no more than 10 per cent could be officers or specialist deck officers, who had to be career sailors serving the colours for 25 years. NCOs and ratings signed on for twelve years. If one thinks of the numbers employed at Staff level and in the numerous shore bases alone, it can be seen how few were left to man the ships—which explains why there were so few vessels in commission in the earlier years. With the arrival of the new light cruisers and the twelve new torpedo-boats in the mid to late 1920s, the personnel situation became desperate, and as early as 1924–25 the first attempts were made to introduce a clandestine short-term volunteer force of 600 men contrary to the Versailles Treaty. The SPD (Social Democratic Party) ensured that nothing came of this.

In the naval rebuilding plan of November 1932, the Reichswehr Minister approved an increase of 1,450 lower rates in the standing force and expressed the urgency for the officer corps, and the manpower situation generally, to be strengthened. Staffing was

---

* The author lists the following Imperial Navy vessels retained as 'destroyers': V 185, V 190 and G 196 (built 1910–11), V 2, V 3 and V 5 (1911), G 7, G 8, G 10 and G 11 (1911–12) and S 18 and S 23 (1912–13), plus V 1 and V 6 (1912) in reserve—a flotilla of twelve plus two reserves. Retained as 'torpedo boats' were S 139, S 141, S 143, S 146, S 148, S 149, V 151, V 153 and V 154 (built 1906–07), V 156, V 157 and V 158 (1908) and S 168 (1911) plus S 144, V 152 and V 155 (190–08) and G 175 (1910) in reserve. This is thirteen plus four reserves and one assumes an erroneous listing here of a 'destroyer' in reserve—probably T 168 or T 175, the two newest ships. Tr.

the most important naval question, but it was not until the declaration of military sovereignty in March 1935, and the signing of the Anglo-German Naval Agreement three months later, that the way was cleared to resolve the problem. From this point, however, time was of the essence, for Fleet rearmament was continuing with haste, and this adversely affected the training of the new generation of military seafarers. The Warrant Officers Corps—formed from the erstwhile 'deck officers' of the former Imperial Navy and the backbone of the Fleet—had been broken, and the best of them (and there were many) had been given commissions. Thus a new and well-qualified NCO corps had to be trained, but time for schooling ashore, and training aboard ship, had to be cut back ruthlessly. This applied to all ranks.

Referring to a speech he made on 21 September 1934, Admiral Raeder remarked, 'Promotions permitting, all appropriate servicemen in their twelfth and last year of service with the Reichsmarine [the contractual period for professional naval men] were kept back. The personnel situation was especially tight in 1935. The shortage of destroyers and torpedo boats in commission in 1937 was directly attributable to our lack of personnel in certain career fields (particularly engine room, radio and signals and weapons). This had its effect on the completion of new ships, the commissioning of numbers of which had to be postponed.' There were shortages everywhere, and there was no time to strike the necessary balance between quality and quantity. It was symptomatic of a Wehrmacht in a fast and impetuous reconstruction in a relatively pleasant period of peace. On the outbreak of war, these gaps would open up painfully.

Applications to join the Navy were insufficient, and the quality of officer candidates in the two or three years before the war had deteriorated markedly as evidenced for example by a report, H.11202 Ia: 'Education and Training of the October 1938 Officer Candidate Entry', signed by Vizeadmiral Schuster, Head of the Naval Training Inspectorate at Kiel and issued on 17 July 1939 to, inter alia, the commanders of all destroyers, torpedo-boats and E-boats, in which he remarked that pre-military training in the RAD (compulsory six-month labour service), Hitler Youth and Naval Hitler Youth had not borne the desired results: 'Whereas the generally very good physical assessment, the interest in sports, physical efficiency, sense of comradeship and, amongst a number of candidates, the desire to serve, toughness and goodwill must of course be recognised, with a relatively large number of them it has, nevertheless, needed a protracted effort to get them to appreciate the moral demands made of the soldier, in particular the need for the uncompromising fulfilment of all—even the most insignificant—duties. A number showed great skill in evading unpleasant tasks and adopted from the outset a highly critical attitude. What was lacking here, primarily, was the ability to integrate unconditionally and a respect for authority and their seniors, coupled with an inability to take heed of warnings and advice.' Conceding that the 1938 entry was better than that of the year before, Schuster concluded that 'the young candidate of today does not always possess those attributes and character values which were generally considered in the past to be a precondition for admission as a Wehrmacht Officer Candidate. This is undoubtedly due to the relatively high admission quotas of recent years in which candidates were successful where in earlier years they would have been rejected. Moreover the "Führer problem"—especially in the Hitler Youth—has not been resolved. As regrettable as it may be to say so, we do have to allow for that in training.' In conclusion, the writer advised the commanders of vessels that cadets showing 'gross character defects, a negative disposition towards the military calling allied to a delight in criticising, an adverse influence on comrades, a continuing standard of under-achievement due to retarded physical or psychological development, a lack of interest and indifference, a lack of pride, enthusiasm or self-confidence, denigration of those in authority over them and failure to follow orders' were to be weeded out and failed as officer candidates. This document throws an intriguing light on the situation regarding personnel in the Kriegsmarine shortly before the war and shows how burgeoning rearmament—in every sense of the word—had resulted in a deterioration rather than an improvement in the quality of human resources.

The same story was repeated amongst promotion candidates in the lower rates. At least two years before the war the training of engine-room personnel at the naval technical schools and other educational institutions had been deteriorating. The pace of rearmament was forcing reductions in the time allowed for training: for example, in 1928 an officer spent 26 months under instruction ashore and 28 months in shipboard training before receiving his commission, but by 1938 this had been reduced to thirteen months ashore and eighteen afloat. During the Second World War a month was clipped off both periods. In 1938 there were 1,800 seaman branch officers, 475 engineer, 26 medical officers, 130 administrative officers and 1,025 *Ergänzungsoffiziere* (a supplementary officers' corps time-served in the Reichsmarine and re-contracted to the Kriegsmarine). These 3,876 officers amounted to 5.8 per cent of a Kriegsmarine numbering 56,000 men. Whereas engineer NCOs of the Reichsmarine spent a three-year apprenticeship afloat and could then be selected for further training, in 1938 the shipboard training period averaged only a year, and about 48 per cent of trainees were selected for further NCO training. Even the shipyard construction familiarisation course was counted as time afloat.

The situation was worse for warrant officers. To fill the gaps left by promotions, the contracts of the veteran warrant officers were extended and the training of suitable junior NCOs accelerated. In the last two years before the outbreak of war in particular, there was a continuous change-round of personnel. This took place practically every six months and affected about 25–30 per cent of naval personnel overall. At watch and battle stations the changeover involved 50–60 per cent.

The destroyers, with their overcomplicated machinery, suffered particularly, and this problem continued into the war. Between September 1939 and October 1940 the destroyer Z 10 *Hans Lody* took part in seventeen operations, and during this period the engine room had a turnover of 100 per cent of the officers, 41.6 per cent of the warrant officer ERAs, 34 per cent of the NCOs and 62.3 per cent of other rates. On 23 September 1937, in Report 5713M to the BdA (C-in-C Cruisers) entitled 'Training in Boiler Rooms', Kapitän zur See Kummetz, FdT, wrote, with reference to two earlier papers: 'The aim of training is to release boiler-room watchkeeping NCOs from supervising any particular machinery or valve, for only then can they accept full responsibility for the room. This aim is coming up against the greatest difficulties because of the physical layout of boilers and the inaccessibility of the installations: (a) The boiler rooms are too small. Particularly restricted is the control stand from where individual pieces of auxiliary machinery and valves are so inaccessible that the instruments have had to be re-positioned on a board because they could not be seen. (b) It is impossible to see the fire in the Saacke burners from the central position. The feedwater regulators do not work automatically and the water level has to be

controlled almost constantly by hand. The lubrication of the boiler supercharger is poor, and it is necessary to shut down the supercharger at 800rpm to permit some degree of lubrication to be carried out. Parallel running of superchargers is not possible because there is no common steam valve. If setting up the changeover for operating the supercharger valves takes too long, they run separately and have to be constantly regulated manually. (c) About 20,000hp is housed in each boiler room. The installation is comprehensive and complicated. The vast and rapid changes in pressure require correct handling of these modern boiler systems by highly qualified personnel who understand the interrelatedness of steam pressure, feedwater supply, superheater temperatures and airflow and have the practical experience enabling them to identify and rectify problems as and when they arise. The prescribed staffing level for each boiler room is one NCO and four stokers. Because the feedwater regulator is so inaccessible, two stokers have to be at the central stand at all times. One stoker has to be ready to shut off the water level and regulate the supercharger atomiser, while the other waits to close down the burn valve immediately should the Saacke burner flame go out since there is then a risk of explosion. The 1+4 staffing is insufficient to guarantee the safe working of the boilers under all conditions.'

The report then described in detail the problems encountered operating the three modes—automatic, semi-automatic and manual. Kummetz concluded: 'Running the boilers manually requires one NCO and six men. The idea of having one man replace the NCO so that he is free in the sense suggested in OKM paper 7340 A IVg of 3 December 1936 is impractical: what is needed is an additional NCO for each boiler room. However, all attempts to introduce this measure aboard destroyers have foundered on the accommodation problem. To summarise: because of the present layout and inaccessibility of the boiler plant, the boiler-room NCO is tied to the control stand precisely as is the NCO at the operating valve of a main engine, and especially when operating the boiler manually. The present staffing level of 1+4 per boiler room is too low. The only alternative would be to broaden training, particularly as regards semi-automatic and manual operation, in a calm training atmosphere, for which up to the present little or no opportunity existed.'

On 2 November 1937, Korvettenkapitän Max Fechner, Commander of Z 6 *Theodor Riedel*, stated in Report

B 752, addressed to 2nd Destroyer Division Command at Wilhelmshaven and referring to Fregattenkapitän Kummetz's paper, that the possibility of releasing the boiler-room NCOs had not been satisfactorily achieved because of 'the inexperience of NCOs, the too brief training period generally and deficient technical instruction of auxiliary machinery operating procedures'. Although criticising some aspects of the FdT's report—particularly the high level of expertise suggested for NCOs (marginal note in the report: 'O-ho!')—and pointing out that there was no need to have all four Saacke burner flames in full view of the central stand at all times, Fechner also concluded that at least one extra man was essential for each boiler room. This would mean an increase of nine in crew numbers, and six of these would have a secondary task of acting as ammunition handlers in combat, but accommodation difficulties could not be avoided.

Both reports mentioned the too-brief training (the result of the forced pace of naval rearmament) and the lack of personnel. Destroyers and their crews were granted only a few years and months of peace. At the outbreak of war many were undergoing trials and working up; others had terminated the prescribed training and were joining the Fleet; and some had taken part in manoeuvres and exercises, even in the Mediterranean. However, the crews were always being chopped and changed, and disruption prevailed: as new destroyers became available, veteran sailors were transferred to them to form the core company, leaving raw, inexperienced men to be trained from the very beginning as replacements.

All was flux, with no period of consolidation. That may have been in some ways justifiable for the seaman and specialised branches such as telegraphy, signals and gunnery, but in the engine rooms the highly developed boiler and turbine systems, linked up to numerous units of auxiliary machinery, often of different manufacture—virtually the entire engine-room domain—demanded a highly qualified workforce and practical training to provide it. In peacetime, these courses lasted for months. When war came, training went by the board, for men were needed to crew the ships. They stood their watches at sea in filthy weather or, when aircraft could get up, kept watchful eyes on the sky from where the chief danger was increasingly liable to come and which was to take a high toll in their blood. Meanwhile, below decks, the engineering branch showed an unflagging devotion to the job of keeping the machinery running despite the ever-increasing number of breakdowns. The concept of 'service' took on a new meaning: everybody was seized by the ambition to keep his own corner up and running. The exigencies of the service—interrupted only rarely for periods of rest and recuperation—drove men to the limits of physical and mental endurance. What they accomplished during the war years in the narrow, twisting confines of these destroyers, particularly towards the end of the war in the conscious knowledge that it was lost, was remarkable and speaks well for the comradeship aboard each individual ship.

The total number of shipboard deaths on board German wartime destroyers was about 2,600. The last Flag Officer Destroyers and Torpedo Boats, Vizeadmiral Kreisch, took leave of his men on 10 May 1945 with the following Order of the Day: 'Following completion of your final mission, I thank you, my dear comrades, for your proven readiness for action and for your loyalty and comradeship over six years of war. Our proud war flag flew during many famous and victorious voyages. Five thousand of our comrades fell aboard our boats. Long live the Destroyer and Torpedo Boat Arm!'

The Destroyer in German Naval Strategy

The Treaty of Versailles had prohibited the building of German warships in private yards. As Danzig no longer formed part of the German Reich, the Kaiserliche Werft there closed its doors, while its subsidiary at Kiel was split up into the state-owned Deutsche Werke and the Naval Arsenal, the latter now being the Reichsmarine repair yard. The other subsidiary, at Wilhelmshaven, became the naval shipyard, and the Uto Yard at Wilhelmshaven was transferred to the control of the Deutsche Werke.

Germany retained seventeen large torpedo boats (two in reserve) and sixteen small torpedo-boats (four), and the ages of these remaining Imperial Navy units was so close to the fifteen-year mark that a start could be made almost immediately on the construction of replacement units—as was the case with the light cruisers. The shipbuilders would be Wilhelmshaven Yard and, under certain conditions, Deutsche Werke at Kiel. The early start in the warship rebuilding programme—the light cruiser *Emden* leading the way—suffered a violent setback in time as a consequence of the developing hyperinflation and devaluation of the German currency.The Washington Naval Agreement signed by the five major powers (the United States,

Britain, France, Japan and Italy) in 1922, aimed to limit the naval arms race, especially with regard to capital ships and cruisers. Germany was not invited to attend this conference, which decided amongst other things the numbers and sizes of future warships based on displacement. The Imperial (or long, or Washington) ton—equivalent to 1,016kg— became the basis of a ship's standard, or type, displacement. This standard displacement was the weight of the ship equipped to sail, with all ammunition and armament, her machinery ready, plus water for the crew, in boilers and in piping but excluding fuel and feedwater. The previous standard as understood by German naval architects, designed displacement, had also included approximately one-third to two-fifths of the fuel and water aboard. The effects of the two changes for smaller warships gave German naval architects a few extra tonnes to play with.

By 1925 twelve former Imperial Navy torpedo boats declared by Germany as 'destroyers' under the Versailles Treaty became due for replacement. The designs, to a standard displacement of 800 long tons, began in 1923. That few former Imperial Navy naval architects remained in harness influenced the decision to place orders for the new vessels with Wilhelmshaven rather than the Deutsche Werke at Kiel.

The 1930 London Naval Conference had set a binding maximum destroyer displacement at 1,830 tonnes, with an armament calibre not exceeding 13cm (5.1in). Two years later the disarmament talks in Geneva held by members of the League of Nations proposed that all nations should disarm. As a result of Versailles, Germany had been forced in that direction and was prepared to make further concessions (for example, to renounce the construction of large *Panzerschiffe*—the pocket battleships of the *Deutschland* class). As the major powers—in particular the victors in the Great War—were now split into two mutually antagonistic camps preparing to fight each other, the conference broke up on 2 February 1932 without having achieved its purpose, and on 26 July that year Reichswehr Minister Schleicher announced that Germany no longer felt bound by the Versailles Treaty. On 15 November 1932 the rebuilding plan for the Reichsmarine was approved, and this was expanded by the National Socialists after their seizure of power in 1933. A homogeneous fleet was proposed, including six half-flotillas of destroyers or torpedo boats. On 19 October 1933 Germany left the League of Nations.

The first designs for pure destroyers had been invited in 1932, and two shipyards, Stettin Vulcan and Schichau, submitted plans. Stettin proposed an 1,100-tonne vessel capable of 35 knots and armed with three 12.7cm (5in) and four AA guns and two triple torpedo sets. The Schichau sketch, for a 1,500-tonne ship with a speed of 38 knots and mounting four 12.7cm guns, bore strong similarities to the final Type 1934 destroyer, although all vessels were built to official designs signed by the Kriegsmarine Naval Architects' Office. The Type 1934/1934A was developed from the 1932 sketches, and the various Types 1936 from the official designs drawn up that year.

The signing of the Anglo-German Naval Agreement on 18 June 1935 cleared the way for the first true destroyers. Germany was permitted a destroyer fleet of 52,200 tonnes, on which work was commenced at once. According to the 1932 Fleet Rebuilding Plan, OKM declared its intention to build sixteen destroyers with a standard displacement of 1,625 tonnes and a 12.7cm main armament. The Treaty of Versailles now ignored, Germany decided to observe the Washington (1922) and London (1930) Treaties instead.

Destroyer construction proceeded according to the Plan, but in making up for the lost time between 1918 and 1935 the work was rushed and, under close examination, appears not to have been well thought out. Initially six destroyers were expected to be laid down, but eventually Deutsche Werke at Kiel received building contracts for the first destroyers, Z 1 to Z 4. These were Type 1934, with an official standard displacement of 1,625 tonnes. Specifications included great strength of hull, good seakeeping qualities, a high maintained speed (even in heavy seas), a large radius of action and a powerful armament. The purpose of the design was to provide a fighting vessel which could double as a small cruiser—a type in which the German Navy was deficient—exceeding the 1,378-tonne French and 1,540-tonne Polish counterparts (these nations being the presumed potential opponents in war). This line of reasoning explains the jump in displacement for tendered destroyer designs from 1,100 tonnes to 1,500 and even 1,800 tonnes.

The specifications imposed by the Kriegsmarine became ever more comprehensive. The 1934 Shipbuilding Replacement Plan, which spoke of 48 destroyers, was discarded by the Admiralty Office in May that year in favour of ordering four more destroyers, followed by a building pause of two years. Doubts had been voiced during the yard work about the projected seakeeping qualities of the first four ships in high seas or heavy swell. The shortish foredeck and the poor lateral flare of the frames forward had come under particular scrutiny, for this was an area where the torpedo boats and the light cruisers *Karlsruhe*, *Köln* and *Königsberg* had all demonstrated weaknesses. Accordingly, it was decided to introduce modifications to the second series of four ships involving a redesign of the foreship and forecastle frames, and so the Type 1934A showed a number of improvements to the original plans. Z 5 to Z 8 were built in the private yard at Deschimag (AG Weser), Bremen.

Over the next few years the Office of Naval Architecture filed many modified plans for destroyers of different sizes and armament, but the design of a really useful type within the 1934 specification eluded them. All this endeavour might profitably have been invested in settling for a good standard type. Z 9 to Z 13 came off the stocks at Germania Werft Kiel and Z 14 to Z 16 at Blohm & Voss Hamburg. The Type 1936, Z 17 to Z 22, was outwardly different and displaced 1,811 tonnes. The ships were completed at Deschimag, the yard which stood at the forefront of destroyer construction. All subsequent vessels (except Z 37 to Z 39) were built there—Types 1936A, 1936A (Mob) and 1936B (Mob), plus the diesel-driven Z 51. Type 1936B (Mob) was the last design to which a destroyer actually came off the slip, although one light cruiser of the *Spähkreuzer* type, SP1, a 6,000-tonne scaled-up destroyer based on 1938 projections, was laid down in August 1941 at Germania Werft and work also advanced on the diesel-driven Z 51, a Type 1942 fleet torpedo boat originally intended to be T 43, Yard No 1109 at Deschimag.

All destroyers were built to the main frame/longitudinal bulkhead system using ST 52 steel and a lighter metal for the superstructure and innards. The first 22 were in commission in September 1939, but no further destroyers entered service for almost a year, by which time twelve of the original fleet had been sunk. At the end of World War II Germany had twelve destroyers left intact, plus one on the stocks and two—Z 44 and Z 45—launched but incomplete. The total number in commission during the war was 40, plus two foreign confiscations. Forty-eight torpedo-boats entered Kriegsmarine service, of which twelve survived intact. A large number were under construction in Baltic yards when the war ended.

Casting a jaundiced eye over the ships of the surface fleet, a senior German Admiralty official remarked after the war, 'We Germans knew how to build outstanding freshwater ships.' Naval building in Germany—in which destroyers were of course included—reached a stage in 1938 which led to a fresh strategy, set out in a memorandum by Fregattenkapitän Heye, Operations Officer of the Seekriegsleitung (Naval Warfare Office). Entitled 'Die Seekriegführung gegen England und die sich daraus ergebenden Forderungen für die strategische Zielsetzung und den Aufbau der Kriegsmarine', it was a decisive and important historical document which, read with the battle instructions of May 1939, set out naval policy in the event of war. The memorandum recognized that a 'balanced' Fleet was required, since, if Britain were the enemy, the German Navy would concentrate the weight of its offensive on the trade routes, thus attracting the might of the Royal Navy away from an expected blockade of Germany as had been imposed so effectively in the Great War. This thinking created the 'Z Plan'.* Once drawn up, a Z Plan wargame was held, resulting in the following opinion delivered by Vizeadmiral Schniewind, SKL Chief of Staff:

'1. Focus of German naval operations is on the oceans. The task here is to get our units on the trade routes. This objective serves domestic naval policy, primarily in the North Sea.

'2. All possible theatres of war in the assumed scenario are closely linked. Successes and losses immediately affect the situation in another war area.

'3. The war against the trade routes can be supported in Europe by the Luftwaffe focusing attacks against the enemy coasts.

'4. Britain's weakest point is tonnage, since supply will always be available. For Germany, the keeping open of the supply line will be more important than ships.

'5. If Germany had naval bases on ocean coasts, the prospects for the success of an offensive naval policy against Britain/France would improve decisively. As long as we do not have our own bases, we have to resort to getting neutrals to collaborate and build up supply bases overseas.

'6. Oceanic warfare requires the development of specific types of German naval unit and involving the mercantile marine in the aims of military policy.

---

* See Conclusions for the make-up of the Z Plan.

'7. I consider it certain that to develop the concept of oceanic warfare, linking all suitable means to this goal—to which I would add the heavy ships if necessary—would give us good prospects on the enemy trade routes. In the situation assumed in the wargame,* these prospects increase commensurate with the growth in naval forces which is not to be expected until 1943. I believe that in the then prevailing widespread nature of ocean warfare, operations promising success will present themselves for the deployment of the numerous smaller vessels: the theatre of possible localised conflict will not be limited to the North Sea, but to the high seas of all parts of the world.'

With this document Schniewind, in recognition of Germany's naval inferiority but against his better judgement, set the course for the future. This fact was all the more obvious from the report of 20 January 1939, 'Grundlagen und Probleme des Seekrieges, Aufgaben der Marine, Möglichkeit und operative Verwendung der Seekampfmittel', which stated: 'The idea of a "fleet in being" must be deleted for ever from German Navy manuals. It grew from a pessimistic foundation which took account only of purely intellectual, calculated factors. Pessimism weakens and is destructive of the fighting man. The history of all wars proves that, apart from certain material basics, the precondition for great success lies not so much in the human intellectual faculty as in the firm belief in one's own strength of character, that is to say, in moral qualities.' In conclusion, the report predicted: 'Confidence in the leadership of the State is so great, allowing no doubt to arise but that at the right time the present enormous difficulties of the political kind can be overcome in order to place the German Fleet numerically in the position to do justice to all such tasks as may fall to it.' What a fallacy!

The advent of the Second World War took the German Navy aback and laid bare the weaknesses of the German Fleet. The Kriegsmarine was simply not in a position to take on its major opponent, the Royal Navy, in terms of either ships or trained personnel—particularly in the marine engineering branch. Destroyer operations in the first months of the war began with an extension of the Westwall or Siegfried Line, from the Dutch coast northwards to the Skagerrak, by means of a defensive mine barrage. Occasional anticontraband controls were carried out in the narrow coastal waters of the Skagerrak and Kattegat. The destroyer's role was generally conceived to be escort, patrol and scouting duties in accordance with the description 'workhorses of the Fleet'.

In November 1939 offensive minelaying operations began off the British coast. These required a high state of readiness of ship and machinery, for a relatively high speed had to be maintained despite the heavy cargo of mines, and this could only be guaranteed if the engine plant worked as it should. That this was achieved was attributable to a marked degree to the training of the NCOs and stokers and the preparedness of chief engineers to cut corners, knowing they could rely on the men under them. 'Old hands know the ropes' was the saying: in the German Navy everything depended on the few veterans in any team while the 'new boys' struggled to familiarise themselves with a confusing mass of piping, valves and stopcocks amidst the main and auxiliary machinery. Everything had to be absorbed in a short time—there was something new every day.

The Norwegian operation, although brilliantly handled, exposed the limits of German sea power. The occupation of France and the Low Countries brought valuable Channel bases, but these lost strategic significance once Operation 'Seelöwe', the proposed invasion of Britain, was given up. After a few early skirmishes in polar waters and a single successful Atlantic operation, the surviving battleships remained in port or fjord. Forays demanded an escort force which was needed more urgently elsewhere.

The idea of a substantial and enduring Luftwaffe involvement proved illusory. Russia and all the many other far-flung fronts proved that the shirt was too short. The Mediterranean theatre, the vast expanses of the Soviet Union and, the early collaboration between Britain and the United States asked too much of the Kriegsmarine in a naval strategic sense. Finally, all rested on the U-boat war. During 1941 the belligerent attitude of the neutral United States reduced its effectiveness, and with the American entry into the war the pendulum swung in favour of the Western powers. The 'tonnage war' could only be successful if the tonnage sunk exceeded the capacity to replace it, and that possibility no longer existed with the United States as an additional enemy.

---

*At the time the wargame was held, nobody was seriously thinking of war, and certainly not against Britain. Wargames of all types, including military manoeuvres, are commonplace and belong to the normal military programme of all nations. The situations assumed are theoretical, as are the resulting plans and counter-measures. In earnest they count as underlying preparation.

By 1942, a Navy designed for economic warfare on the oceans had become a fleet of primarily medium and small active units, with the U-boats providing the main punch, and in January 1943 Hitler ordered the decommissioning of the big ships from light cruisers upwards. With this decision, Raeder, Naval C-in-C, stepped back. His successor, Dönitz, managed to have the instruction trimmed, but otherwise could do nothing. In June 1943 the Naval Building Programme was revised and naval armaments were tailored to the general war situation. Contracts could only be placed for vessels up to destroyer size, and the output of U-boats increased. Although the idea was good, this new programme stood in the shadow of the economic situation.

By the summer of 1943 the Kriegsmarine—with the exception of the U-boats—was for practical purrposes limited to coastal waters stretching from Biarritz to the Gulf of Finland, from Kiel to the White Sea. A striking factor throughout the war as a whole was the overall low destroyer availability for sea duty, at 40 per cent. On the 2,069 days between the outbreak of war and the end of April 1945, Z 15 *Erich Steinbrinck* was laid up under repair for 1,325 days, spending about 64 per cent of the war in the dockyard.*

Vizeadmiral Friedrich Ruge, after the war the first Inspector of the new Bundesmarine—and a widely respected historian—arrived at the following verdict: 'The Second World War was won by those states which controlled the sea lanes. Even in the future these will play a decisive role . . . there is little argument [however] that our small fleet accomplished more than could reasonably have been expected of it.'

Naval Construction

German shipbuilders made no giant leaps forward with their destroyer designs. Studies involving theoretical calculations relating to weapons, machinery and equipment followed in the train of the military specifications. Once these were presented, there began the departmental struggle. The weapons specialists wanted a powerful armament with numerous barrels, superior to a supposed opponent they had in mind. Steadfastness, the ability to take punishment and the steaming range had to be good. This gave rise to discussions about the type and quality of the ship's machinery. Finally, an overall decision was taken, the construction plans were drawn up and approved and the contract was placed with a yard.

So far as the first German destroyers—the Type 1934s—were concerned, it was recognised early on that these ships, built to the initial 1932 designs, did not measure up, and from the beginning they were spoken of as 'reserve destroyers'. They were not very seaworthy, and they were generally unsuitable for deployment away from local waters because of their poor range—and seaworthiness and range were the very qualities which had been requested. Minor modifications to the bows of the Types 1934 and 1934A did little to alleviate the problems of poor sea-keeping and instability, and the Type 1936, which was a larger vessel fitted with an 'Atlantic' or 'clipper' bow, was not noticeably better. A larger main calibre weapon was introduced aboard the Type 1936A, and it was seen fit to mount two of these on the forecastle deck in a twin turret. This had a further adverse effect on stability and sea-keeping—and the ship had also to carry aloft the burden of several cumbersome radar aerials.

One is prompted to ask whether German naval architects had forgotten that a war was in progress. Design after design came pouring out of their offices. Wouldit not have been more sensible to have designed a relatively economic standard destroyer type suitable for mass production? The large German shipyards could be counted on the fingers of one hand—Germania Werft at Kiel and Blohm & Voss, Hamburg and Deschimag (AG Weser) at Bremen. Destroyer production was finally concentrated at the latter.

The war had taken a course in direct contrast to the flights of fancy exercised at the green table, and the reasons for the delay in naval building were listed in an OKM letter of 28 September 1940 as being (i) a lack of workers; (ii) a shortage of raw materials; (iii) problems in *matériel* supply; (iv) new types of yard work being introduced, such as craft for Operation 'Seelöwe', the construction and fitting out of mine destructor vessels and increasing ship repairs; (v) transport difficulties; (vi) the suspension of work because of air raids, blackout etc; and (vii) the unusually fierce winter of 1939/40.

---

* These periods are listed in this destroyer's career section, in order to highlight the problems involved. Also included are the number of missions sailed and casualties sustained. A 'mission' was any voyage from port to port, an period escort duty, a patrol, a minelaying operation or an engagement with the enemy. Points were awarded for involvement in an action and were the basis for the award of the Destroyer Badge and Iron Cross First and Second Classes. The leading five destroyers for missions sailed were Z20 *Karl Galster*—131; Z 4 *Richard Beitzen*—104, Z 14 *Friedrich Ihn*—89; Z 6 *Theodor Riedel*—66; and Z 25—also 66. All had a negligible casualty list.

On 6 July 1940 Admiral Schniewind wrote that individual ship types exhibited a limited seaworthiness only and demanded 'an improvement in design to guarantee trouble-free running and sea-keeping: therefore no high demands, but a high and reliable endurance of ship and machinery.' This criticism included the destroyers. The individual destroyer classes of the Royal Navy, by comparison, had been built almost uniformly. From the 'A' class to the 'H' class, all had twin funnels, three triple-drum Admiralty boilers (wet steam with superheater) and two sets of turbines and could make about 36 knots; none had a standard displacement over 2,000 tons (on the contrary, all were well below this limit); and the gun calibre was 4.7in (12cm). With the 'J' class, the number of boilers was reduced to two, enabling one of the funnels to be dispensed with, creating more deck space for anti-aircraft weapons. Speed, size and performance remained unchanged. The 'Tribal' class, developed in the 1930s, were too expensive, had no advantages over the others and were not further developed. The 2,000-ton limit was first exceeded with the 'Battle' class, but the purpose was solely to increase bunkerage for greater range, the vessels having been planned for use in the Pacific. It must be added that Britain had a large number of yards that built for the Royal Navy, and, contrary to the German experience, their output was not affected by the initial enemy air attacks.

In the Reich it became increasingly difficult to fulfil orders. This was partly becvause of a shortage of skilled workers: in September 1940 the Naval Armaments Office, Department Wirtschaft V, reported a shortfall of 13,303 workers in the 65 most important supply industries and yards, and a further 7,050 vacancies were unfilled.

Not only had the bows of the new destroyers revealed deficiencies: the sterns were also unsatisfactory. A deflector wedge was added to the flat bottom, but it proved to be no solution: the design was simply bad. In comparison, the American *Fletcher* class destroyers, which had a similar stern form, proved totally successful despite increased weight demands arising from additional anti-aircraft weapons, depth charges, etc), and the same was true for other American, and British, destroyer classes. The typical stern shape of the German destroyer was chosen because substantial propulsion was needed for the heavy after section. It was also assumed that this would give a higher speed and improve sea-keeping at the bow. That a special

bow design would be required in this case was unfortunately forgotten. It was rationalised that the 'V' form was better than a flat stern, but in practice it was very quick to 'suck under'. The fitting of *Totholz** and tunnelling above the propellers was only partially successful, for the stern now sat too high, creating too much turbulence and destroying the jet effect. Propellers are most efficient in a calm and steady waterflow, and much energy was lost in the turbulence, moreover, besides a stronger cavitation observed about the propeller blades, the rudder effect was also lessened.

Comparing the German destroyer types with the American *Fletcher* class side-on and through the frames, one observes how on the US type the draught begins to decrease from abaft No 3 gun. Screws and rudder work freely in a steady flow of water. On the US type the distance between No 5 gun and the end of the deck is shorter, and the *Totholz* stretches as far aft as the rear of No 5 gun. This design was so successful that it was used in cruiser construction up to and including the *Alaska*s. For a dry ship and better sea-keeping the forecastle had considerable sheer, which was evident to a lesser degree at the stern of larger types and later classes (see Hadeler, Friedman etc).

Weapons and Radar

The 12.7cm gun was the standard destroyer weapon and was located in five single gunhouses—No 1 gun on the foredeck with No 2 superfiring, No 3 gun on the after deck, and Nos 4 and 5 superfiring from mounts on the aft deck housing. The anti-aircraft (*Flak*) outfit was the standard 3.7cm and 2cm issue of the time, but this proved insufficient and during the course of the war numerous 3.7cm twin and 2cm quadruple mountings were embarked. As this extra weight topside added to the general instability and poor sea-keeping of the ships, one of the 12.7cm or 15cm main turrets was unshipped in compensation.

A wartime measure beginning with new Type 1936A destroyers was an increase in the main calibre to 15cm (5.9in). However, as by April 1940 Germany had available only four light cruisers—*Emden, Köln, Leipzig*

---

* The *Totholz* is that part of the hull forward and aft below the waterline which contributes to the broadside or lateral plan while having a negligible effect on displacement. The term originates from the time when wooden full-rigged ships required a large lateral plan for sailing with the wind on the beam, the additional resistance being provided by heavy board (hence 'deadwood'), which took up no interior space.

and *Nürnberg*, the last three being such poor sea boats that they were not permitted beyond coastal waters in bad weather—the thinking behind the larger calibre was almost certainly to 'cruiserise' these later destroyers to the extent that, if necessary, they could take on British light cruisers in battle. The straight changeover of calibre retaining the designed single-gunhouse layout would not have caused problems in itself, but it was then considered—against the stated opinion of sea-going destroyer officers—to be a good idea to increase the number of guns on the first three Type 1936A ships (Z 23 to Z 25) from four 15cm in single gunhouses to five 15cm, three in single gunhouses aft and two in a twin turret on the forecastle deck. Inevitably this extra weight forward brought more sea-keeping problems, stability was impaired and a speed restriction had to be imposed during inclement weather.

The later projected designs returned to the 12.7cm calibre. Other projects included the 12.8cm multi-purpose KM 41 gun in a twin turret, for use against aircraft as well as surface targets, which would, had it ever been developed, have led to a reduction in numbers of the less effective 3.7cm weapon on board ship; a 45kg salvo was, theoretically, possible every five seconds. The other weapon was the fully automatic, air-cooled, gas-pressure-loaded 5.5cm Flakgerät 58, the first designs of which from Naval Ordnance Office sources bear the date 9 October 1944. Several prototypes were completed and, according to unconfirmed reports, were tested aboard a destroyer. Rate of fire was 120–150 rounds per minute, and single-round firing was also possible.

At the end of the 1930s Germany led the field in radar. There were numerous developments, and many well-known scientists and companies were involved in pushing ahead with the technology. They found little approval from the highest levels, however, and shortly after the outbreak of war Hitler ordered that all investigation in the field of radar should be halted. Before 1938 the Luftwaffe leadership had come down heavily against the usefulness of researching radar, and it was not until well into the war that British progress was discovered—thanks to a set which used the lower-centimetre wavelengths being found in the innards of a crashed bomber; this explains the difference in size between the small British antennas and the gigantic steel 'mattresses' carried aboard German warships.

Although German firms and scientists had continued their work in secret despite the prohibition, even now they still ran up against absolute official disinterest and a lack of coordination between not only the various fighting arms (the U-boat arm being the most co-operative) but also the multitudinous experimenters in radar development—there were more than a thousand different models occasionally available for inspection—most of whom, intent on profiting from their research, continued their own projects in circumstances of the most exaggerated secrecy. That there was a war on, and that the need for co-operation was therefore paramount, was not understood.

Machinery

During the design and planning stage of the destroyers the question of the right machinery became acute. The 'pocket battleships' had broken new ground with the introduction of pure diesel drive, but the majority of the other new vessels had made do with the usual (if somewhat improved) wet-steam plant. The exceptions were the light cruisers *Leipzig* and *Nürnberg*, and it is incomprehensible why they should have been fitted with diesels to complement an out-of-date (respecting the steam pressure and temperature) wet-steam plant.

The plans for the first four destroyers were completed early in 1932 to specifications for a high-pressure/hot-steam installation with turbines, two shafts and a 12.7cm armament. Demands for a heavier anti-aircraft battery and more torpedo tubes, a higher speed, a greater range and better engine output led to a greater displacement. Because of the demand for high output, diesels were not considered: at that time insufficient data was available respecting the performance of diesels aboard the large warships which had them (the pocket battleship *Deutschland* and the gunnery training ship *Bremse*). Accordingly, the Wagner High Pressure Company received an order for a 26,000hp turbine plant as a project, the size of the output forcing the greater displacement. Violent controversy ensued between 'K' (the Konstruktionsamt, or Office of Naval Architecture) and 'Ing' (the military marine engineering department) on the question of steam pressure and temperature: the architects were cautious whereas the naval engineers wanted to go the whole hog. 'K' was also uninterested in a further development of the proven Wagner boiler with its natural circulation and expected much of other boiler types—Benson, La Mont and Velox.

A supernumerary Benson boiler had been installed in 1930 aboard the freighter *Uckermark* for experimental purposes; it had a steam pressure of 225 atmospheres and a temperature of 450°C. The plant included a number of innovations and proved successful. The point here is that a merchant ship at sea maintains generally much the same engine output and speed from leaving one port to arriving at the next; there is hardly any change in the pressure. In a warship, on the other hand, one expects constant changes in engine speed as the result of proceeding in formation, in manoeuvring and in the daily training schedule, and the engine room has to satisfy the requirement. Because of this, great demands are made of the machinery, particularly the boilers. Taken overall, the question of boilers was the decisive consideration leading to the selection of high-pressure, hot steam: the guarantee of performance was paramount.

The gunnery training ship *Brummer*, commissioned in 1936, had trouble-free Wagner boilers but her auxiliary machinery proved very prone to breakdown. To save space and weight these were mostly driven by small turbines or had electrical motors (the feed for which came from the turbo-generators), which were thoroughly uneconomical because of the constant demand for steam to keep them running. This meant that steam had to be maintained permanently in some form of boiler, and this increased the ship's fuel consumption. The fuel consumption of wet-steam machinery was 0.6–0.7kg/shp, for high-pressure, hot-steam machinery 0.3–0.4kg/shp. With diesels the figure was 0.25kg/shp. A compromise was finally reached in which some of the destroyers had Wagner and the others Benson boilers. The Wagner was a water-tube boiler with natural water circulation; the Benson had forced circulation, wherein the feedwater is forced through the boiler tubes, where it is superheated and evaporated. The system was ideal for a warship, but the weakness lay in the ability to manoeuvre—which led later to the addition of a steam collector.

To resolve the boiler problem it was decided to test out the three newer types—the Velox on a minesweeper and the similar La Mont system aboard the old battleship *Hessen*, while Blohm & Voss would report on the Benson. The difficulties the early destroyers had experienced with the Wagner were documented for comparison. Their future wartime use was questionable, but at the time nobody was thinking of war. The main advantage was recognised as being high engine output in the smallest area (about 10kg/shp). Diesels had not achieved this at the time, the value aboard the

pocket battleships being much greater. The high-pressure, hot-steam system seemed ideal for destroyers in view of their assumed role mainly in coastal waters, for (i) economic use of space, (ii) tolerance of pressure changes, (iii) rapid readiness for use, (iv) resistance to hits striking the ship, (v) reliability, (vi) low noise output and (vii) resistance to shock. In the event, however, the impetuous pace of development brought serious drawbacks. Personnel at all levels lacked a well-founded theoretical knowledge of the machinery and the expertise to master it. The new boilers required the maximum technical understanding of procedures, for the automatic regulating installations did not necessarily respond appropriately to sudden increases in output, which then required manual intervention. The new system had a mass of extra piping and armatures and was very susceptible to breakdown in the vacuum (condenser parts), often resulting in salting up. Oil and lubricant supply piping was also frequently affected. Fuel consumption was not drastically diminished, and the materials question began at high temperature.

Another of the really important demands of the new destroyer that was never fulfilled was the yearned-for great range. In the original specifications, 5,000–6,000nm at 20 knots and 7,000nm at 17 knots had been desired, but in practice the Type 1934 made 3,100nm at 19 knots and only a hundred more at 15. An SKL memorandum of February 1941 observed: 'The few ships available would have been able to undertake much more had they measured up to specification and had they been deployed accordingly.' This referred to the high susceptibility to breakdown of the new hot-steam engine plant, which, by reason of its complicated design and inaccessibility, required a long period in dock for even the minor types of repair. The memorandum also complained about limited range and poor seakeeping, which brought into question whether the vessels were actually battleworthy; for future new construction it was necessary to lay down clearly that the steam pressure and temperature had to be reduced. In general it was a strident criticism of the ships and their machinery.

This criticism was naturally not without its influence on shipboard officers. Many chief engineers set out deliberately to spare boilers and tubes by 'working measures' involving lower boiler pressures. Commanders were usually prepared to connive with the chief engineer, even if it involved a breach of regulations. In the shipyard while under repair, destroyers were often given structural and other 'improvements' without the knowledge of the powers above. This explains how Z 4 *Richard Beitzen*, one of the first four new-build German destroyers, could enter the yards in May 1943 for a refit having remained operational for 524 days and steaming 32,000 miles since the previous visit.

Compared to other systems, high-pressure/hot-steam had indisputable advantages for turbine drive, particularly the reduction in time needed to raise steam and an improvement in manoeuvrability, both of which matched expectations (the Benson boiler proving superior in this respect). In the Battle of the Bristol Channel on 17 October 1940 involving the German destroyers *Hans Lody*, *Karl Galster*, *Erich Steinbrinck* and *Friedrich Ihn* and a mixed force of British cruisers and destroyers, an engine room NCO aboard one of the Type 1934As had the turbines running full out only nine minutes after firing two cold boilers. The system required numerous auxiliary equipment, and this add-itional demand for steam brought so many disadvantages in its train that the military value of the system as a whole was considered questionable.

The possibility of a basic improvement preoccupied many veteran sea-going chief engineers, one of whom was Kapitänleutnant (Ing) Illies; he had been a member of the destroyer construction permanent instruction staff, was involved in the sea trials of the first destroyers and had been chief engineer of Z 2 *Georg Thiele* at Narvik. He took a keen interest in the problem of steam consumption, particularly that relating to auxiliary plant, and his deliberations resulted in the development of a system of control comparable to the accelerator pedal of a motor car combined with electric drive for all auxiliary machinery. This created an altogether simpler system of construction, better reliability, easier hand-ling and a reduction in repair time and thus in the queue for repair. He amassed additional data during the work-up of the battleship *Tirpitz* as a member of the Warship Testing Branch. In order to force through his ideas, he made contact with household names in industry and the universities to clarify points of doubt and finally prepared a memorandum which the Warship Testing Branch (EKK) received in January 1942, from where it was passed upwards with a positive recommendation to the OKM Warship Construction Headquarters. He also gave a copy to a functionary involved in military economics, from which source Speer's Ministry for

Armaments and Munitions received it. When this came to the attention of the EKK, they demanded the return of the paper and Illies was reprimanded for passing an official document to an unauthorised recipient. Unabashed, he compiled another paper, 'Entwurf einer Zerstörerantriebsanlage' (Design for a Destroyer Pro-pulsion System), and submitted it to EKK. The func-tionary in military economics also came into possession of a copy by unknown means and, relying on a new *Führerbefehl*, forwarded the memorandum to a Ham-burg shipyard owner.* This was too much for the OKM, however, and Illies was hauled before Admiral Raeder and sentenced to fourteen days' confinement to quar-ters for breach of confidence. Illies' second paper came to light at OKM through the normal channels in July 1942 while the first memorandum remained a thorn of contention between the ship machinery department (KIV) and the naval designers (KII).

As interest elsewhere grew in Illies' proposal, he was invited to attend a conference at the end of 1942, as a result of which it was decided that 'for the clarific-ation of hitherto uncertain questions the firm of Schich-au will receive a contract to design a fleet torpedo boat incorporating the suggestions of Kapitänleutnant Illies. The results of this investigation will be made known at the appropriate time.'

Following the resignation of Admiral Raeder in January 1943, Illies was transferred to the Schichau yard, where work was beginning on the I-S Anlage project. All naval armament schemes received a boost on 22 July 1943 when they came under the umbrella of the new Shipbuilding Commission at the Speer Minis-try. The I-S system was first tested on 8 January 1944 and listed for installation aboard the new Type 44 torpedo boat. None of these was completed by the war's end, however. The Schichau shipyard was taken over by the Soviets in January 1945: what documents were confiscated there is not known.

Diesel Drive for Destroyers

The economy of a steam engine—compared to diesel plant—depends not so much on pressure as on the temperature of the steam entering the turbines. The machinery simply transforms heat into mechanical energy, and the hotter the steam the more the energy

---

* According to the Führer directive, all inventions and improvements in the weapons and military-economy field could be sent by any German to a special field post-office box within the Speer Ministry.

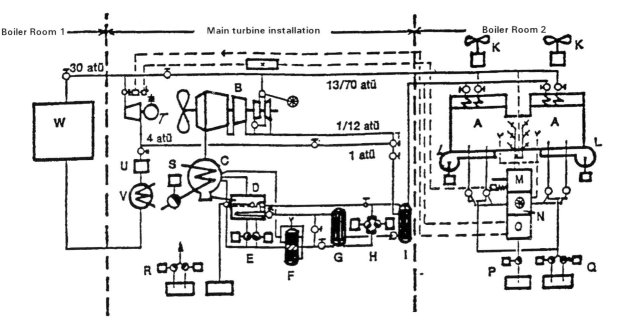

The I-S Engine Plant: Scheme of the Testbed Layout
Key: A Main boiler. B Main turbine installation. C Main condenser. D Regulator box. E Condenser pumps. F Main distributor. G Condenser re-cooler. H Main feedwater pump. I Feedwater pre-heater. K Boiler supercharger. L Atomiser supercharger. M Steam pressure/air mixture boiler regulator. N Air mixture/heating oil boiler regulator. O Feedwater/steam differential pressure boiler regulator. P Regulator oil pump. Q Heating oil pump. R Turbine oil pump. S Main cooling pump. T Turbo-generator. U Steam suppressor. V Auxiliary condenser. W Auxiliary boiler. X Turbine control stand. (From files of F. Schichau AG, Elbing 1944: Bröckow, *Geschichte des deutschen Marine-Ingenieur-Korps*)

produced. The temperature of so-called saturated steam—that is, steam before superheating, is about 200°C at 15atms, 235°C at 30atms and 340°C at 150atms, and the critical point is reached at 225atms with a temperature of 374°C. Thus the temperature rises much more slowly than the pressure—in other words, only a higher temperature can bring about an increase in output, by superheating. At this stage the problem of materials comes into play—steel alloys must be used—and the expected fuel saving (at least, on a warship) becomes debatable owing to numerous auxiliary engines all consuming steam. High-pressure/hot-steam has significant advantages—smaller boilers, fewer personnel, clean fuel—but its disadvantages are the high temperatures. Steam plant of this kind can only be run with efficient regulating machinery, and this has to be supervised, which requires more personnel. There is also an intense demand for feedwater.

The diesel motor needs none of this regulating equipment and therefore demands fewer personnel. It is also instantly ready. A diesel ship has great range,

but it requires fuel of a better quality fuel, which is more expensive. In the period between 1928 and 1935 MAN Augsburg built a light, double-acting, two-stroke diesel motor to German Navy specifications which had proved satisfactory aboard ship after initial teething problems, and it was the exaggeration of these problems by the steam lobby that led to the abandonment of diesel drive for large warships in favour of high-pressure/hot-steam for the critical rebuilding period from 1935 onwards.

From about 1938 there was a revival of Kriegsmarine interest in diesel-driven warships, but with the advent of hostilities it was all placed in abeyance and contracts were subsequently placed for only one ship, a Type 1942 experimental destroyer, Z 51. The order for six diesels was placed with MAN at the beginning of 1943, and four had been built by the war's end. Test work on the prototypes was abandoned for lack of fuel in February 1945. The 24-cylinder (2 ×12), 320mm-bore, 440mm-stroke motor, designated V12 Z32/44, was a V-form, fast-running, double action, two-stroke motor of

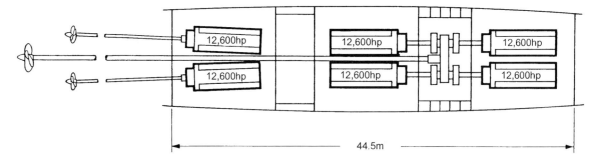

Above: Layout of main diesels aboard Z 51 (1942).

welded steel construction. Maximum revolutions were 600 per min, piston speed 8.8ms, maximum output was 12,000hp, medium effective pressure 5.52kg/cm² and fuel consumption at maximum demand 185g/hp/hr. The dry weight of the engine, including auxiliary machinery but excluding the oil cooler, was 67 tonnes.

If the work on Z 51 had been seen through to completion, the ship would have represented a great stride forward for the German Navy. There was, behind the design, a marked 'oceanic' thinking, caused by the dearth of light cruisers, for with diesel drive this type of destroyer would have had a range to equal not only that of the the pocket battleships but also of the U-boats.*

The monthly *Wehrtechnischen Monatsheft*, in its 4/56 issue, concluded on the eternal controversy between high-pressure/hot-steam and diesels: 'It was the tragedy of German warship construction that faith

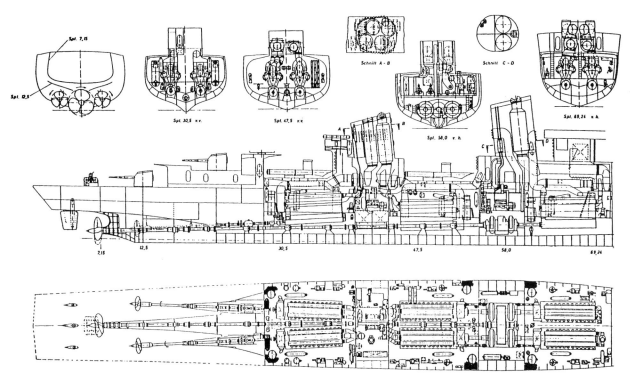

Above: Stern section and machinery of destroyer Z 51 (1942). (MAN Archive).

[in diesels] was lost during the battle against high-pressure/hot-steam, and was accordingly renounced by the military side. It was a further tragedy that this struggle occurred at a time when the Naval Architect's Office had a technical chief not up to the high demands of the post. (And it must be noted that the choice of the person to fill the post was made not on the recommendations of the engineers, but of the military.)

The *Spähkreuzer* Programme

Mention should be made here of the twenty-two 5,000-tonne small scouting cruisers known as *Spähkreuzer*, envisaged under the 'Z Plan'. Orders were placed with Germania Werft for the first three in February 1941. SP 1 (ex Z 40) was laid down as Yard No 642 on 20 August 1941 and Nos 643 and 644 were allocated for SP 2 (ex Z 41) and SP 3 (ex Z 42). The ship was basically a scaled-up destroyer to a Blohn & Voss design based on variations of the projected Type 1938 Type. The entire *Spähkreuzer* programme was abandoned in late

Left: The MAN V-form V12Z 32/44 diesel at the firm's Historical Museum, now located in the Auto und Technik Museum, Sinsheim, Kraichgau. This was one of the four motors built by MAN on contract for the Type 1942 destroyer Z 51.

1941, although the six engine plants remained on order in December. Displacement: 4,589 tons standard, 5,900 tons full load. Dimensions: 152.2m × 14.62m × 4.66. Seventeen watertight compartments. Machinery: turbines (77,500shp) plus diesels (14,500hp). Speed 35.5 knots (turbines). Bunkerage 820 tonnes max. Range 8,000nm at 17 knots. Five ship's boats. Complement 18 officers and 520 men.

In this general connection it may also be of interest to remark that the German Navy showed no interest in a Brown Bovery & Cie gas turbine and diesel mixed system for destroyers offered in 1939. The Type 1940 destroyer, which got no further than the drawing board, was designed to mount sixteen diesels providing 60,000hp for a speed of 40 knots. Range would have been 10,500nm at 19 knots.

---

* Z 51 was laid down at Deschimag Bremen on 25 November 1942, Yard No 1109. Displacement: 2,041 tons standard, 2,328 tons designed, 2720 tons full load. Dimensions: 114.3m × 11m × 4.37m (max); freeboard 6.5m. Armament: 4 ×12.7cm in single gunhouses, two forward and two aft; 8 × 3.7cm and 12 × 2cm AA; 2 × 3 torpedo tubes; up to 50 mines. Fifteen watertight compartments. Machinery: six diesels developing 57,120hp; 3 shafts; 3 rudders. Speed 36 knots. Bunkerage 553 tonnes max. Range 5,200nm at 19 knots (much greater at lower cruising speeds).

Technical Data

CONSTRUCTION DETAILS

Type*	Desig-nation	Name	Contract placed	Builder	Yard No	Laid down	Launched	Commissioned
1934	Z 1	LEBERECHT MAASS	07.04.34	Deutsche Werke, Kiel	242	10.10.34	18.08.35	14.01.37
	Z 2	GEORG THIELE			243	25.10.34	18.08.35	27.02.37
	Z 3	MAX SCHULTZ			244	02.01.35	30.11.35	08.04.37
	Z 4	RICHARD BEITZEN			245	07.01.35	30.11.35	13.05.37
1934A	Z 5	PAUL JACOBI	09.01.35	Deschimag, Bremen	899	15.07.35	24.03.36	29.06.37
	Z 6	THEODOR RIEDEL			900	18 07.35	22.04.36	02.07.37
	Z 7	HERMANN SCHOEMANN			901	07.09.35	16.07.36	15.09.37
	Z 8	BRUNO HEINEMANN			902	14.01.36	15.09.36	08.01.38
	Z 9	WOLFGANG ZENKER	04.08.34	Germania-Werft, Kiel	535	22.03.35	27.03.36	02.07.38
	Z 10	HANS LODY			536	01.04.35	14.05.36	17.03.38
	Z 11	BERND VON ARNIM	10.11.34		537	26.04.35	08.07.36	08.06.38
	Z 12	ERICH GIESE			538	03.05.35	12.03.37	04.03.39
	Z 13	ERICH KOELLNER			539	12.10.35	18.03.37	28.08.39
	Z 14	FRIEDRICH IHN	19.01.35	Blohm & Voss, Hamburg	503	30.03.35	05.11.35	09.04.38
	Z 15	ERICH STEINBRINCK			504	30.05.35	24.09.36	08.06.38
	Z 16	FRIEDRICH ECKHOLDT			505	14.11.35	21.03.37	02.08.38
1936	Z 17	DIETHER VON ROEDER	06.01.36	Deschimag, Bremen	919	09.09.36	19.08.37	29.08.38
	Z 18	HANS LÜDEMANN			920	09.09.36	01.12.37	08.10.38
	Z 19	HERMANN KÜNNE			921	05.10.36	22.12.37	12.01.39
	Z 20	KARL GALSTER			922	14.09.37	15.06.38	21.03.39
	Z 21	WILHELM HEIDKAMP			923	14.12.37	20.08.38	20.06.39
	Z 22	ANTON SCHMITT			924	03.01.38	20.09.38	24.09.39
1936A	Z 23		23.04.38		957	15.11.38	15.12.39	15.09.40
	Z 24				958	02.01.39	07.03.40	23.10.40
	Z 25				959	15.02.39	16.03.40	30.11.41
	Z 26				960	01.04.39	02.04.40	09.01.41
	Z 27				961	27.12.39	01.08.40	26.02.41
	Z 28				962	30.11.39	20.08.40	09.08.41
	Z 29				963	21.03.40	15.10.40	25.06.41
	Z 30				964	15.04.40	08.12.40	15.11.41
1936A (Mob)	Z 31		19.09.39		1001	01.09.40	15.05.41	11.04.42
	Z 32				1002	01.11.40	15.08.41	15.09.42
	Z 33				1003	22.12.40	15.09.41	06.02.43
	Z 34				1004	14.01.41	05.05.42	05.06.43
1936B (Mob)	Z 35		17.02.41		1005	06.06.41	02.10.42	22.09.43
	Z 36				1006	15.09.41	15.05.43	19.02.44
1936A (Mob)	Z 37		19.09.39	Germania-Werft, Kiel	627	00.00.41	24.02.41	16.07.42
	Z 38				628	00.00.41	05.08.41	20.03.43
	Z 39				629	00.00.41	02.12.41	21.08.43
1936B (Mob)	Z 43		17.02.41	Deschimag, Bremen	1029	01.05.42	00.09.43	31.05.44
	Z 44				1030	01.08.42	20.01.44	–
	Z 45				1031	01.09.43	15.04.44	–

Above: Z 2 *Georg Thiele* after her first conversion, with 'box' type bridgework and spray deflectors at the bows.

---

* It was planned originally that Z 23 to Z 36 should all be in service much earlier than eventually was the case. Yard contracts were placed on 1 April 1937 for Z 23 to Z 25 at Deschimag and for Z 26 to Z 28 at Blohm & Voss, Hamburg but these were cancelled following a change of plan in the autumn of 1937. Prewar, Z 29 to Z 39 were intended to enter commission in May 1945 but were brought forward by two to three years.

The series Z 31 to Z 42 inclusive was initially Type 1938B. Contracts were placed for Z 31 to Z 36 on 28 June 1939 and given yard numbers 663 to 668 at Deschimag, Bremen and Wesermünde. Oderwerke Stettin received contracts for the remainder—Z 37 to Z 39 (Yard Nos 822 to 824) on 28 June 1939; and Z 40 to Z 42 (Yard Nos 825 to 827) on 21 July 1939. On 19 Septmber 1939 the plans for the 1938B Type were discarded. The yard contracts for Z 31 to Z 34 at Deschimag were placed as Type 1936A, then cancelled and replaced as Type 1936A (Mob); those for Z 35, Z 36 and Z 43 to Z 45 at Deschimag were placed as Type 1936A (Mob), then cancelled and replaced as Type 1936B (Mob). The yard contracts for Z 37 to Z 39 at Oderwerke, Stettin, were placed as Type 1936A, cancelled, and replaced as Type 1936A (Mob) at Germania-Werft, Kiel. Yard contracts were also placed for Z 40 to Z 42 at Oderwerke, Stettin, as Type 1936A, but these were then cancelled and replaced as Type 1938A/Ac at Germania, Kiel, Z 40 on 19 September 1939 (Yard No 642) and the other two on 13 October 1939 (Yard Nos 643 and 644). Z 40 was then cancelled in June 1940, the other two in October 1940. The 1938A/Ac programme was scrapped on 1 February 1941.

Contracts were placed at Deschimag for five destroyers of the 1936C type, Z 46 and Z 47 on 8 October 1941 (Yard Nos 1071 and 1072) and the other three on 12 June 1943 (Yard Nos 1157, 1158 and 1159). It was decided initially to build Z 46 and Z 47 as Type 1936B (Mob). Because of shortages and air raids neither were launched and the material was broken up on the stocks in 1945. It does not seem that the last three

were laid down. Z 51, a unique Type 1941, was given yard number 1160 and then redesignated Type 1942 under yard number 1109, replacing T 43, a Type 1942 fleet torpedo boat, the building contract being placed on 25 November 1942. Z 51 was the all-diesel oceanic destroyer mentioned earlier in the text.

Types 1936D and E were an alternative project to the 1936A Types should the 15cm twin turret on the forecastle be found impractical; the design plans were destroyed in an air raid. The Type 1945 destroyer was a development of the 1936D and E Types. Types 1937 J I, II, III and IV were project studies, the last two for scaled-up destroyers displacing over 5,400 tons full load.

The Types 1938A and B were projects which laid the foundations for Types 1938Ac and Ad, the design for the *Spähkreuzer* or 'Z Plan' small cruisers. The *Spähkreuzer* were scaled-up destroyers with mixed steam/diesel drive and really belonged in the light cruiser category; none was launched. Mention is made of them as a footnote earlier in the text. The Type 1940 was a project study. Types 1941A to D were drawn up following the cancellation of the *Spähkreuzer* programme, but ultimately the designers went back to the 1936C design. Type 1942A to C, at Deschimag, had originally been the torpedo boats T 44 to T 47 (Yard Nos 1110–1113). The contract was briefly redesignated Type 1941 when Z 51 was ordered on 25 November 1942, then changed to Type 1942.

The Type 1942A was the 'groundwork' for the diesel-driven Z 52 to Z 56, which would have displaced about 3,700 tons full load and have been capable of 38 knots with a huge range. Eventually it was redesignated Type 1942B and C and finally Type 1944. Contracts for these five ships were placed at Deschimag in 1944 (Yard Nos 1110–1114 but cancelled on 6 November 1944.

The Type 1942/43 was a project study for an escort destroyer, while Types 1943, 1943A and 1943A (Mod) were project studies for a small destroyer based on the 1936C design.—Tr.

DESTROYER TYPES

		1934	1934A			1936	
		Z 1–4	Z 5–8	Z 9–13	Z 14–16	Z 17–19	Z20–22
Displacement	Official	1625 tonnes				1811 tonnes	
	Standard	2,619 tonnes (2,223 tons)	2,574 tonnes (2,171 tons)	2,270 tons	2,619 tonnes (2,239 tons)	2,806 tonnes (2,411 tons)	
	Full load	3,156 tons	3,110 tons	3,190 tons	3,165 tons	3,415 tons	
Length	pp	114.0m					
	waterline	116.25m				116.5m	
	overall	119.0m				123.4m	125.1m
Beam		11.31m				11.75m	
Draught		3.82–4.23m				3.77–4.5m	
Freeboard		6.4m				6.6m	
Watertight compartments		15					
Machinery		Turbine drive					
Output		60,000–70,000hp					
Speed		36–38.7 knots					
Fuel*		Benson boilers, 670 tonnes / Wagner boilers, 770 tonnes				787 tonnes	
Range at 19 knots		Benson: 1,530nm / Wagner: 1,900 nm				2,090 nm	
Ship's boats		3				4	
Complement†		10 officers + 315 men‡				10 officers + 313 men‡	

* The fuel calculated on the designed displacement was 299 tonnes for 1934 Types and 310 tonnes for 1936 Type. The amounts were variable between the ships and the values given above are averages.
† During hostilities, ships' companies received a War Supplement of extra crewmen.
‡ Plus a further four officers and nineteen men as flagship.

		1936A				1936A (Mob)
		Z 23–24	Z 25–27	Z 28	Z 29–30	Z 31–34, 37–42
Displacement	standard	2,603 tons	3,079 tons	2,596 tons	2,603 tons	3,083 tons (2,757 tonnes)
	full load	3,605 tons	3,543 tons	3,519 tons	3,597 tons	3,691 tons
Length	waterline	121.9m				
	overall	127.0m				
Beam		12.0m				
Draught		3.92–4.65m	3.91–4.43m	3.72–4.38m	3.92–4.62m	3.92–4.62m

Freeboard		6.6m			
Watertight compartments		15			
Machinery		Turbine drive			
Output		60,000–70,000hp*			
Speed		36–38.5 knots			
Fuel	designed	308 tonnes	321 tonnes	318 tonnes	318 tonnes
	maximum	801 tonnes	769 tonnes	825 tonnes	835 tonnes
Range at 19 knots		2,174nm	2,087nm	2,239nm	2,239nm
Ship's boats		4			
Complement†		11–15 officers + 305–321 men‡	12 officers + 315 men†	11–15 officers + 305–321 men‡	

* Short-term maximum output (Z 29–34) 71.915hp at 388rpm per shaft, (Z 37–42) 75,638hp at 391rpm per shaft.
† During hostilities, ships' companies received a War Supplement of extra crewmen.
‡ Plus a further four officers and nineteen men as flagship.

		1936B (Mob)		1936C	1936B*
		Z 35–36	Z 43–45	Z 46–50	Z 31–42
Displacement	standard	2,954 tonnes (2,519 tons)		3,071 tonnes (2,636 tons0	2,200 tonnes (1,969 tons)
	full load	3,542 tons		3,683 tons	2,747 tons
Length	waterline	121.5m		121.44m	108.0m
	overall	127.0m		126.2m	117.0m
Beam		12.0m		12.2m	11.3m
Draught		3.54–4.32m		3.62–4.45m	3.19–4.03m
Freeboard		6.6m			6.75m
Watertight compartments		15			13
Machinery		Turbine drive			
Output		60,000–70,000hp†			50,000hp
Speed		36–36.5 knots		37.5 knots	36 knots
Fuel	designed	341 tonnes	318 tonnes	340 tonnes	423 tonnes
	maximum	835 tonnes	825 tonnes	822 tonnes	
Range at 19 knots		2,600nm	2,950nm	2,500nm	3,350nm
Ship's boats		4			2
Complement		11–15 officers + 305–321 men			8 officers + 231 men

* Alternative sketch design for Type 1936A in case of unavailability of 15cm twin turret.
† Short-term maximum output (Z 35–36) 71,510hp at 390rpm per shaft.

WEIGHT GROUPINGS (tonnes) (after Witte)

Type		1934	1936	1936A	1936B	1936C
Length (m)	waterline	116.5	120.0	121.9	121.44	121.44
Beam (m)		11.36	11.75	12.0	12.0	12.15
Freeboard (m)		6.4	6.6	6.6	6.6	6.05
Draught (m)	designed	3.72	3.67	3.95	3.83	3.91
Engine output (hp)	maximum	60,000	70,000	70,000	70,000	70,000
Building steel		ST 52	ST 52	ST 52	ST 52	ST 52
Hull		820	943	1,064	1,045	1,047
Main machinery with equipment		758	901	958	983	986
Aux. machinery with equipment		193	175	177	140	169
Guns		106	106	174	116	194
Torpedo tubes		38	38	50	43	50
Mine launchers		5	5	15	13	2
General equipment		58	58	58	54	55
Nautical equipment		5	2	5	4	2
Rigging			3			
Wireless equipment etc		1	1	1	16	7
Ballast and stabiliser installation		–	–	–	2	2
Empty ship, with equipment		1,984	2,232	2,499	2,416	2,514
Gun ammunition		53	53	82	73	41
Torpedoes		14	14	6	4	6
Mines			5	56	8	6
Consumables		6	6	6	13	11
Crew		24	24	24	24	24
Crew effects		16	17	17	16	16
Provisions		10	10	10	5	10
Standard displacement (excluding fresh water)		2,112	2,361	2,650	2,559	2,678
Drinking water		22	23	23	9	9
Washing water		27	27	27	14	14
Feedwater		70	76	76	31	37
Fuel oil		285	222	293	323	313
Diesel fuel		5	5	5	8	9
Lubricating oil		8	9	9	10	11
Designed displacement		2,529	2,723	3,083	2,954	3,071
Feedwater		20	20	20	27	25
Fuel oil		429	444	491	470	500
Diesel fuel		11	13	13	12	13
Lubricating oil		13	14	14	15	16
Reserve fresh water		40	35	35	35	35
Full load displacement		3,042	3,249	3,656	3,513	3,660

CONSTRUCTION WEIGHT GROUPINGS TYPE 1936A (after Witte)

		tonnes		%				tonnes		%
M I	Turbines, inc. drive gear	170.04	=	17.8		M II	Auxiliary drive machinery	154.62		
	Condensers	66.38	=	7.0			Equipment in M II	3.65		
	Shafts	53.0	=	5.6			Oil and water in M II	19.38		
	Propellers	13.63	=	1.4		M II	Total	177.65	=	18.6*
	Pumps and superchargers	60.29	=	6.2						
	Pipework	128.26	=	13.5		*Or 16.4% of S				
	Smoke extractors	22.69	=	2.4						
	Equipment in M I etc	37.27	=	3.9		Percentage of double-bottom in relation to ship's length: 47				
	Boilers and instrumentation	279.37	=	29.2						
	Oil and water in M I	123.37	=	12.9						
M I	Total	954.35	=	100.0						

WEIGHTS (TONNES) AND PERCENTAGE WEIGHTS OF SUB-GROUPS (after Witte)

Type	1934	1936	1936A	1936B (original)	approx %
Length (m)　　　　　　waterline	116.5	120.0	121.9	108.0	
Beam	11.36	11.75	12.0	11.3	
Watertight compartments	15	15	15	15	
Crew	315	313	321	231	
Weights (tonnes)					
Keel and frames	89.3	108.6	122.3	89.3	14
Stem, rudder, shaft bearers	29.2	27.7	28.4	24.6	4
Heavy bulkheads	94.3	119.8	130.8	119.0	14
Inner bottom and engine bearers	52.4	69.2	75.0	58.5	8
Decks	136.5	174.6	195.1	125.7	21
Outer plating	135.7	147.2	160.4	120.0	20
Light bulkheads, masts, protective plating	11.8	13.6	17.1	9.2	2
Deckhouses etc	47.0	51.4	53.4	37.2	6
Stanchions, ammunition lockers, chain lockers, supports	35.5	38.1	43.0	29.1	5
Bridges and gangways	9.9	8.4	9.8	4.0	1
Miscellaneous	24.6	36.2	57.7	27.4	5
S I = Ship construction	657.2	794.8	839.0	644.2	83
Doors, fittings, handrails, ladders etc	10.1	10.1	10.2	7.2	11
Water fittings	33.2	41.1	41.1	31.9	39
Equipment for helm, anchors, boats	21.5	23.7	23.7	18.5	23
Equipment for ventilation, washrooms, etc	11.9	13.4	13.5	10.6	15
Weapons equipment	25.4	7.6	9.5	6.8	12
S II = Metalworkers	102.1	95.9	98.0	75.4	10.9
Officers' cabins	6.4	6.0	7.0	4.5	19

Crews	14.9	9.8	15.7	6.5	37
Storage rooms, etc	13.7	13.1	16.3	10.8	44
S III = Carpenters	35.0	28.9	39.0	21.8	3.3
S IV = Painters	26.2	23.1	34.0	18.8	2.8
S (S I–IV) = Ship excluding Constructor's Reserve	820.5	942.7	1,064.0	760.0	100.0

FORM VALUES (after Witte)

Type		1934	1936	1936A
Freeboard (m)	amidships	2.68	2.9	–
	forward	–	–	–
Length:beam ratio		10.25	10.21	–
Beam:draught ratio		3.05	33.18	3.02
Length:freeboard ratio		18.2	18.2	–
Longitudinal prismatic coefficient (δ)		0.515	0.513	0.514
Midships section coefficient (β)		0.816	0.84	–
Coefficient of fineness of waterplane (α)		0.724	0.734	–

The longitudinal coefficient is the ratio of the volume of displacement to the volume of a prism having a length equal to the length between perpendiculars and a cross-sectional area equal to the midships sectional area. The fineness of waterplane coefficient is the ratio of the area of the waterplane to the area of its circumscribing rectangle. The midships section coefficient is the ratio of the midships section area to the draught and beam extreme amidships.

METACENTRIC HEIGHTS (GM) (after Witte)

Type	Displacement	50% supplement
1934/1934A	0.79m	0.6m
1936	0.96m	0.81m
1936A	0.88m 0.78m 0.83m respectively	

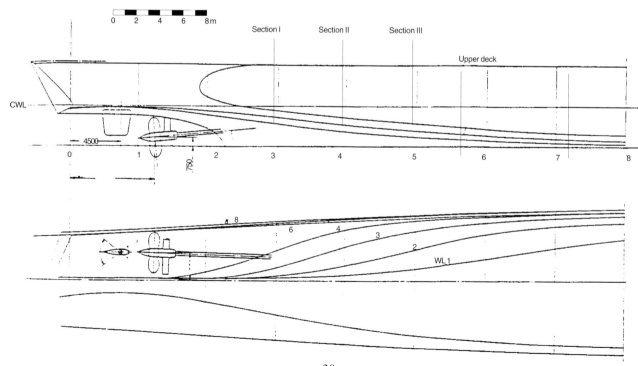

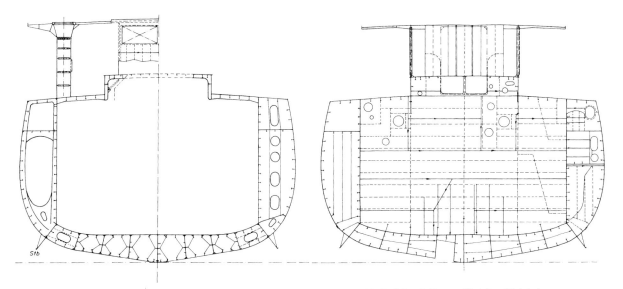

Above: Z 35: Main frame (after Hadeler).

Above: Z 35: Bulkhead, Frame 54 (after Hadeler).
Left and below: Type 1936A: Lines and frames (after Hadeler).

Type 36A: Dimensions

Length (designed waterline):	121.5m
Length (between perpendiculars):	120.0m
Beam:	12.0m
Freeboard:	6.6m
Draught (designed):	3.3m

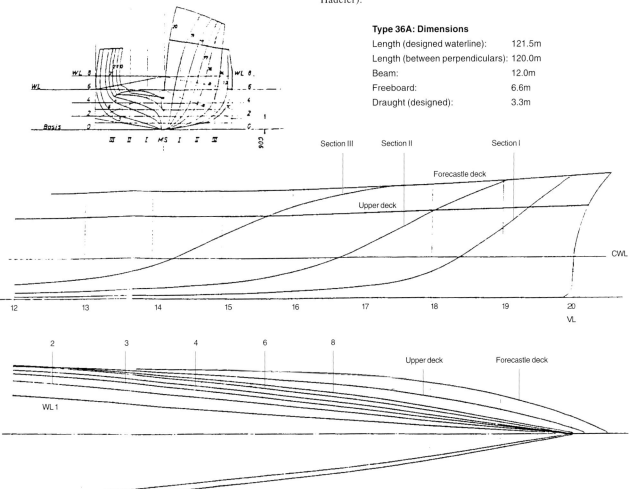

Differences, Modifications, Conversions

During their intensive trials the four Type 1934 destroyers manifested so many weaknesses—especially basic design weaknesses—that their relegation from Fleet to training duties was seriously discussed from an early stage, although the debate was abandoned on the outbreak of war. The naval reconstruction plan taking effect in 1939 foresaw Z 1 *Leberecht Maass* being replaced by Z 29 as *Führer der Torpedoboote* (FdT) flagship on 1 April 1941. The creation of the post of *Führer der Zerstörer* (FdZ) restored Z 1 to her flag role, although she was now listed for attachment to the torpedo school as a training ship from 1 October 1941. Z 2 *Georg Thiele* and Z 3 *Max Schultz* were to be removed from Fleet duty between 1 July and 1 November 1941 for the torpedo-school training role, and Z 4 *Richard Beitzen* would be attached to the *Flugzeugträgergeschwader* (Aircraft Carrier Squadron) from 1 August 1942. These three vessels would be replaced in front-line service by Z 37–39.

Although there is a certain uniformity in the outward appearance among the destroyer types, there were many differences, large and small, visible in peacetime and emphasised as the war progressed. They are so numerous as to defy comprehensive description, and only the most important differences, modifications, conversions and peculiarities are listed here.

Types 1934/1934A

Sea trials showed that because of excessive topweight the freeboard was inadequate. For this reason the general stability was borderline and poor longitudinally, while the decks shipped a lot of water. In the course of scheduled refits after the destroyers entered commission, the decks and inner bottom were strengthened and the anti-roll equipment was unshipped and replaced by stabiliser keels. From 1935–36 a wooden wedge was fitted at the stern abaft the rudder, although this was removed between 1940 and 1942. In 1938–39 a bow protection device with an extensible pole was installed, and at the same time the foreship was length-

ened by about a metre and raised by 50cm. On Z 7 and subsequent vessels the *Totholz* (deadwood) added to the lateral plan below the waterline was increased in order to improve the turning circle.

On Z 1–4 the hull form forward below the waterline had a quadrant profile either side and from 1938 a spray deflector was added to the ships' sides between the anchor cluse and No 1 gun. The thickness of the deflector added to Z 2 in 1937–38 was broader than in the other three units. The first half-rounded bridges were made square during conversion work (this applied also to Z 5–7).

Z 5–16 had a more angular form below the waterline and the frames forward had a more pronounced outward flare. Two large-diameter steam pipes were fitted to the forward surface of the after funnel and Z 5–8 and 9–13 received a thinner steam pipe to the rear of the fore-funnel. Z 14–16 had two thick, and between them four thin, steam pipes on the forward surface of the after funnel.

Between 1939 and 1941 the destroyerts of this type had a degaussing coil installed above the waterline. From 1940 the searchlight platform on the mainmast was removed, although the bracing struts for the mast remained. In 1941–42 a 2cm quadruple mounting was installed on the after deckhouse.

On Z 4–6, Z 10 and Z 14–15 the cowl of the fore-funnel was reduced in height by between 1.2 and 0.7m and the after funnel cowl by 0.7. From 1944, to enable the huge FuMO radar antenna rotate, the lower section of the foremast aboard Z 5, Z 10 and Z 15 was removed and replaced by a 'goalpost', what remained of the foremast mast being fitted to the 'crossbar'.

During the course of the war, Z 5 and Z 15 received an 'Atlantic' bow with anchor cluses, and No 3 12.7cm gun was landed in favour of a new platform for the 3.7cm AA mounting. The mainmast was brought forward and given two bracing struts. In 1944 radar ranging equipment was installed abaft the after funnel, replacing the searchlights there on Z 5, Z6 and Z 10.

Type 1936

Six large-diameter and one or two small-diameter steam pipes were fitted to the surface of the forefunnel of Z 17–22. A slightly modified arrangement of the propellers improved the ships' turning circle. The problem of topweight that afflicted the earlier destroyers was also apparent in the Type 1936.

In 1939 a forward-projecting adjustable pole was fitted at the forefoot for the bow protection gear. Except in Z 20 *Karl Galster*, which retained it for experimental purposes, the anti-roll equipment was abandoned and replaced by stabiliser keels. Z 20–22 were refitted with an 'Atlantic' bow, and in 1942 bracing struts were added to the foremast aboard Z 20 and FuMO radar was installed on top of the bridge and abaft the after funnel. A degaussing coil was added below the level of the main deck and the forecastle deck.

Types 1936A, 1936A (Mob) and 1936B (Mob)

The fitting of the 15cm twin turret (adding about 65 tonnes topside) resulted in the Type 1936A destroyers being poor sea boats and subject to speed restrictions in heavy seas, and as a result of complaints by commanders, the Type 1936B (Mob) reverted to the original 12.7cm armament. Two rudders in the propeller stream gave better turning qualities, wooden add-ons below the waterline assisting in course-keeping. A different arrangement of bunkers and tanks provided better stability, and the restrictions on fuel consumption (from the point of view of stability) were lifted, despite the remaining problem of the twin turret. On the other hand the redesign of the frames forward brought no benefit. The pole at the foot of the stem was removed from Z 25 and Z 28 as the war progressed, and Z 25 received a modified, more rounded stem.

Z 25, Z 28–30, Z 33–36 and Z 43 were fitted with FuMO radar, and a second FuMO set was installed aboard Z 25, Z 28–30 and Z 33–34 in place of the searchlight abaft the after funnel. Differing tripod masts and funnel caps were evident among the type. Z 25 and Z 28 had temporarily, Z 39 permanently and Z 38 finally a second degaussing coil along the forecastle forward, although on Z 39 this encircled the ship, covered at the level of the main deck by the spray deflector. Until 1943 Z 30 had flying bridges above her torpedo tubes.

Right: Z 5 Paul Jacobi (far left), with Z 29, Z 8 Bruno Heinemann and Z 4 Richard Beitzen, at Hoplaelven near Trondheim, 17 January 1942. All four have radar.

On Z 28 the mainmast was originally at the aft end of the enlarged deckhouse erected for the FdZ staff.

Some destroyers had distinguishing emblems: on the bridge face Z 30 displayed a four-leafed clover and Z 38 a black panther in flight with a rolled umbrella beneath its armpit. Z 39 carried the Greek royal coat of arms on the side of the 15cm twin turret, while on the side of the Z 43's bridge was a springing jaguar.

Weapons

All the destroyers were fitted with eight 53.3cm torpedo tubes in two quadruple sets, to port and starboard of the after funnel. Up to sixty mines were carried—the Type 1936B (Mob) carried only 32–36 mines—along with paravane-type minesweeping gear for the ship's own protection. All units had depth charges and throwers.

In November 1944 it was decided to upgrade the ships' anti-aircraft battery in a gradual programme, by, for example, fitting two additional 3.7cm twins at the level of No 2 gun forward of the bridge, two more twins replacing the singles amidships and three further twins replacing No 3 gun; 3.7cm-calibre guns would supplant the 2cm singles aboard destroyers fitted with a 15cm main armament, and additional light AA mountings would be positioned on the bridge.

As the borders of the Reich became increasingly compressed, the programme could only be partially completed. Only a few destroyers were re-armed fully in accordance with the plan, and the additions are described below, though others acquired extra mountings during dockyard refits and fitted them according to the 'Barbara' instructions.

Armament

Types 1934, 1934A

Five SK 12.7cm L/45 in single gunhouses, two forward three aft.* No 3 gun aboard Z 5 *Paul Jacobi*, Z 10 *Hans Lody* and Z 15 *Erich Steinbrinck* was unshipped in favour of additional anti-aircraft guns in 1944. As her main armament for a few months after commissioning in 1938, Z 8 *Bruno Heinemann* carried four 'Utof' quick-firing 15cm on a U-boat/T-boat gun mount. The AA battery consisted of four 3.7cm and six (increased in 1942 to eight) 2cm. Under the 'Barbara' programme Z 5 *Paul Jacobi* was equipped with six more 3.7cm in three twin mountings located two abaft No 2 gun, two abaft the after funnel and two replacing No 3 gun. Nine extra 2cm barrels were added, two twins on the forecastle deck either side of the bridge platform together with a 2cm quadruple and a single on the deckhouse roof. Z 10 *Hans Lody* had additional 3.7cms as for *Paul Jacobi*, but two 2cm twins probably replaced two singles as well. Z 15 *Erich Steinbrinck* was given additional 3.7cms as for *Paul Jacobi*, plus an extra twin on a platform enlarged for a quadruple; two 2cm singles were positioned on the forecastle deck either side of the bridge and a 2cm quadruple was placed on the deckhouse aft. Z 6 *Theodor Riedel* ended her war career with fourteen and Z 14 *Friedrich Ihn* with eighteen 2cm AA.

Type 1936

Five SK 12.7cm L/45 in single gunhouses; four 3.7cm; and six (later nine) 2cm. Z 20 *Karl Galster* was the only survivor of the type after Narvik. The outline sketch (q.v.) of the vessel shows a quadruple AA mounting on the after deckhouse, and additional AA weapons grouped around the after funnel and bridge.

Type 1936A

Upon commissioning each destroyer had four TK 15cm L/48 guns in single gunhouses, one forward and three

---

* 'L/' plus a numeral is the barrel length expressed in multiples of the calibre. Thus '15cm L/48' gives a barrel length of 720cm.

aft, but from 1942–43 the forward gunhouse aboard Z 23–25 was unshipped and replaced by one TK 15cm twin turret, increasing the number of 15cm barrels to five. Z 29 was similarly converted under the 1944 'Barbara' rearmament programme. The AA battery comprised originally four, later five and from 1942–43 twelve 3.7cm; and six or seven, and from 1942–43 up to sixteen 2cm. Z 28 and Z 30 had ten of each calibre, while Z 30 later had seven 3.7cm and fourteen 2cm. 'Barbara' additions for Z 25 were two 3.7cm flak twins on the deckhouse roof abaft the turret forward and four 3.7cm singles, two either side of the after funnel and two on the superstructure abreast No 3 gun; sixteen 2cm barrels were also added, two flak twins on both sides of the 3.7cm mounting forward and both sides of the bridge, plus two quadruples on an enlarged platform replacing No 3 gun. Z 29 received twenty additional 2cm, nine more 3.7cm and two 5.5cm experimental guns. Two 3.7cm singles were placed either side of No 3 gun and a 2cm quadruple and a 3.7-cm single were installed on an enlarged platform close to No 3 gun. Two 3.7cm twins replaced the 2cm guns either side of the after funnel, and the 2cm battery was augmented further by two quadruples in front of the bridge structure and three twins, one each on the main deck aft, on the forecastle deck and either side of the bridge. There were probably two 5.5cm prototypes at the midships 3.7cm position.

Type 1936A (Mob)

The standard fit was one TK 15cm twin turret forward and three TK 15cm L/48 in single gunhouses aft, although Z 31 initially had four TK 15cm L/48 in four single gunhouses, one forward three aft. The AA battery consisted of four 3.7cm and ten 2cm. In the 'Barbara' programme Z 39 received fourteen additional 3.7cm guns, two twins forward of the bridge, one twin either side of, and two singles on, a platform abaft the after funnel and two more twins alongside the former of No 3 gun position. Two 2cm twins were located either side of the bridge and two quadruples and two singles on the extended deckhouse near No 3 gun position, making fourteen 2cm barrels in all. Z 33 received no 'Barbara' allotment and made do in 1945 with anti-aircraft weapons from the wreck of the heavy cruiser *Lützow* (ex *Deutschland*), No 3 gun being unshipped and mounted on Z 34. Her 3.7cm suite at the end of the war was ten, two twin mountings before the bridge, two more on a platform amidships and one on the No 3 gun position. One quadruple, two twins and four singles made up the 2-cm battery. Z 34 carried one, and possibly two more, 4cm Bofors guns and two RaG 8.6cm

rocket launchers in addition to six 3.7cm and eighteen 2cm. Z 38 had latterly six 3.7cm and sixteen 2cm. Z 31 ultimately had fourteen 3.7cm and twelve 2cm; her 15cm twin turret forward was destroyed by enemy action in January 1945 and replaced by an SK 10.5cm L/45 in a single gunhouse.

Type 1936B (Mob)
The gun armament comprised five SK 12.7cm L/45 in single gunhouses, four 3.7cm and fourteen to sixteen 2cm.

WEAPONS AS PERCENTAGES OF FULL LOAD DISPLACEMENT (after Witte)

Type	Main armament	Torpedoes	Percentages		
			Guns	Torpedo gear	Mine gear
1936	Five 12.7cm (5 × 1)	Eight 53.3cm (2 × 4)	4.89	1.6	0.31
1936A	Five 15cm (1 × 2, 3 × 1)	Eight 53.3cm (2 × 4)	7.0	1.53	0.57

Data

15cm TK C/36 on C/36 single Lafette mounting

Manufacturer:	Rheinmetall/Borsig	
Gun:	Calibre	149.1mm
	Muzzle velocity	835ms
	Barrel length	L/48 (7,165mm)
	Bore length	L/45.7 (6,815mm)
	Designed gas pressure	3,000kg/m²
	Barrel life	1,000 rounds
	Recoil force at 0° elevation	58,000kg
	Length of grooving	5,587mm
	Type of grooving	Cubic parabola, 45/30cal
	No of grooves	44
	Weight of gun plus breech	8,564kg
	Maximum range	21,950m
Ammunition:	Weight of projectile	45.3kg
	Weight of powder	6kg
	With nose fuse	3.89kg
	Type of powder	Fp 02
	Length of projectile	700kg
	With nose fuse	678.9mm
	Weight of cartridge	23.5kg
	With nose fuse	24kg
	Length of cartridge	865mm
	Fuse type	Time S/30, impact C/27

Mounting:	Elevation/depression	+30°/–10°
	Training	±360° = 720°
	Manual elevation, 1 turn handwheel	1° 52'
	Manual training, 1 turn handwheel	3°
	Weight of cradle	1,730kg (from 1942; earlier 1,500kg)
	Weight of gun bed	2,400kg
	Weight of pedestal	3,885kg
	Weight of sights	650kg
	Weight of electric drive	450kg
	Weight of shield	3,185kg
	Total weight	16,100kg
Armour:	Front	10mm
	Sides	6mm
	Roof	6mm

Variations for C/38 twin mounting (turntable mounting, 15cm turret:

	Barrel elevation	+65°/–10°
	Manual elevation, 1 turn handwheel	1° 30'
	Manual training, 1 turn handwheel	4° 30' or 3° 45'
	Weight of cradle	4,300kg
	Weight of pedestal	22,250kg

	Weight of sights	650kg
	Weight of electric drive	2,400kg
	Weight of shield	13,750kg
	Total weight	60,400kg
Armour:	Front	30mm
	Sides	20mm
	Roof	20mm
	Rear	5mm

12.7cm C/34 on C/34 centre pivot mounting

Manufacturer:	Rheinmetall	
Gun:	Calibre	128mm
	Muzzle velocity	830ms
	Barrel length	L/45 (5760mm)
	Bore length	L/42.5 (5,430mm)
	Barrel life	1,650 rounds
	Recoil force at 0° elevation	38,000kg
	Length of grooving	4,536mm
	Type of grooving	Cubic parabola, 35/30cal
	No of grooves	40
	Weight of gun plus breech	3,645kg
	Maximum range	17,400m
Ammunition:	Weight of projectile	28kg
	Weight of powder	8.5kg
	Type of powder	Fp 02
	Length of projectile	564.7mm
	Weight of cartridge	16kg
	Length of cartridge	732mm
	Propellant	RPC/32
	Fuse (nose)	C/27
	Fuse (nose + time)	S/60
Mounting:	Elevation/depression	+30°/–10°
	Training	±360° = 720°
	Manual elevation, 1 turn handwheel	2.95°
	Manual training, 1 turn handwheel	3.08°
	Weight of cradle	1,320kg
	Weight of gun bed	2,605kg
	Weight of sights	530kg
	Weight of electric drive	260kg
	Weight of shield	1,870kg
	Total weight	10,220kg
Armour:	Front	8mm
	Sides	8mm
	Roof	8mm

10.5cm SK C/32 on C/32 centre pivotal mounting

Manufacturer:	Rheinmetall/Borsig	
Gun:	Calibre	105mm
	Muzzle velocity	780ms
	Barrel length	L/45 (4,740mm)
	Bore length	L/42 (4,400mm)
	Designed gas pressure	2,850kg/cm^2
	Barrel life	4,100 rounds
	Recoil force at 0° elevation	22,600kg
	Weight of gun plus breech	1,765kg
	Maximum range	15,175m
Ammunition:	Weight of projectile	15.1kg
	Weight of powder	3.8kg
	Length of projectile	459mm
	Weight of cartridge	24kg
	Length of cartridge	1,050mm
Mounting:	Barrel elevation	+70°/–10°
	Manual elevation, 1 turn handwheel	3°
	Manual training, 1 turn handwheel	3°
	Weight of cradle	655kg
	Weight of gun bed	2,100kg
	Weight of sights	350kg
	Weight of electric drive	210kg
	Weight of shield	1,670kg
	Total weight	6,750kg
Armour:	Front	12mm
	Sides	4mm
	Roof	4mm

3.7cm SK C/30 on C/30 twin mounting

Gun:	Calibre	37mm
	Muzzle velocity	1,000ms
	Muzzle energy	38 megatonnes
	Barrel length	L/83 (3,074mm)
	Bore length	L/80 (2,960mm)
	Designed gas pressure	3,450kg/cm^2
	Barrel life	7,500 rounds
	Recoil force at 0° elevation	1,000kg
	Length of grooving	2,554mm
	Type of grooving	Cubic parabola, 50/35cal
	No of grooves	16
	Weight of gun plus breech	243kg
	Maximum range:	
	Horizontal	8,500m
	Vertical	6,800m
	Tracer	4,800m
Ammunition:	Weight of projectile	0.742kg
	Weight of powder	0.365kg
	Type of powder	Fp 02
	Length of projectile	162mm
	Weight of cartridge	0.97kg
	Length of cartridge	381mm
	Propellant	RPC/32
	Fuse	C/30 (C/34 for tracer C/34)
	Tracer burn time	12sec
	Rate of fire:	
	Theoretical	160rds/min
	In practice	80rds/min
Mounting:	Barrel elevation	+85°/–10°
	Training	±360° = 720°
	Manual elevation, 1 turn handwheel	3°

	Manual training,	
	1 turn handwheel	4°
	Weight of cradle	152.5kg
	Weight of moving mass	243kg
	Weight of gun bed	2,162kg
	Weight of base	71kg
	Weight of sights	87kg
	Weight of electric drive	630kg
	Total weight	3,670kg

3.7cm M/42 on LM/42 mounting
Manufacturer: Rheinmetall/Borsig

Gun	Calibre	37mm
	Muzzle velocity	
	(HE shell)	850ms
	Muzzle energy	24.4 megatonnes
	Barrel length	L/69 (2,568mm)
	Barrel life	7,000 rounds
	Recoil force at 0°	
	elevation	1,240kg
	Length of grooving	2,289mm
	Type of grooving	Constant radius, 7° = 25.6cal
	No of grooves	16
	Weight of gun plus	
	breech	109kg
Ammunition:	Weight of projectile	
	(HE shell)	0.61kg
	Weight of cartridge	0.51kg
	Total weight	1.3kg
	Fuse type	Nose fuse 40
	Fuse ignition	Double fuse case
	Magazine contents	8 rounds

3.7cm 43/M
Gun:	Calibre	37mm
	Muzzle velocity:	
	HE shell	870ms
	AP shell	770ms
	AP 40 shell	1,150ms
	Muzzle energy	21.8 megatonnes
	Barrel length	L/57 (2,109mm)
	Designed gas pressure	2,900kg/cm^2
	Barrel life	8000 rounds
	Recoil force at 0°	
	elevation	1,500kg
	Length of grooving	1,838mm
	Type of grooving	Kupa 3°/5°
	No of grooves	20
	Weight of gun plus	
	breech	127kg
	Maximum range:	
	Horizontal	6,400m
	Vertical	4,800m
Ammunition:	Weight of projectile:	
	HE shell	0.625kg
	AP shell	0.685kg
	Total weight	1.5kg

	Total length	368mm
	Detonator	Nose fuse
	Fuse type	Double fuse case
	Magazine contents	8 rounds
Mounting:	Barrel elevation	+90°/–10°
	Train	360°
	Weight	c. 1,900kg

2cm C/30 on single-mounted C/30
Manufacturer: Rheinmetall

Gun:	Calibre	20mm
	Muzzle velocity	835ms
	Barrel length	L/65 (1,300mm)
	Bore length	L/65 (1,300mm)
	Designed gas pressure	2,800kg/cm^2
	Barrel life	22,000 rounds
	Recoil force at 0°	
	elevation	250kg
	Length of grooving	720mm
	Weight of gun plus	
	breech	64kg
	Maximum range:	
	Horizontal	4,900m
	Vertical	3,700m
Ammunition	Weight of projectile	0.134kg
	Weight of powder	0.0395kg
	Length of projectile	78.5mm
	Rate of fire:	
	Theoretical	280rds/min
	In practice	120rds/min
Mounting:	Barrel elevation	+85°/–11°
	Weight of moving parts	43kg
	Weight of mounting	
less sights		282kg
	Total weight	420kg

2cm C/38 on C/30 mounting
Gun:	Details as for 2cm C/30 except:	
	Recoil force at 0°	
	elevation	290kg
	Weight of gun plus	
	breech	420kg
Ammunition:	Details as for 2cm C/30 except:	
	Rate of fire	
	Theoretical	480rds/min
	In practice	220rds/min

2cm Flak 35 on C/38 quadruple mounting
Manufacturer: Mauser/Rheinmetall

Gun:	4 × 2cm C/38	
Ammunition:	Details as for 2cm C/38 except:	
	Rate of fire	
	Theoretical	1,800rds/min
	In practice	880rds/min
Mounting:	Weight of moving parts	410kg
	Weight of mounting	
	less sights	828kg
	Weight of sights	96.6kg
	Weight of electric drive	500kg
	Total weight	2,150kg

4cm Flak 28 (Bofors) L/60

This weapon was originally a 1924 Krupp development. The *Reichswehr* was not interested, and the gun was apparently sold to Sweden.

Manufacturer:	Krupp (from about 1928)	
Gun:	Calibre	40mm
	Muzzle velocity	854ms
	Barrel length	L/65.225
	(2,249mm)	
	Barrel length with flash suppressor and ground tackle	3,700mm
	Length of extension	1,910mm
	Length of grooves	1,932mm
	No of grooves	16
	Type of grooves	Ascending right-hand spin
	Maximum range:	
	Horizontal	11,850m
	Vertical	6,200m (in 11.5sec)
	Rate of fire:	
	Theoretical	240rds/min
	In practice	120–150rds/min

Recoil loader, falling block wedge breech, liquid brake, spring feed, screw-in muzzle-flash suppressor

Mounting:	Single	
	Elevation/depression	+90°/–5°
	Traverse	360° to either side
Ammunition:	Four-round feed	
	Type	HE or tracer
	Weight of explosive	45g
	Type	Trotyl
	Length of projectile	365mm

5.5cm Flak/Gerät 58

This fully automatic, air-cooled gun was a gas-pressure loader and was manufactured in land and naval versions. It was intended for the Type 1942C destroyers; some prototypes were completed, and according to unconfirmed reports one

Below: The early sketches of the Gerät 58 (5.5cm Flak) released by the *Marinewaffenamt* (Naval Ordnance Office) on 9 October 1944.

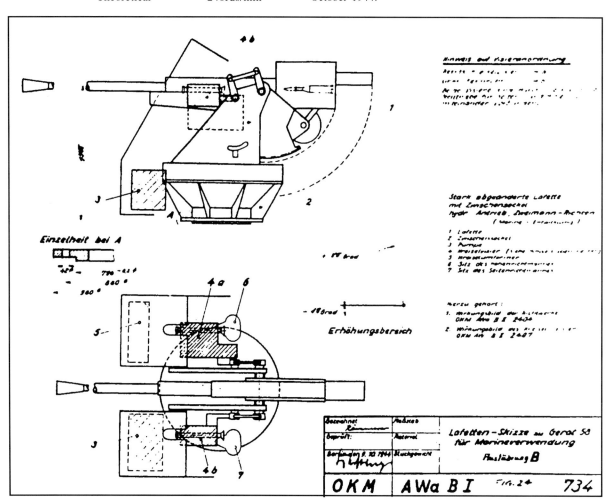

or another of them were tested aboard Z 29. Further details are not known.

The gun was triaxially or even quadriaxially stabilised, and it had the same twin mounting as that used by the Army. The magazine held five rounds and the rate of fire was between 120 and 150 rounds per minute. Single-round firing was also possible. The following data are theoretical.

Gun:	Calibre	55mm
	Weight of gun	650kg
	Weight of barrel	350kg
	Length overall	6,000mm
	Length of barrel	4,220mm
	Length of grooving	3,750mm
	No of grooves	20 (depth 0.75mm, breadth 4.34mm)
	Spin	Increasing towards muzzle
	Weight of projectile	2kg
	Weight of charge	1.1kg
	Length of projectile	665mm
	Muzzle velocity	1,020ms
	Explosive content	25%
	Total weight of salvo (full magazine)	5.3kg
	Flight times:	
	Range 1,000m	1.1sec
	Range 2,000m	2.5sec
	Range 3,000m	4.34sec
	Range 4,000m	6.75sec

Torpedoes

The standard torpedo was the G7a.

	Calibre	533mm
	Drive	Compressed air
	Warhead	
	Range:	
	At 30 knots	15,000m
	At 40 knots	5,000m
	At 45 knots	4,500m

Mines

The standard mines were the EMC (contact) and EMF (magnetic) types.

	EMC	EMF
Explosive	300kg	350kg
Diameter	c. 1.1m	c. 1.1m
Overall height (inc regulator	2.1m	–
Thickness of casing	3mm steel alloy	7mm aluminium
Weight plus anchor seating	1,110–1,300kg	–
Normal anchor-warp length and thickness	100m × 12.5mm ∅ 200m × 11.5mm ∅ 500m × 8mm ∅	200m × 11mm ∅ 300m × 9.5mm ∅ 500m × 8mm ∅
Detonators:	7 horns	–
Normal depth setting	3–6m	12–15m
Detonation by	Contact	Magnetic field

Depth Charges

Two types were normally carried—WBF (*Wasserbombe F*) and WBG.

	WBF	WBG
Weight of explosive	60kg	350kg
Total weight	139kg	180kg
Used for depths to	15, 25, 45, 60 and 75m	20, 35, 50, 70, 90 and 120m
Minimum depth	6m	6m
Effective areas:	Destructive zone 0–5.6m	
	Danger zone 5.6–17m	
	Damage zone 17–28m	
	Safety zone Beyond 28m	
Shortest release interval	–	30m

8.6cm Rocket Launcher (Abschußgerät M42/43)

Launcher:	Calibre	86mm
	Length of launcher	c. 1270mm
	Weight of launcher	c. 27kg
	Weight of mounting	c. 36kg
	Train	360°
	Maximum elevation	90°
Ammunition:	8.6cm rocket casing (HE)	
	Weight	c. 8.4kg
	Length	417mm
	Propellant	Black powder
	Range	400, 600 or 800m
	Warhead	Corresponding to an 8.8cm shell

Guidance equipment (parachute-/wire-steered) R.Dg.400/R.Dg.1000:

	Weight	5kg (R.Dg.400) 5.3kg (R.Dg.1000)
	Length	392mm (R.Dg.400) 426mm (R.Dg.1000)
	Propellant	Black powder
	Range	400 or 1,000m
	Deployment altitude	300–400m (R.Dg.400) 800–1,000m (R.Dg.1000)
Flare:	Weight	4.3kg
	Length	392mm
	Propellant	Black powder
	Range:	
	Horizontal	1,100m
	Vertical	350m at 40° elevation
	Burn period	30sec

Fire Control and Sensors

The standard fire direction instrument for the 15cm and 12.7cm main armament was a 4m rangefinder located one on the bridge superstructure and another on the after deckhouse. A 1.25m rangefinder served the 3.7cm anti-aircraft guns and a portable 70cm unit was used for the 2cm AA. Rangefinding radar (FuMO) was used in combination with gunlaying optics for running calculations of aircraft altitude and bearing. The fire control units functioned independently. They were electrically driven and triaxially stabilised against ship movement.

In 1942 the Hazemeyer/Hengelo company offered the OKM a quadraxial stabilised chassis for the 5.5cm AA gun. The system was designed for multi-purpose batteries aboard battleships, cruisers and destroyers; for various reasons, in automatic AA weapons the quadraxial-based gun is the most advantageous, the fourth axis being the vertical. The project was forced through in combination with SAM and Rheinmetall, but although a few prototypes were tested it came to nothing as a result of the winding-down of research projects towards the end of the war.

Locating Devices

Destroyers were equipped with *S-Anlagen* (hydrophone systems), the 36 receiver microphones being arrayed on either side of the foreship below the waterline.

Radar

The individual radar sets, installations and aerials were of the standard Kriegsmarine type, but there were variations between destroyers. The external location of radar 'mattresses' was as follows:

Z 4 *Richard Beitzen*: After mid-1941: FuMO 24/25 and FuMO 63 Hohentwiel

Z 5 *Paul Jacobi*: In 1941 a non-rotatable FuMO 21 aerial, 4m × 2m, on bridge. In 1944 this was replaced by FuMO 24/25 to allow rotation–the foremast being remodelled into a 'goalpost'-type mast–and FuMO 63 Hohentwiel replaced the searchlight on the after funnel. FuMB Metox was also installed.

Z 6 *Theodor Riedel*: A FuMO 21 non-rotatable aerial on the bridge was later replaced by FuMO 24/25. From 1944 a FuMO 63 ireplaced the searchlight on the after funnel and FuMB Metox was installed

Z 10 *Hans Lody*: In 1944 the foremast was rebuilt as a 'goalpost' for a 6m × 2m rotatable FuMO 24/25 aerial. FuMO 63 Hohentwiel replaced the searchlight on the after funnel and FuMB Metox was installed.

Z 14 *Friedrich Ihn*: After April 1941 the ship was fitted with FuMO 24/25 and FuMO 63 Hohentwiel. FuMB Metox was also added.

Z 15 *Erich Steinbrinck*: In 1944 the foremast was converted to a 'goalpost' for a rotatable FuMO 24/25, and FuMO 63 Hohentwiel was fitted.

Z 20 *Karl Galster*: In 1942 the ship received a FuMO 24/25 on the bridge, two FuMO 63 Hohentwiel—one aerial replacing the searchlight abaft the after funnel—and FuMB Metox.

Z 24: FuMO-21 and FuMB Metox installed.

Z 25: In 1944–45 a FuMO 63 Hohentwiel replaced the searchlight on the after funnel. A FuMO 24/25 installed on the bridge had the necessary clearance not to require the 'goalpost' conversion. The unit was replaced in 1944 by a FuMO 21, a FuMB 6 Palau located above it and a FuMB-3 Bali at the masthead. A FuMB Metox was installed.

Z 31: In 1944/45 a FuMO 63 Hohentwiel replaced the searchlight on the after funnel and a FuMB Metox was fitted. In 1945 an experimental FuMO 231 Euklid AA radar was installed.

Z 33: A FuMO 24/25 was installed, as were a FuMB 31, a FuMB 4 Palau plus one FuMB 4, 9 or 10 aerial and one FuMZ 6. At the masthead were an FuMB 3 Bali and FuMB 26 Tunis. A FuMB 6 Palau and FuMB 4 Sumatra were added atop the bridge. In 1944–45 a FuMO 63 Hohentwiel replaced the searchlight on the after funnel.

Z 34: A FuMO 24/25 and FuMB 34 were installed. In 1944–45 a FuMO 63 Hohentwiel replaced the searchlight on the rear funnel.

Z 37: The ship was fitted with a FuMB Metox.

Z 38: A FuMO 21 was fitted on the bridge and four FuMB 4 Sumatra aerials were located around the foremast searchlight platform.

Z 39: A FuMO 21 was fitted on the bridge and four FuMB4 Sumatra aerials were located around the foremast searchlight platform. At the masthead were FuMB 3 Bali and FuMO 81 Berlin-S. The ship also received a FuMO 63 Hohentwiel.

Z 28, Z 29, Z 30: The ship was fitted with a FuMO 24/25 and in 1944–45 a FuMO 63 Hohentwiel replaced the searchlight on the after funnel

Z 35, Z 36, Z43: Fitted with a FuMO 24/25.

Unidentified unit: From 1942 one ship was fitted with a 1.9m × 6.4m FuMO 32 with Radattel beam (so-called because the two halves of the receiving aerial were connected by a lead and the electric motor which ran the device made a noise which gave rise to the nickname).

Machinery

The destroyers of all types were fitted with six Wagner boilers (except Z 9–16, which had Benson boilers). Two sets of turbines provided the drive. Types 1934, 1934A and 1936 had an electrical plant with two turbo- and three diesel generators, and had two shafts and one rudder. Type 1936B (Mob) had one turbo-generator, and 1936A and 1936A (Mob) two; and these three types were equipped with four diesel generators and had two shafts and two rudders.

Boilers

The Wagner was a high-pressure, hot-steam boiler with natural water circulation, equipped with exhaust gas and feedwater preheaters (two steam-heated and one fresh-steam stage), and had an effective operating level of 83 per cent. The working pressure was 70atm, with steam temperature at 480°C (later reduced to 450°C).* Between 35 and 46 tonnes of steam was raised per hour. The boiler was constructed as both a single- and double ender and had two Saacke burners.

The Benson was a forced-flow boiler, the feedwater being forced through the boiler tubes, evaporated and then superheated. The operating level was 77 per cent, the working pressure 110atm and the working temperature 510°C. The Benson boiler did not perform well and was liable to break down, and it was not until another drum as a steam collector was added in the late 1930s that it was finally made manageable. As these boilers were a Blohm & Voss/Benson development, they were dubbed 'Blohmson' during the continuing debate about the La Mont boiler.

The six boilers installed in the Type 1936A destroyer were of two different sizes, four producing 54 tonnes of steam per hour and two producing 48 tonnes. There were three boiler rooms; later projects had two. The exhaust pipes of boiler rooms 2 and 3 were trunked through the forefunnel, the after funnel serving boiler room 1.

---

* The steam temperature for the Type 1936B (Mob) was only 426°C, and it was even lower for the planned Type 1945.

BOILERS

	Z 30	Z 1–8
Type/manufacturer	Wagner	Wagner-Deschimag
Construction	Double-ender with two Saacke burners	
Heating surface, per boiler:		
Vaporiser	392m^2	400m^2
Superheater	100m^2	100–120m2
Air preheater	564m^2	536m^2
Output	54.6 tonnes/hr	46 tonnes/hr
Operating pressure	70 atm	70 atm
Steam temperature:		
Hot steam	465°C	450°C
Saturated steam	284°C	284°C
Feedwater temperature	170°C	170°C
Boiler operating level	76.5%	77%
Weight and water content	46.78 tonnes	46.5 tonnes
Heat production	608kcal/kg	621.7kcal/kg
Exhaust gas temperature	520°C	520°C
Air preheating	350°C	350°C

INTERVENTION PRESSURE OF SAFETY VALVES OF BENSON AND WAGNER BOILERS

Benson-Kessel (Z 10, 13, 14–16):
Working pressure	110 (125) atm
Approved pressure	140atm
Drum intervention pressure	140–145atm
Hot-steam production area intervention pressure	135–140atm

Wagner-Kessel (Z 1–8):
Working pressure	70 (75) atm
Approved pressure	80atm
Drum intervention pressure (steam collector)	80 81.5atm
Wet-steam production area intervention pressure	86–86.5atm

Z 17–30:
Working pressure	70 (75) atm
Approved pressure	80atm
Steam collector/hot steam production area	78.5–60atm

Turbines

Turbines for the destroyers were built by Deschimag, with the exception of Z 9–16, where the manufacturer was Blohm & Voss. The first four ships received an extra cruising turbine with gearing and Vulcan coupling. Tests proved that the coupling loop was too large, and eventually the cruising turbine was unshipped; it did not reappear. The turbines had individual HP, IP and LP housings. The reverse turbine had a two-stage Curtis wheel and was situated at the end of the LP turbine. Blohm & Voss put the HP and LP turbines on one axle, the IP being coaxial with the second LP turbine. In the battle between the two suppliers, Deschimag and Blohm & Voss, the German Marine finally accepted a modified plant built by Deschimag. The output weights were 13.8kg/hp for the Deschimag and 12.3kg/hp for the Blohm & Voss plant.

Taken as a whole, the engine room occupied a large proportion of the hull: for example, in the Types 1934, 1934A and 1936 it occupied compartments IV–X and accounted for 48 per cent of the total length.

The turbines were located in two turbine rooms, one set per room.

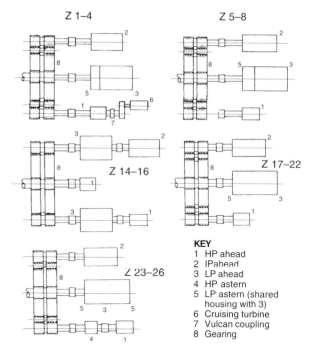

Above: Scheme of turbine arrangements.

Propellor Shafts and Rudders

All completed destroyers had two shafts each with a three-bladed propeller. The Type 1934 had one rudder, the remainder two, and some of the later projects were designed for three shafts and three rudders.

From the outset, the OKM laid down the main dimensions for propellers, and Deschimag prepared the workshop designs and submitted them for approval in the usual way. During the further course of development, when Dr W Schmidt became the official respon-

WEIGHTS AND SPACE REQUIREMENTS FOR ENGINE ROOMS (after Witte)

	Type 1934	Type 1936	Type 1936B
Type of machinery	HP	–	IP
Full load displacement (tonnes)	3,042	3,249	3,513
Length waterline (m)	116.5	120.0	121.9
Freeboard (m)	6.4	6.6	6.6
Output for full load displacement (shp)	65,000	70,000	70,000
M I weight (tonnes)	758	901	983
M II weight (tonnes)	193	175	140
M III as percentage of M I	25.5	19.4	14.2
Length of boiler room as percentage of length wl	23.8	24.5	24.6
Length of turbine room as percentage of length wl	15.2	16.0	16.4
Length of auxiliary machinery room as percentage of length wl	6.9	6.7	6.6
Remarks	Many pipes, reserve circuits; 3 boiler rooms	–	–

42

TYPE 1934 ENGINE ROOM (after Witte)

Output for drive:		
	Total	60,000shp
	117%	70,000shp
	Astern (25%)	15,000shp
Number of shafts		2
Turbine performance at 70,000shp:		
	HP	7,600rpm
	IP	4,000rpm
	LP	3,600rpm
Shaft revolutions (70,000shp)		450rpm
Turbine manufacturer		Deschimag
Turbine type		HP/IP/LP; triaxial; astern turbine in LP section; cruising turbine IP; Vulcan coupling; emergency connection facility
Turbine room:		
	Length	8.75m + 11.25m
	Surface area	157m^2
	Volume	883m^3
Weight of turbine plant		270 tonnes (= 38.5% M I)
Boiler manufacturer		Deschimag
Boiler type		HP hot-steam, six double-enders, small-tube
	Heating surfaces	4 × 320m^2, 2 × 429m^2; 2,138m^2 total (exc. super-heating component)
	Steam production	4 × 54 tonnes/hr; 2 × 44 tonnes/hr
Boiler room:		
	Length	27m
	Suurface area	224m^2
	Volume	1,337m^3
Weight of boiler plant		369 tonnes (= 52.6% M I)
Turbine start-up		60atm/460°C
Boiler cut-out		70atm/480°C
Weight of shafts and propellers		57 tonnes (= 8% M I)

sible for propeller design, the OKM increasingly took over the whole complex affair, evaluating sea trials and experimental work on free-running scaled-down models. Even sketches had to be drawn up in a particular manner approved by OKM. The result of this control is that no useful theoretical or practical documentation can be found today in the shipyard archives.

The sets for the first destroyer series were ordered simultaneously and were later discovered to be inadequate or at variance with specifications. A period of experimentation with blade angles and thicknesses led to improvements, and eventually to the final propeller form. In order to avoid the same procedure for the whole series, the optimum diameters and pitch were worked out to establish the most favourable relationships. For Z 1–22 about eight, and for Z 23-44 about six, different sets were trialled before the final design was approved. For the earlier destroyers various turning speeds, to port and starboard, were tested in order to obtain different pitch settings that would enable port and starboard screws to be run at the same revolutions. The reason for the difference proved to be the effect of the stern cool water discharges on the mid-flow, and the openings were modified to permit the same pitch settings for both propellers.

From the beginning, all propellers were manufactured with radially variable pitch, maximum pitch being about half the diameter, gradually decreasing towards the root and tip. The pitch of the first destroyer series was tangentially constant, however. After the discovery in 1940 of French results for the 'mussel shell' propellers—so-called for their concave form—a proposal was made to develop them for German destroyers on the grounds of promising advantages offered by the cavitation effect. A study of the 'mussel shell' propellers for Z 17 showed that the initial benefits did not occur until 33.5 knots, contrary to a calculation of 29 knots by Schmidt and Lerbe, but that the type was superior in some respects to the constant or radially variable-pitch propeller. These measures to reduce cavitation led to an improvement in the degree of effectiveness.

The material employed was initially the usual special brass. It was proven in practice and could be poured to make the required form without great difficulty. However, as a result of the shortage of tin, stainless steel was tried. Krupp V2A steel propellors had already been installed on the fast passenger ship *Europa*, but the material required a special production process because of casting problems. Krupp then developed a steel designated P125 which contained 22 per cent chrome and 7 per cent nickel. This proved more suitable, but manufacture took time—six months as compared to one month for bronze—and was costly. Germania Werft at Kiel and later the Kriegsmarine Werft at Wilhelmshaven ordered special milling machines. In urgent cases it had become necessary meanwhile to turn to bronze.

The finished stainless steel castings were good. Whether or not they were inferior to bronze—in terms of cavitation and efficiency—is not known, since the circumstances of the time did not allow comparisons.

Towards the end of the war, some destroyer propellers were made of the usual V5M material. All steel propellers for destroyers were cast by Krupp, whereas those in bronze were manufactured principally by Atlas Werke, Zeise. Others came from Blohm & Voss and Germania Werft.

Electrical Plant

A varying number of generators with different outputs supplied the shipboard electricity—turbo-generators for the main current and diesel generators for use when the ships were in harbour. Brief details were as follows:

Types 1934/1934A: Electrical generating stations (*E-Werk*) Nos 1 and 2 were located in turbine rooms 1 and 2 respectively and had two 200kW turbo-generators each. In Z 1–8, *E-Werk* 3 was located in compartment VIII, with two 60kW diesel generators and one of 30kW; Z 9–16 had three 50kW diesel sets.

Type 1936: As above, but with one 40kW and two 80kW diesel generators in *E-Werk* 3.

Type 1936A: Two generating stations. The turbo-generators produced 200kW each, the four diesels 80kW each.

Type 1936A (Mob): As the foregoing, but with only one 200kW turbo-generator.

Type 1936B (Mob): No details available, but probably as for Type 1936A (Mob).

Other Machinery and Equipment

Besides the maze of pipes and valves of the main engine machinery with its feedwater, heating oil, water coolant and lubricating oil and reserve pumps, many other installations were to be found aboard—the fresh water distillation unit with pumps, the auxiliary boilers with feedwater and heating oil pumps, the water ballast installation, the damage control organisation, including the fire extinguishing installations and auxiliary pump unit with numerous interchangeable pumps; the magazine flooding equipment, the sea water, washing-water and fresh water units with their circulation pumps, and the refrigeration machinery, to mention just a few.

Z 1–22 were fitted with an anti-roll device (an electrically run system based on flooding two trim tanks amidships) which—as also aboard ships up to *Panzerschiff* size—proved next to useless and were removed during routine overhauls and replaced by stabiliser keels. The exception was Z 20 *Karl Galster*, which retained the device for experimental purposes. (The unit did not possess any known advantages, but it was kept alive for the benefit of other projects.)

The destroyers had a bow anchor which weighed between 1,850kg and two tonnes. The anchor cable, comprising nine lengths, had a link thickness of from 42mm to 54mm. The cable portside had an additional three reserve lengths

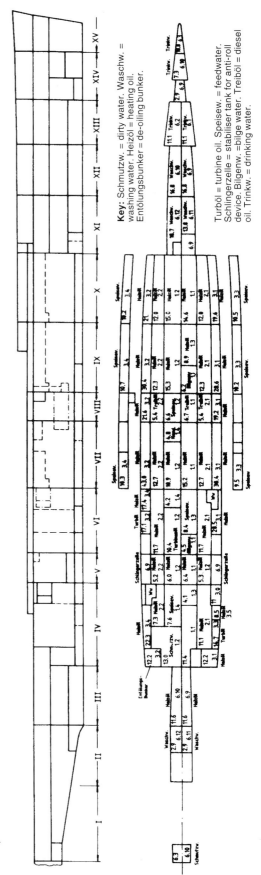

Key: Schmutzw. = dirty water. Waschw. = washing water. Heizöl = heating oil. Entölungsbunker = de-oiling bunker.

Turböl = turbine oil. Speisew. = feedwater. Schlingerzelle = stabiliser tank for anti-roll device. Bilgenw. =bilge water. Treiböl = diesel oil. Trinkw. = drinking water.

Above: Bunker, tank and trimming plan (from Z 5–8 Sketchbook)

Flotillas, Flotilla Commanders and the *Führer der Zerstörer*

The enforced and, in many respects, over-hasty rebuilding of the *Kriegsmarine* led to numerous changes in command structure during the war. Until 1939, destroyers came under the umbrella of the FdT (*Führer der Torpedoboote*, literally 'Torpedo-Boat Leader'), whose flagship was Z 1 *Leberecht Maass*. On 26 October 1939 the destroyer command organisation came into being under an FdZ (*Führer der Zerstörer*, or 'Destroyer Leader'). In the period from 26 October 1939 until the time of 'Weserübung' (the Norwegian campaign), the FdZ was *Kommodore* Friedrich Bonte; he was lost with his Staff aboard Z 21 *Wilhelm Heidkamp* on 10 April 1940.

These destroyers were originally organised in three-ship divisions, as follows (note that not all the divisions had been formed by the time the first two flotillas had been drawn up):

1. Z-Division: Z 2, Z 3, Z 4 (formed 1 December 1937)
2. Z-Division: Z 5, Z 6, Z 7
3. Z-Division: Z 14, Z 15, Z 16
4. Z-Division: Z 20, Z 21, Z 22
5. Z-Division: Z 17, Z 18, Z 19
6. Z-Division: Z 8, Z 9, Z 11
8. Z-Division: Z 10, Z 12, Z13

1. Z-Flotilla was formed of 1. Z-Div. and 3. Z-Div. on 26 October 1938 and was based at Swinemünde in the Baltic. The flotilla commander until 24th October 1939 was Kapitän zur See Wilhelm Meisel; the post remained vacant until 11 December, when Fregattenkapitän Fritz Berger took over.

2. Z-Flotilla was raised under Kapitän zur See Friedrich Bonte on 1 November 1938 from 2. Z-Div., based at Wilhelmshaven; ships of 4. Z-Div. joined the flotilla as and when they entered service. Following the appointment of Bonte as FdZ on 19 October 1939, Fregattenkapitän Rudolf von Pufendorf became Flotilla leader.

4. Z-Flotilla, based at Wesermünde and commanded by Fregattenkapitän Erich Bey, was set up in April 1939 and embraced 6. Z-Div. and 8. Z-Div. The post of FdZ came into effect on 26 October 1939. Z 1 *Leberecht Maass* was attached to 4. Z-Div. of 2. Z-Flotilla, thereby releasing Z 21 *Wilhelm Heidkamp* for duty as FdZ flagship.

3. Z-Flotilla was formed on 1 December 1939 at Swinemünde and comprised 5. Z-Div., plus Z 20 *Karl Galster* and Z 22 *Anton Schmitt* from 4. Z-Div. The flotilla commander was Fregattenkapitän Hans Joachim Gadow.

Tactical Numbers

In peacetime destroyers displayed a large white-painted tactical number on both sides of the hull below the bridge. The first numeral indicated the division and the second the tactical position of the ship within it. Occasionally the divisional organisation was changed, or a destroyer was attached to another division, resulting in a a change in the tactical number. Details are as follows:

Ship	Name	Tactical no(s)
Z 1	*Leberecht Maass*	–
Z 2	*Georg Thiele*	13
Z 3	*Max Schultz*	12
Z 4	*Richard Beitzen*	11
Z 5	*Paul Jacobi*	21
Z 6	*Theodor Riedel*	22
Z 7	*Hermann Schoemann*	23
Z 8	*Bruno Heinemann*	63, 61
Z 9	*Wolfgang Zenker*	61, 62, 63
Z 10	*Hans Lody*	81, 62, 61
Z 11	*Bernd von Arnim*	62
Z 12	*Erich Giese*	82
Z 13	*Erich Koellner*	83
Z 14	*Friedrich Ihn*	32, 33, 31
Z 15	*Erich Steinbrinck*	31, 32, 33
Z 16	*Friedrich Eckholdt*	33, 32, 31
Z 17	*Diether von Roeder*	51
Z 18	*Hans Lüdemann*	53
Z 19	*Hermann Künne*	52
Z 20	*Karl Galster*	42
Z 21	*Wilhelm Heidkamp*	43
Z 22	*Anton Schmitt*	41

The Second World War

From 1938 to Narvik

The launching of the heavy cruiser *Prinz Eugen* was the one of the greatest showpiece events for the German Navy since the First World War. On 22 August 1938, in the presence of Adolf Hitler and other high-ranking guests, Dr Seyss-Inquart, Reich Governor of Ostmark (as Austria had then been renamed), delivered the pre-launch speech. The attendance of the Hungarian Regent, Vice-Admiral Nikolaus Horthy de Nagybanya—from 24 November 1917 to 1 March 1918 commander of the Austro-Hungarian battleship *Prinz Eugen*, and subsequently the last fleet commander of the Austro-Hungarian Navy—lent the launching the character of a state occasion of special significance. *Prinz Eugen* was launched by Horthy's wife.

For the Kriegsmarine to bestow this particular name was a sign that the tradition of the once-proud Austro-Hungarian Navy had been absorbed into that of the German Navy. Originally it had been intended to name the cruiser *Tegetthoff*. A battleship of this name had taken part in the annihilation of the Italian Fleet at the Battle of Lissa on 20 July 1866, but as fascist Italy and National Socialist Germany were now close allies, it was decided not to risk offending Mussolini. The launching was followed by the greatest—and last—Naval Review in Kiel Bay. Every destroyer in commission and not under repair was present.

Although several of the vessels exercised with fleet units in Spanish waters during that country's civil war, the only show of force involving German destroyers prior to the Second World War was the two-day mission commencing on 23 March 1939 to reoccupy the former East Prussian territory of Memel, which had been incorporated into Lithuania under the terms of the Treaty of Versailles. The three 'pocket battleships' (Hitler was aboard *Deutschland*) and the light cruisers *Leipzig* (flagship of *Admiral* Raeder for the occasion) and *Köln*, plus the destroyers Z 1 *Leberecht Maass*, Z 2 *Georg Thiele*, Z 3 *Max Schultz*, Z 4 *Richard Beitzen*, Z 14

Friedrich Ihn, Z 16 *Friedrich Eckholdt*, Z 17 *Diether von Roeder* and Z 19 *Hermann Künne* and nine torpedo boats put into Memel without incident.

On the outbreak of war with Poland on 1 September 1939, Germany had sixteen destroyers available for duty. Of the 21 in commission, Z 3, Z 5, Z 7 and Z 21 were in dock and Z 13, recently commissioned, had not yet joined the Fleet. Six destroyers—Z 6, Z 12, Z 17, Z 18, Z 19 and Z 20, were based on the North Sea coast. The remaining ten were in the Baltic, where, following manoeuvres there in August 1939, Z 1 (flag, FdT Vizeadmiral Lütjens) assembled with Z 2, Z 4, Z 14, Z 15 and Z 16 of the 1st Flotilla and Z 8, Z 9, Z 10 and Z 11 of the 4th Flotilla, at Pillau naval base on the eastern side of the Bay of Danzig, in the final days of the month in preparation for the attack on Poland. On 1 September the destroyer squadron formed up off the Gulf of Danzig near Hela for anti-contraband duty off Polish coast. During the day several ships—Greek and Norwegian neutrals—were examined and released. Polish submarines were active in the area and a number of sightings were made, *Leberecht Maass* avoiding torpedoes fired by the submarine Wilk.

Early in the morning of 3 September, off Gotenhafen, *Leberecht Maass* and *Wolfgang Zenker* encountered the destroyer *Wicher* (1,920 tons 4 × 5.1in guns, 6 torpedo tubes, 33 knots) and the Polish flagship, the minelayer *Gryf* (2,250 tons, 6 × 4.7in, 20 knots). Against a combined armament of 10 × 5in and sixteen torpedo tubes, the Poles were evenly matched, but the German destroyers quickly drew the fire of the Cyplowa battery. A 15cm round hit *Leberecht Maass* on the starboard side by No 2 12.7cm gun, killing four—the first Kriegsmarine shipboard deaths of the war—and wounding four. The action was broken off at 0735 hours. Stukas were called up, and the aircraft sank *Wicher* and forced *Gryf* ashore near Hela. *Leberecht Maass* put into Swinemünde on 4 September for repairs.

At the end of August 1939 Konteradmiral Densch (flag, light cruiser *Nürnberg*) had spread a task force of 38 warships, including *Leipzig*, *Köln*, destroyers, torpedo boats and numerous support vessels, across the western and central Baltic to prevent the escape of Polish naval units. No hostile action had been permitted before 1 September, however, and in the last remaining hours, as the destroyers *Grom*, *Burza* and *Blyskawica* made their way across the Baltic bound for Britain, the German naval force could do nothing but shadow them. On 2 September Densch entered the North Sea, and on the 3rd, in company with *Leipzig*, destroyers and torpedo boats, began work mining the German Bight from the Dutch coast to the Skagerrak so as to extend the defensive Westwall seawards. On the 4th and 5th the state yacht *Grille* and more destroyers and torpedo boats joined the force. The operation, based on Wilhelmshaven, continued until 20 September.

The first offensive mining operation by German destroyers against the coast of Britain took place on 17/18 October 1939 when Z 16, Z 17, Z 18, Z 19, Z 20 and Z 21 laid 300 mines off the Humber estuary. On 7 November 1939 the newly appointed FdZ, Kommodore Bonte, raised his pennant aboard Z 21 *Wilhelm*

Heidkamp and prepared to set out from Wilhelmshaven with Z 5, Z 6, Z 7, Z 14, Z 16, Z 18 and Z 20 formed in three groups. Z 21 dropped out with engine trouble and the FdZ transferred to Z 20 *Karl Galster*. The next day the operation was postponed because of storm-force winds and heavy seas.

On 9 November, Z 21 was declared ready for sea and the FdZ returned to his flagship. The force at Wilhelmshaven now comprised Z 6, Z 7, Z 12, Z 14, Z 16, Z 19, Z 20 and Z 21. Z 5 and Z 18 had reported defects, and so Z 12 replaced Z 5 and Z 20 shipped the mines from Z 18. However, the meteorologists reported winds force 7 and the vessels remained in port. On 10 November Z 19 had engine trouble but Korvettenkapitän Friedrichs reported Z 18 clear to sail and she loaded mines that night, but the operation was again postponed.

On 11 November Z 21 (FdZ flag) together with Z 6, Z 7, Z 12, Z 14, Z 16, Z 18 and Z 20 lined up in the Schillig Roads. There was thick fog in the North Sea and no fuel replenishment was possible. Korvetten-

Below: Mining operations by German destroyers against the East Coast of England, 1939–40.

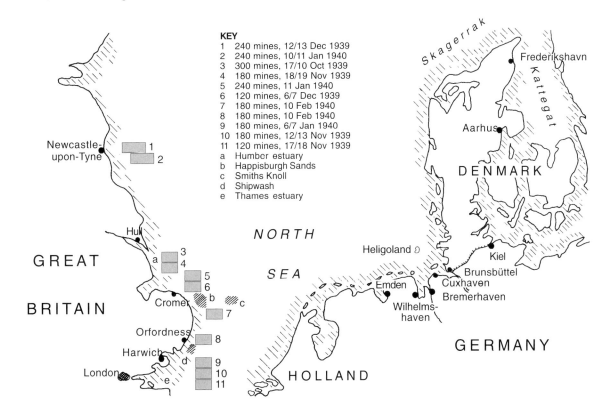

KEY
1   240 mines, 12/13 Dec 1939
2   240 mines, 10/11 Jan 1940
3   300 mines, 17/10 Oct 1939
4   180 mines, 18/19 Nov 1939
5   240 mines, 11 Jan 1940
6   120 mines, 6/7 Dec 1939
7   180 mines, 10 Feb 1940
8   180 mines, 10 Feb 1940
9   180 mines, 6/7 Jan 1940
10 180 mines, 12/13 Nov 1939
11 120 mines, 17/18 Nov 1939
a   Humber estuary
b   Happisburgh Sands
c   Smiths Knoll
d   Shipwash
e   Thames estuary

kapitän Kothe reported Z 19 clear to sail; Z 8, Z 10, Z 14, Z 15 and Z 16 were detached for other duties. The remaining force, consisting of Z 6, Z 7, Z 12, Z 18, Z 19, Z 20 and Z 21 (flag) sailed in two groups. Z 6 and Z 7 soon reported engine problems and were detached, Z 7 requiring Z 12 to act as escort back to port.

During the night of 12 November 1939 four destroyers set out and laid 180 mines off Harwich, being met on the way back by the light cruisers *Nürnberg*, *Köln* and six torpedo boats. Z 10 and Z 15 returned to Wilhelmshaven on the 13th to replace Z 6 and Z 7. A low degree of engine readiness meant that no operation was possible on 14 November, and the destroyers moored in the Schillig Roads in fog so thick that it was decided unsafe even to attempt to find them.

The force put into Wilhelmshaven on 15 November. Z 10, Z 19 and Z 21 loaded with mines, but Z 18 reported engine trouble and was held in reserve. Marinegruppe West ordered a rest day for the crews as urgently necessary. On the 16th Z 11 joined the group.

On 17 November Z 11, Z 19 and Z 21 laid 120 mines off the Thames estuary, escorted by two light cruisers on the return voyage. Z 16 re-joined the group that night, and the next evening Z 10, Z 15 and Z 16 laid 180 mines off the Humber estuary.

There was now a brief pause in mining operations until the 6/7 December 1939, when Z 10 *Hans Lody* and Z 12 *Erich Giese* laid 120 mines off the Norfolk coast

Below: The skirmish with British destroyers off Cromer, 7 December 1939.

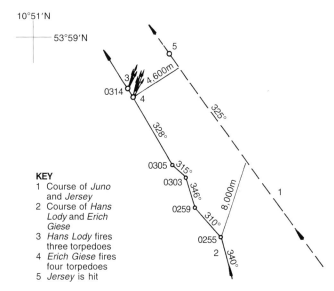

10°51'N

53°59'N

5

3   4,600m

0314   4

325°

328°

0305   315°

0303   346°   8,000m

0259   310°   1

0255

2   340°

KEY
1 Course of *Juno* and *Jersey*
2 Course of *Hans Lody* and *Erich Giese*
3 *Hans Lody* fires three torpedoes
4 *Erich Giese* fires four torpedoes
5 *Jersey* is hit

before making contact with the Royal Navy's 36-knot 'J' class destroyers *Juno* and *Jersey* (1,690 and 1,965 tons respectively, 6 × 4.7in guns and ten torpedo tubes). The British vessels maintained a course of 325°, suggesting that they were not aware of the German ships which were converging on them. At a range of 5,000yds seven torpedoes were fired, and *Jersey* was hit and badly damaged.

A fiasco occurred following the minelaying operation of 12 December 1939. Z 4 *Richard Beitzen*, Z 8 *Bruno Heinemann*, Z 14 *Friedrich Ihn*, Z 15 *Erich Steinbrinck* and Z 19 *Hermann Künne* (flag, FdZ) sortied in two groups to lay 240 mines off the Tyne, after which they headed for a rendezvous in the German Bight with three light cruisers to escort them home. *Heinemann* had an engine malfunction and wallowed for an hour and a half in sight of the English coast with *Steinbrinck* standing by. Three British aircraft which arrived to investigate at about 1030 the following morning were beaten off.

At 1730 on 12 December *Nürnberg*, *Leipzig* and *Köln* had left Schillig Roads for the north-west corner of the Westwall mine barrage. Vizeadmiral Lütjens, who had replaced Vizeadmiral Densch as BdA (CinC Cruisers) on 21 October and was aboard *Nürnberg*, had orders from Marinegruppe West (Naval Command West) to rendezvous there with the five returning destroyers at about 1130 on the morning of 13 December. The wind was variable, force 2–3, with sea state 2, cloudy but with good visibility, and *Nürnberg*'s and *Leipzig*'s shipboard aircraft were catapulted up to fly anti-submarine escort. Since a light cruiser rates more highly than a destroyer, the logic of using three such warships to protect five destroyers seems incomprehensible. As stated by Lütjens in his report, although the proper escort for a destroyer is a torpedo boat, both torpedo-boat flotillas were in the shipyard for refit or engine overhaul; only *Seeadler* and *Jaguar* were operational, and these were in the Baltic. The only destroyers operational in the entire Navy were the five engaged in the minelaying operation, although it was 'hoped' that two more would be 'repaired in time'. Admiral Marschall, Fleet CinC, stated in his 'G.Kdos B. Nr. 296/40 Anlage 2 zu 1/SKl 1745/40' that although it was clear to him from the outset of this operation that the presence of British submarines in the North Sea presented a risk to the cruisers, that risk was justified. Until then British submarines had had no success, and in his opinion it was preferable to have a cruiser torpedoed now and again rather than that destroyers crews gained an impression of cruisers just lying at anchor while smaller units were thrown into action against all manner of superior forces without any support. Moreover, the morale of cruiser crews suffered severely in the long run if they were always ready to sail but never received orders to do so. Thus the drawbacks of this type of operation had to be accepted, there being no successful warfare without risk.*

Lütjens had investigated the Danish freighter *Charkov* sending suspicious radio codes, but he did not have her stopped and examined when he saw she was on the Free List of neutrals. Shortly afterwards a British aircraft began to shadow the cruisers. The five destroyers were sighted bearing north-east by German reconnaissance aircraft, the three cruisers with which they were to rendezvous being north of them and below the horizon. At 1120 their position was about 40 miles west-south-west of the cruisers, and Lütjens ordered the three cruisers to steer 240° to meet the destroyers. Five minutes later *Leipzig* and *Nürnberg* received one torpedo each from a fan of three, the third having missed the latter ship. Four to five minutes after *Nürnberg* was hit, three more torpedo tracks were sighted astern of the cruiser, but the torpedoes exploded harmlessly on the sea bed. Shortly afterwards *Nürnberg* sighted a partially surfaced submarine directly astern about 5,000yds off. The wireless monitoring section reported that the submarine was HM Submarine *Salmon*, with six bow torpedo tubes. Following the hit *Nürnberg* reduced speed to about 18 knots: her AA fire control was out of commission but her seaworthiness was not affected. Meanwhile *Leipzig* had been left alone heading south-east, making 12 knots on her cruising diesel because all her boiler furnaces had been extinguished.

The detonations and smoke had been observed aboard *Hermann Künne* and *Friedrich Ihn*. The bearing was so far off the expected rendezvous point, however, that the FdZ decided that the activity did not involve the cruisers and must be between aircraft and a submarine, and for this reason the destroyers did not approach. A signal '1126 Nürnberg and Leipzig torpedoed grid square 3747. BdA.' had not been transmitted on all bands because of a defective aerial and a simultaneous telegraphist error. The FdZ did not

receive this signal since he had not tuned in on the long-wave close zone in accordance with standing instructions, for which he was later reprimanded. At 1137 Lütjens requested the rendezvous through the Navy short-wave band. For the critical ten-minute period after the attack, complete confusion had reigned ashore, but even now the destroyers remained unaware of what was amiss. Between 1212 and 1222 three Hampden bombers—possibly those beaten off ninety minutes or so earlier by *Bruno Heinemann*—attacked *Nürnberg*, but without success.

More than an hour after *Nürnberg* and *Leipzig* had been torpedoed, the destroyers had still not effected the rendezvous, and as it seemed to Lütjens that a navigational problem existed he decided to wireless the FdZ his position, course and speed and a homing signal as from 1245, and he sent off the aircraft circling *Leipzig* to scout for the destroyers. However, the aircraft failed to establish contact because of poor visibility.

At 1250 the FdZ detached *Friedrich Ihn* (boiler trouble) and *Erich Steinbrinck* (contaminated fuel oil) while he proceeded with *Hermann Künne*, *Bruno Heinemann* and *Richard Beitzen* to the original rendezvous position. A few moments later his telegraphists intercepted a message from an aircraft with the call sign 'S4EH' reporting damage to a light cruiser. This was the first he knew of the incident, and he decided not to recall the two detached destroyers since his force of three would be sufficient to cover the damaged ship. At 1340 the three German destroyers finally steamed up on the casualties. *Beitzen* and *Heinemann* took up station on *Leipzig* while *Nürnberg* received the protection of *Künne*, with *Köln* off the port quarter. Three low-flying aircraft aircraft circled the group. Strict radio silence was imposed since it was considered possible that enemy submarines or destroyers might infiltrate the German Bight behind the mine barrier for a night attack.

Nürnberg could make 15 knots and reach coastal waters by nightfall and thus was sent on with only *Hermann Künne* for escort, the two ships steering 135° and homing in on the Hornum coastal beacon.

At 0702 Marinegruppe West ordered *Leipzig* to make for Wilhelmshaven. The two destroyers led, with *Köln* astern. When *Friedrich Ihn* and *Hermann Schoemann* arrived directly from the dockyard, *Köln* took station ahead of *Leipzig* with the four destroyers abeam. Between 0730 and 0815 the escort was further strength-

---

* For further details of this incident see *German Light Cruisers of World War II* by the same authors (Greenhill Books, 2001).

ened by F 7, F 9, six motor minesweepers of the 3rd R-Boat Flotilla, four boats of the 2nd Minesweeping Flotilla and several aircraft.

At 0951 *Köln* was ordered by Marinegruppe West to make for Wilhelmshaven at once and was detached at high speed with *Friedrich Ihn* and *Hermann Schoemann* as escorts. At 1235 the British submarine *Ursula* fired successive torpedoes at *Leipzig*; one missed and the other hit the escort vessel F 9. *Leipzig*'s diesel was restarted for full ahead. F 9 foundered quickly on her port beam, the motor minesweepers R 36 and R 38 picking up 34 survivors.

At 1429 the convoy passed Lightship H and at 1728 anchored in the roadstead at Brunsbüttel. The cruiser proceeded to Deutsche Werke shipyard at Kiel for repair. Later, Admiral Raeder, CinC *Kriegsmarine*, observed: 'The use of cruisers to escort destroyers or other light forces in the manner undertaken on 13 December 1939 proved unsuitable and inappropriate.'

Offensive mining operations off the East Coast of England were resumed on 6 January 1940 when 180 mines were laid near the Shipwash by Z 4, Z 7, Z 14, Z 15, Z 16 and Z 20; four nights later Z 4, Z 14, Z 20, Z 21 and Z 22 laid 240 off Newcastle, and on the 11th of the month Z 8, Z 9 and Z 13 mined Cromer. The last of these missions took place on 10 February 1940 when a total of 480 mines were sown off Happisburgh and the Shipwash by a force consisting of Z 21 (flag, FdZ), Z 1, Z 4, Z 6, Z 7, Z 8, Z 9, Z 13 and Z 16.

Loss of Z 1 and Z 3

The first wartime German destroyer losses occurred allegedly as the result of a Luftwaffe error. On 21 February 1940, KG 26/II's *4. Staffel*, based at Neumünster in Schleswig-Holstein, received orders to fly a mission against shipping between the estuaries of the Thames and Humber. Crews were to be at readiness from 0600, and the first aircraft took off at 1600 on 22 February. Visibility over the North Sea was 30 miles, with a full moon to the south-east. Aircraft of 4. Staffel followed one another into the air, oriented on the south point of the island of Sylt and then at an altitude of 1,000m headed for the Humber.

The He 111 in question had a crew of four—a sergeant pilot and three NCOs as observer, radio operator and air gunner. Towards 1900 the gunner reported a distinctly visible wake in the water to port. The pilot drifted the aircraft to starboard and saw below him a ship running at high speed and bearing north-

west. It was the crew's first night mission and hence their first sight of a ship at night, and the pilot somehow came to the conclusion that it must be enemy. According to his report, he brought the aircraft to 1,500m and made a bombing run, dropping a stick of four. The ship replied with her AA. Two bombs went into the water, a third hit full amidships with a large explosion and the fourth was not observed. The attack was timed at 1945. The stricken ship lost speed but remained afloat. A second bombing run resulted in another hit and the ship sank.

The aircraft turned at once for Neumünster, where the crew made their report. These papers were sent from Gruppe to Geschwader headquarters and from there to Fliegerkorps in Hamburg. The same evening the crew was summoned to Hamburg for a personal interview with X. Fliegerkorps Chief of Staff, Major Harlinghausen. They set out in high spirits, dreaming perhaps of some sort of recognition in the form of a small decoration, and if so it must have hit them all the harder to discover that the ship they had sunk was a German destroyer. What passed for the full circumstances were later determined by a Committee of Inquiry composed of Generalmajor Coeler, Kapitän zur See Heye, commander of the cruiser *Admiral Hipper*, and Oberstleutnant Loebel, commodore of KG 30.

For some time the German Navy had suspected that British fishing vessels north of the Dogger Bank were really spy trawlers. On 22 February 1940, the destroyers Z 1 *Leberecht Maass*; flag, Flottillenschef Fregattenkapitän Berger), Z 16 *Friedrich Eckholdt*, Z 4 *Richard Beitzen*, Z 13 *Erich Koellner*, Z 6 *Theodor Riedel* and Z 3 *Max Schultz* were assembled to investigate. A number of prize crews were embarked and the six destroyers sailed to raid the British trawler fleet. As the German Westwall defensive minefield lay across their path to the south of the Dogger Bank, they had to navigate through a clear channel. In the evening of 22 February the flotilla was steering 300° at relatively high speed through the channel when the attack came from the air, as a result of which two destroyers sank.

The OKW had laid down unequivocal instructions for Luftwaffe–Kriegsmarine co-operation regarding operations at sea, which in this case affected Marinegruppe West and X. Fliegerkorps. In essence, all operations had to be declared between themselves, and with sufficient advance warning to ensure that there was no overlapping or other activity to endanger the other arm of service. This meant, for example, that the

Luftwaffe could not attack any ship east of the Westwall mine barrier unless Marinegruppe West requested it, or the ship was definitely known to be the enemy. With the exception of attacks on submarines, which could not be identified with any degree of certainty, any attack west of the mine barrier was permitted even if Marinegruppe West had its own units at sea in the area. But this would have to be reported. So far the arrangement had worked well. Unfortunately, on this occasion the responsible Admiral staff officer had not relayed X. Fliegerkorps's declaration, and the destroyer flotilla remained unaware that there would be friendly aircraft in the area. This error should have become apparent when Marinegruppe West requested X. Fliegerkorps in the afternoon of 22 February to supply an air escort for the destroyers returning to port on the 23rd.

A telephone call at about 1800 on the 22nd made with the authority of Admiral Ciliax, Chief of Staff, Marinegruppe West, requested X. Fliegerkorps to order the aircraft airborne only to attack shipping off the coast of England, but this could not be done because Fliegerkorps did not have the codes. There now began a wrangle in which Marinegruppe West insisted that the Luftwaffe order the aircraft by radio, while the Luftwaffe wanted Marinegruppe West to instruct the destroyers—and in the event neither occurred.

Late in the evening of the 22nd, X. Fliegerkorps received the report from KG 26 that one of their aircraft had attacked a steamer about 20nm north of the Terschellingerbank lightvessel. The aircraft had been fired on and had probably sunk the steamer. The report was sent at once to Marinegruppe West and Göring, head of the Luftwaffe, and almost at once Generaloberst Jeschonnek, Chief of the Luftwaffe General Staff, asked whether there could be any connection between the bombing of the steamer and the sinking of the destroyers *Leberecht Maass* and *Max Schultz*.

The various eyewitness and logged accounts of what happened do not tally. None of the destroyers—the aircraft crew always spoke only of one steamer—fired a recognition flare. The destroyer commanders stated that the first, fiery explosion occurred beneath *Leberecht Maass*'s forecastle; all thought it was a mine. The second explosion was amidships. There was flame, and a large column of water reared up, and, again, it was thought that the cause was a mine. The explosion which sank *Max Schultz* almost immediately was very powerful. A mine or torpedo hit was suspected; there

had been a number of submarine sightings with torpedo tracks, all false. Strangely, on a night of the full moon, none of the commanders had seen or heard an aircraft, and the 'bomb hits' on Z 1 and Z 3 had not been observed, while on that same brightly moonlit night, with visibility all around for 30 miles, the crew of the He 111 crew saw only the rear destroyer—which they thought was a merchant ship—in a formation of six such ships steaming in line ahead, each vessel no more than two or three lengths apart. How could it have been possible for an aircraft to have crept up on six warships in line and dropped a stick of four bombs on and around one of them unnoticed?

The question of whether the aircraft was fired on was not resolved. Here the story was that an anti-aircraft gun had opened fire on a suspected submarine, and the other flak crews then joined in. There had been no aircraft recognition signal because the presence of friendly aircraft in the area had not been advised by Marinegruppe West. The commanders, including the Flottillenchef, were quite adamant that the cause of the sinking had been mines or torpedoes and that an aircraft being responsible was 'impossible'. This belief was underscored by the reports of torpedo tracks and periscope heads causing the rescue operation to be abandoned, resulting in many more deaths.

Commanders and crew members interviewed at a later date made statements which contradicted the earlier evidence. The flagship -indeed heard, and then sighted, an aircraft at 1913. As it flew past the squadron the fifth and sixth destroyers in line—*Max Schultz* and *Leberecht Maass*—opened fire on it. At 1921 it was heard again and the air raid alarm was given. As it flew past the squadron, it dropped bombs which exploded with great fountains of water near the third and fourth destroyers, *Erich Koellner* and *Theodor Riedel*, according to crewmen from those two ships. Between 1922 and 1927 an ultra short-wave conversation ensued involving *Friedrich Eckholdt*, the lead ship, *Erich Koellner* and *Max Schultz* as to whether this was a friendly or an enemy aircraft. The explosions at 1921 were described as 'bomb explosions'.

At 1944 or 1945 the first explosion occurred aboard *Leberecht Maass*, forward. This time coincides precisely with that of the first attack made by the Heinkel on a 'fast-moving ship'. Similarly, the time of the aircraft's second attack, 1958–2000, is very close to the time when the second explosion occurred aboard *Leberecht Maass*.

The Committee of Inquiry finally came to the conclusion that the reports about submarine sightings, the wild firing of the anti-aircraft guns and the general excitement all contributed to the air of uncertainty about times and so forth. It was determined that there had been four bombing attacks: (i) at 1921 three bombs fell about 400m abeam of *Max Schultz*; (ii) at approximately 1944 *Leberecht Maass* was bombed and hit forward; (iii) at about 1956 there was a huge explosion on board *Leberecht Maass* amidships; and (iv) at 2004 *Max Schultz* broke up and sank following a massive explosion. The contradictory evidence of the aircraft crew was that only two bombing runs were flown, at 1945, apparently scoring a hit on the forecastle, and between 1958 and 2000, apparently resulting in two hits amidships.

The reason for the discrepancy between these accounts remains unresolved, as do many questions about what really happened that night. The Heinkel crew was absolved from all blame. They had not been warned of the destroyer movements, no recognition signal had been fired from below, and they had, accordingly, made the justifiable assumption that the target was hostile.

The Gruppe West War Diary for 22 February 1940 recorded that at 2255, 'as FdM West has already mentioned in his War Diary, the mine situation in the approaches to the Heligoland Bight is very serious. The lack of minesweepers makes regular or even infrequent passages impossible.' It is now known that on the night of 10 January 1940 the British destroyers *Ivanhoe* and *Intrepid* laid 120 anchored mines

Right: The sinking of Z 1 *Leberecht Maass* and Z 3 *Max Schultz*, 22 February 1940.

approximately where Z 1 and Z 3 foundered. It is therefore certain that *Leberecht Maass* was damaged by the bomb at 1945 but that the second explosion, at 2000, was a mine. *Max Schultz* also hit a mine, for she turned with the remaining four destroyers to render assistance to Z 1 just outside the swept channel. Altogether 286 crewmen from *Leberecht Maass* and all aboard *Max Schultz*—over 320 men—were lost.

The tragedy had far-reaching consequences: there were no more destroyer operations in the North Sea. The next mission was 'Weserübung', the invasion of Norway in April 1940, when ten more were sunk. Of the 22 name-bearing destroyers in commission before the

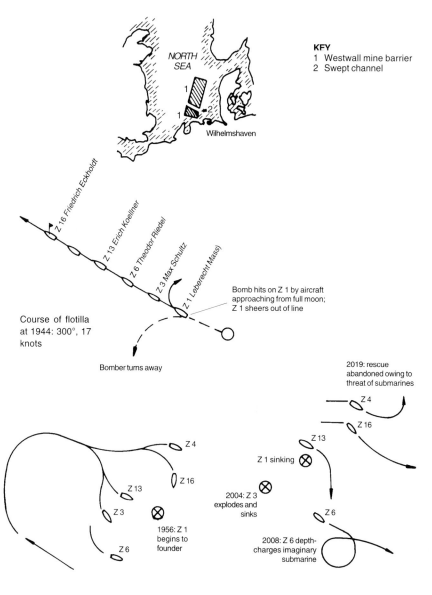

KFY
1 Westwall mine barrier
2 Swept channel

outbreak of war, only ten would still be afloat on 13 April to patrol a coastline that stretched for thousands of miles around Norway, and from the Westwall to Estonia—to which would soon be added the coastlines of the Low Countries and France. Three new destroyers entered service in 1940, but it would be the second half of 1943 before the number had risen once more to 22.

'Weserübung': The Invasion of Norway

At the beginning of April 1940 fourteen destroyers were put on notice to transport occupation troops to Norway in two warship groups. The six units which took no part in the operation were Z 4 (in reserve in the German Bight for escort duty to the heavy ships on their return), Z 7 (originally listed for Group 2 but replaced by Z 16 because of suspect machinery and put on standby with Z 4), Z 10 (under repair at Wesermünde), Z 14 (at the disposal of the Torpedo Test Branch and in dock): Z 15 (laid up under repair at Blohm & Voss) and Z 20 (in dock at Wilhelmshaven). The heavy cruiser *Admiral Hipper* was at the Steubenhöft, Cuxhaven, where, at the beginning of April, she began to embark Army units for Operation 'Weserübung', the occupation of Norway. This cruiser and the destroyers Z 5, Z 6, Z 8 and Z 16 formed Group 2, which had been given the objective of taking Trondheim.

Z21 *Wilhelm Heidkamp* was the flagship of Group 1, which consisted of the ten destroyers destined for Narvik. The FdZ, Kommodore Bonte, and his staff were embarked aboard Z 21 together with Generalmajor Dietl, CO 3rd Gebirgsjäger" Division. In Group 1 were Z 18 (lead ship, 3. Zerstörerflottille), Z 22, Z 2 (lead ship, 1. Zerstörerflottille), Z 11, Z 9 (lead ship, 4. Zerstörerflottille), Z 12, Z 13, Z 17 and Z 19.

Troops and equipment were embarked at Wesermünde and Wilhelmshaven on 6 April and the operation began the following day when the two groups joined up in the German Bight and forged northwards. The battleships *Scharnhorst* and *Gneisenau* were to sail at the centre of the armada to provide cover for the troop-laden convoy, making it arguably the largest and most formidable German naval force to put to sea in the Second World War. A gale set in from the northwest and strengthened later to storm force, and the destroyers began to find the going rough, experiencing frequent engine breakdowns. The sailing orders had to be relaxed, and stragglers were left to cope as well as they could.

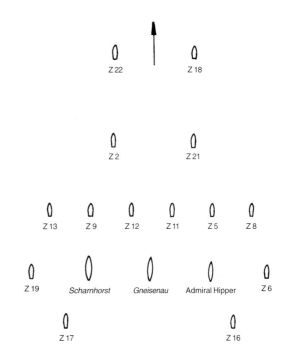

Above: Steaming order of Kriegschiffgruppen (Warship Groups 1 (Narvik) and 2 (Trondheim), 7April 1940. During the day the wind increased, and near-hurricane conditions set in during the night. The armada gradually began to drift apart, some destroyers losing contact altogether. The group re-formed on 8 April. Those ships destined for Trondheim—*Hipper*, Z 5, Z 6, Z 8 and Z 16—had their hulls painted black.

HMS *Glowworm* (Lt-Cdr G. B. Roope) was one of four escort destroyers accompanying the battlecruiser *Renown* as part of Operation 'Wilfred', the objective of which was to mine the Norwegian inshore waters. *Glowworm* had a man washed overboard in heavy seas on 6 April and, having abandoned the search, now found herself west-north-west of Trondheim and attempting to re-join the British group. She was a 'G' class destroyer of 1,345 tons, capable of 35½ knots and armed with five 4.7in guns and ten torpedo tubes.

Passing through the Shetland Narrows at 0900 on 8 April in a south-westerly gale 7–8 with gusts of near-hurricane force, Z 11 *Bernd von Arnim* suddenly sighted *Glowworm* about 7,000yds abeam on her starboard side. At 0922, when the range had closed to some 6,000yds, *von Arnim* opened fire. The action was reported by Z 18 *Hans Lüdemann*, which with Z 5 *Paul Jacobi* changed course to assist Z 11. Z 5 heeled to 55° in the enormous seas, five men were swept overboard (though subsequently rescued) and water came into the boiler room through the ventilation shafts, extinguishing five boilers and putting the port turbine out of action.

Despite the conditions, Z 11 scored hits on *Glowworm*, but the British destroyer was also shooting well and forced *von Arnim* to increase speed and make smoke. At 35 knots her bows drove under in the mountainous seas, damaging the bridge and forward command stand coamings and smashing the wheelhouse windows. No 2 gun became jammed in the hard a-starboard position and the torpedo aiming gauge on the port side became unseated. Two men disappeared overboard. The bridge was awash to knee height, and only after stopping both engines and putting the rudder hard over did the destroyer begin to recover. Her top speed was by now reduced to 27 knots.

Following receipt of the signal from *Lüdemann*, the Fleet Commander had ordered *Admiral Hipper* to detach and search for *von Arnim*, and at 0950 a lookout in the cruiser's foretop reported mastheads off the port bow; a second destroyer was soon made out to starboard. Neither ship could be identified, but at 0956 the starboard ship blinked a string of 'A's to *Admiral Hipper*, this being the standard British request for a ship's identity. Lt-Cdr Roope had been misled by *Hipper*'s lofty mainmast and, as no German units were expected in the area, had erroneously assumed that he had spotted a British cruiser.

Admiral Hipper opened fire on the British destroyer at 0959, eventually sinking her after a difficult struggle in which the cruiser was rammed and damaged, in position 67°12′N 06°28′E.

The Trondheim Group Detaches

Group 2, Trondheim-bound, re-formed and detached from the main force. At 1450 on 8 April, and in position 64°12′N 06°25′E, *Admiral Hipper* and her four destroyer escorts were reported by an RAF Sunderland flying boat, but the intruding aircraft was shot down by the cruiser.

The blacked-out ships entered the fjord at Frohavet at 0030 the following morning, two destroyers leading with anti-mining gear streamed from the bow and *Hipper* following in their wake, escorted by the other two destroyers as anti-submarine escort on either flank. The five passed Flesa Light at the entrance to the dangerous Kragvagfjord at 0255 in line astern and, having been warned that the Norwegians were about to extinguish all coastal lights, increased speed to maximum revolutions.

At 0404, when leaving Kragvagfjord, the Germans set navigation lights when a Norwegian patrol vessel came out from Beian on the port side. *Admiral Hipper* responded to the demand for her identity with the delaying routine of a small Varta lamp. She was posing as the British battleship *Revenge*—which she vaguely resembled—and stated that she had the permission of the Norwegian government to pursue a German steamer. A short distance ahead lay the mouth of Trondheimfjord: the channel had a 90-degree bend at its mouth, and at Brettingnes, on the east bank, were a searchlight battery and a number of coastal guns two 21cm, two 15cm and three 6.5cm coastal guns); further down, at Hysnes, was the master battery with a similar complement of weapons.

The Norwegians seem to have hesitated, for at 0404 Brettingnes fired up some red starshell, enabling the Germans to identify the gun emplacements, and it was not until 0412 that the Hysnes guns opened fire on the German destroyers, to which *Admiral Hipper* replied. The shells threw up large clouds of dust, dirt, sand and smoke, and in the resulting confusion the German formation picked up speed and broke away. At 0525 on 9 April the cruiser dropped anchor at Trondheim. Z 5 *Paul Jacobi* had suffered storm damage and engine trouble and was short of fuel; Z 6 *Theodor Riedel* required repairs to her port turbine and had gone aground while disembarking her invasion troops; Z 8 *Bruno Heinemann* was otherwise engaged until about 14 April; and Z 16 *Friedrich Eckholdt* reported limited readiness.

During the course of 9 April Kapitän zur See Heye, *Admiral Hipper*'s commander, attended a situation conference. The picture presented was a gloomy one, and afterwards he signalled Marinegruppe West that he was proposing to make the run home alone, at least as far as the German Bight, sailing on the 10th. Initially permission to do so was withheld, but, after the coastal batteries fell into German hands and four U-boats entered the fjord, Gruppe West ordered that all fleet units able to sail were to leave—and by night. *Riedel* and *Jacobi* had 40 tonnes of fuel between them, and after this had been pumped aboard *Eckholdt* the cruiser and destroyer weighed anchor at 2130.

At 2320 *Hipper* fired on U 32 in error and forced her to dive. On account of the submarine threat, Heye had taken the decision to exit via Ramsöyfjord, one of the most dificult channels in Norway for a ship to negotiate. Once this had been achieved he released *Eckholdt*,

Korvettenkapitän Schemmel having signalled that his ship could not maintain the required speed of 29 knots. Off Trondheim the destroyer survived an attack by torpedo aircraft from the carrier *Furious* intended for *Hipper*. The cruiser rendezvoused in German waters with *Scharnhorst* and *Gneisenau*, and all three made Wilhelmshaven without incident at 2300 on 12 April.

On 14 April *Heinemann* and *Eckholdt* returned to Wilhelmshaven. *Paul Jacobi* completed repairs using her own facilities by 21 April and then landed her contingent of *Gebirgsjäger* at a location up-fjord. She eventually sailed for home on 8 May, docking at Wilhelmshaven for repairs on the 10th. *Theodor Riedel* was beached in shallow water in Strömmen Bay on 10 April for use as a defensive battery against a British landing force, but ten days later she was refloated and towed to Trondheim, where she was patched up and became the first German destroyer to be fitted with radar. On 7 June she sailed for Wilhelmshaven to undergo permanent repairs.

The Main Group Heads for Narvik

The epic voyage of the German destroyers to the north was described in a memoir *by Kapitänleutnant (Ing) Heye*, chief engineer aboard Z 13 *Erich Koellner*:

Our destroyer was one of those fitted with the sophisticated Benson boiler. The pressures and temperatures made great demands of the ship—and just as much of the engine room personnel. During our trials the Engineering Director at the shipyard told me, 'I am familiar with how this boiler system works, but I wouldn't have any confidence that I could get it running and put to sea with it.'

Every Benson boiler room had more than thirty auxiliary machines, all driven by the main turbines, and, because of the narrowness of the room, access to some of them could only be gained by crawling . An unusually high level of expertise was required by the entire engine-room staff, expert technical knowledge having to make up for a lack of experience. In January 1940 Z 13 joined the front-line fleet. The North Sea operations proved the great power of the machinery, but also exposed its extraordinary susceptibility to the least irregularity in service. Leakages, split tubes, fires and other breakdowns had to be overcome on every voyage.

I will give an example. We stood by anxiously, impotent in the face of a seemingly insoluble riddle. We had a high, inexplicable loss of boiler feedwater. When you think that at high speeds feedwater circulated at the rate of 200 cubic metres an hour, the allowance of 120 cubic metres was not much. There was no reserve, and the slight but unavoidable steam losses had to be made up for by the sea water evaporating equipment. On Z 13,

however, the feedwater content reduced so rapidly that after about 36 hours at sea the engines were practically unserviceable. This meant that [the ship's] range was only a few hundred miles. All the searching revealed nothing—not the least clue existed to explain the huge feedwater loss. That was how we stood twenty-four hours before we were due to sail for Narvik, a voyage of about 1,000 miles.

Converting fuel bunkers to feedwater tanks was not allowed, and, in any case, instead of the usual 85 per cent load per bunker, they were to be filled to the very top. The day before we went, the Chief Engineer of a sister ship advised me to reinforce the tubes in the boiler at the joints: he had had the same problem. It was an insidious leak which hadn't been spotted. That same night I got the shipyard to the look at the reinforcing and—lo and behold—the problem was solved. We took on almost 800 [cubic] metres of heating oil, but to be on the safe side I filled some of the washing-water tanks with additional feedwater.

On the morning of 6 April we were clear to sail. We came through the locks and made fast at the Columbus Quay in Wesermünde, where 200 mountain troops came aboard. At 2300 we left for the Weser. For the required top speed of 27 knots only two boilers were needed, and the other four we left cold.

On 7 April *Fregattenkapitän* Schulze-Hinrichs informed the crew of our mission and our destination. Towards midday it got cloudy and began to blow hard, the sea got up and the first spindrift appeared. Towards 1700 the pumpmaster's mate was washed overboard and lost. At 1800 we got two more boilers fired; with four boilers we could make 32 knots. Shortly before 2300 a superheater tube tore apart with a loud bang. The boiler was shut down, the pressure was released, and we had to crawl in and repair the fault. The boiler was ready by 0200 next morning. Meanwhile we had got the remaining two boilers going, and, having all six, we were now capable of 30 knots.

Outside, huge rollers were running which coursed over the deck. Water was coming into turbine room No 1 through a ventilation shaft like a waterfall. E-Plant No 1 took in water, short-circuited and broke down. This cut the whole electrical output by a third. The ventilation shafts on the upper deck had to be plugged by whatever means available, resulting in an intolerable damp heat in the turbine room.

Suddenly the E-Plant 2's switchboard in the forward turbine room failed, followed at once by all command elements, machine telegraphs and the rudder gear. Z 13 slewed broadside to the sea. All orders had to be relayed by means of a runner making his way over the upper deck—in these seas a breakneck operation. After an hour the cause was identified as a short circuit in the gunnery gyro gear. After disconnecting the gyro we got E-Plant 2 going again.

The damage sustained that night was considerable. The breakdown of a 24V transformer for the telephone installation and the breakdown of electrically driven spring pump No 1. In all machinery spaces the water level rose because of the seas coming aboard. The suction mechanism of the spring pumps in turbine room No 2 and boiler room No 2 was blocked; we tried everything we could to reduce the water in the engine room, including using the cold-water pumps of the condensers. That had to be done very cautiously to make sure the condensers didn't fail with a resultant loss of engine output. We also tried the three big damage control pumps, but No 3 pump wasn't working and the starter valve of another one broke. Finally we opened up the connecting valves in the various compartments to spread the water through the ship and also to get all available pumps involved.

Meanwhile the boilers were having to be supplied from fuel tanks further away, for which two demand pumps were used. A critical situation arose here when boiler room 3 demand pump refused to function on account of the rolling of the ship and the pump shaft of boiler room 1 support pump seized. This had to be removed and repaired on a lathe.

The grey dawn came and the commander tried to re-establish contact with the main convoy, but only Z 19 *Hermann Künne* was nearby. The sea was still running very high and breaking across the ship. In this situation a stoker crawled across the deck to the machinery workshop hatch to repair the pump shaft. He came back the same way a couple of hours later, was caught by a sea but managed to hold on. While returning to the workshop he was not so lucky and this time was washed overboard. The sea seized another stoker on the companionway down to turbine room No 2, and he suffered a fractured coccyx. During the change of watch another was thrown against the superstructure and broke his collarbone.

In the 'tween deck forward the water was ankle deep at this time. The swell had risen, we were shipping more sea, and it was no longer possible to relieve the men on watch. At about 0300 on 9 April we got under the lee of the land and at 0530 began ferrying the mountain troops ashore off Elvegarden north of Narvik. We might have reached our destination, but there was no rest for the crew: we had to repair the storm damage, refuel and get back to operational efficiency. Then a fresh difficulty came along: while on patrol on the night of 12 April we struck an uncharted rock which tore open the hull from forward to amidships. That really sounded the death knell for Z 13, since she could never have made it home in that condition.

And how did other destroyers fare? During the near-hurricane, Z 21 *Wilhelm Heidkamp* yawed up to 40 degrees off her rudder, large amounts of equipment were swept over the side, railings and stanchions proved too weak, both cutters were wrecked and the hoisting tackle for the picket boat and the boat itself were made unusable. Z 22 *Anton Schmitt* yawed up to 40 degrees and heeled, her decks under water as far as the starboard 3.7cm AA guns, the guardrail for which became buckled, preventing the gun from being trained. Fittings, Army equipment and motorcycles went overboard, a cutter was wrecked and one man was washed away. Z 18 *Hans Lüdemann* broached 90 degrees, the starboard guardrail parted and two cutters were destroyed. Three men were lost overboard. Z 19 *Hermann Künne* received damage when she heeled 50 degrees, water pouring through ventilation shafts and into the boiler rooms. Z 17 *Diether von Roeder* lost a man overboard, and her starboard cutter was wrecked when she heeled 50 degrees. With rolls of up to 40 degrees, Z 9 *Wolfgang Zenker* lost one man and the ship's dinghy overboard and most of her rail and stanchions were ripped away. Z 12 *Erich Giese* heeled up to 50 degrees, losing her ship's dinghy and guardrail; fittings, depth charges, boxes of lifejackets and even lashed-down motorcycles went over the side. This was the quantifiable damage: in the engine rooms it was little better.

Once the convoy began to bear down on Narvik, the scattered units gradually re-established contact with the main group. *Giese* was an exception. She was well adrift of the convoy and had water in 90 cubic metres of fuel, her range thereby cut down accordingly. Her chief engineer had calculated that at 21 knots she could reach Narvik in three or four hours. Once he was under the coast a careful sounding revealed that he had more fuel than he first thought, but even so he had to reduce speed to 15 knots and shut down all unnecessary power if he were to make port.

Entering the approaches to Narvik, the ships were cleared for action. Speed was 27 knots, though some destroyers were making up to 36 knots to regain formation. *Von Roeder* suffered rudder failure and only avoided running aground by reversing full out.

As the penetration into the fjord proceeded, a number of Norwegian patrol boats were seen. At 0510 Kommodore Bonte offered talks to the Norwegian coastal armoured vessel *Eidsvold** under a white flag of truce, but an honourable surrender was declined. *Heidkamp* thereupon sank the ship with a single torpedo. *Bernd von Arnim* was confronted by *Norge*, a

---

* *Eidsvold* and *Norge* were 4,233-ton *Norge* class coast defence vessels built in 1900. They could make only 16 knots but outgunned the German destroyers with their two 21cm and six 15cm guns plus two torpedo tubes.

sister ship of *Eidsvold*, and a short exchange of fire occurred in which *Georg Thiele* also became involved. A single torpedo from *von Arnim* was enough to settle the issue.

Meanwhile the scheduled disembarkation of the Army units had begun at preselected places along the fjord. Narvik harbour was full of merchant vessels of all nations, and a number of them—including some German ships, the crews not understanding the naval operation—were scuttled. The destroyer crews began working feverishly to restore their ships to full operational readiness. The most important task was to refuel as soon as possible so that the homeward run could be started at a moment's notice . . . and that was when things began to go sour.

There was only one oiler in the harbour, the *Jan Wellem*, and she had more diesel fuel in her tanks than heating oil, which meant that the destroyers would not receive a complete replenishment. However, the two fuels could be mixed in the right ratio, and this was done as an expedient. Next the actual transfer of fuel presented a problem. Only two destroyers could be refuelled at a time, one on either side of the oiler, or two in line alongside. There were insufficient connections and the pump pressure was too low, with the result that the whole procedure dragged. Another oiler, the 12,800dwt *Kattegat*, was expected: she had left Wilhelmshaven on 3 April for Narvik and was a shade overdue, while on 4 April her sister ship *Skagerrak* had left Wilhelmshaven for Trondheim. Unfortunately, neither would arrive: *Kattegat* was sunk by the Norwegian patrol boat *Nordkapp* on the 9th and *Skagerrak* fell foul of the British heavy cruiser *Suffolk* on the 14th.

Although the Norwegian garrison at Narvik surrendered at 0800 on 9 April, German Army units were in urgent need of heavy weapons, anti-tank guns, tanks and ammunition in order to secure the area against enemy landings. These were aboard the freighter *Rauenfels*, which, on 10 April while en route for Narvik, was scuttled by her crew upon the approach of the Royal Navy destroyer *Havock*. Other supply ships met a similar fate around the fjord entrance, where British warships were congregating.

The timely and rapid departure of the ten German destroyers from the trap of Narvik was becoming ever less likely. Gradually they took on their fuel quota, after which they took up waiting positions in the arms of the fjord or maintained a watch mid-fjord.

Gruppe West was pressing for a rapid departure, but by the evening of 9 April only two destroyers had been fully replenished. If the refuelling had gone as planned, the operation would have been ended towards midnight on 10 April, when the FdZ and his flotilla could have set out straight away. This was indicated in a signal to the CinC Fleet and *Gruppe West* at 1457. A further contributory factor to the impending disaster was the U-boat 'torpedo crisis' of early 1940, when U 51, U 25 and U 48 all made attacks on British vessels off Narvik with torpedoes which proved to be duds.

During 9 April the FdZ called several situation conferences, at which some decisions were made:

1. It is to be expected that the enemy will make a counter-attack. Last evening a British cruiser and destroyer were

Below: The arrival of the German destroyer flotillas at Narvik, 9 April 1940 (after Fechter and Schomakers, *Der Seekrieg 1939/1945 in Karten*, Preetz, 1967).

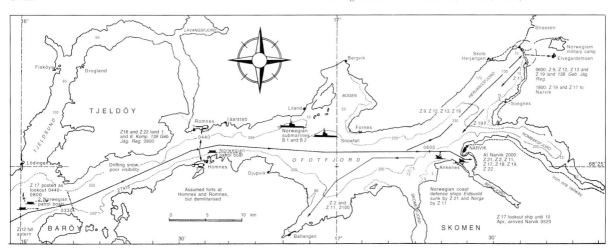

reported in Westfjord. Other enemy units, including battleships and aircraft carriers, may have reached this area in the meantime. At 2100 on 9 April a U-boat reported five enemy destroyers on a south-west heading in Westfjord (i.e., towards the open sea).

2. The enemy may content himself with launching his counter-attack against German ships in the harbour, but it is also possible that an enemy force may attempt to penetrate Ofotfjord with the intention of wiping out the German destroyers. It is not considered very likely that the enemy will attempt to land troops.

3. In any case, it is risky for the German naval units to remain with *Jan Wellem* in Narvik Bay. This massing of targets increases the possibility of air attack alarmingly. The narrowness of the bay itself and the fjord exit also involve loss of time if the German units have to take on enemy naval forces.

4. The assumption that shore batteries were emplaced at the entrance to Ofotfjord as envisaged in the battle plan was incorrect. This fact had escaped the German reporting service, but we cannot rely on the enemy not knowing. This increases the danger of the entry of enemy naval forces.

5. On the other hand, the U-boats inside the fjord offer outstanding protection. They will report enemy naval vessels entering and probably inflict heavy damage on them. Possibly the presence of U-boats may have caused the enemy to abandon any idea of penetrating the fjord.

6. We must not tolerate any more delay in the refuelling operation obstructing the departure of the eight to ten (seaworthy) destroyers.

As regards the refuelling, the Type 1934/1934A destroyers had to have a full load of oil because of their stability problems. Maximum bunkerage was not vital for the Type 1936, and so these ships would be replenished first, to get them out of the way.

That night it began to snow heavily, calling for a high state of vigilance by the destroyers posted on lookout duty. The snow and poor visibility proved favourable for the attack by a handful of British 'H' class destroyers of the 2nd Flotilla—*Hardy* (flag, 1,505 tons, 5 × 4.7in guns, 8 torpedo tubes, 36 knots) and *Hunter*, *Hotspur*, *Havock* and *Hostile* (all 1,340 tons, 4 × 4.7in guns, 8 torpedo tubes, 35.5 knots). They had not been given specific targets, but it was known that German destroyers were alongside the oiler *Jan Wellem* and others at the quay in the inner harbour.

Hardy, the leading British destroyer, fired two fans of torpedoes into the mass of shipping. It was difficult to see clearly what had been achieved, although they were fairly sure of a hit on the stern of one destroyer,

while another sank. The German destroyers were taken completely by surprise, no report having been made by the lookout vessels, perhaps because it was about the time when the watches were being changed.*

The gun and torpedo attack began at about 0530. Before the exhausted German crews could react, the worst had already occurred: a torpedo hit Z 21 *Wilhelm Heidkamp* in compartment III astern, the after magazine exploded, the stern was torn off as far forward as No 1 turbine room and the destroyer's hull settled to her upper deck. The Führer der Zerstörer, his staff and 83 crewmen died in their sleep. Z 22 *Anton Schmitt* was torpedoed amidships, broke in two, capsized and sank. Her stern collided with Z 19 *Hermann Künne*, which, after casting off the lines and pumps from *Jan Wellem*, lay motionless in the harbour with heavy smoke pouring from her innards. Z 17 *Diether von Roeder* suffered a serious fire as a result of a shell hit but was under sufficient control to take part in the ensuing battle, while Z 18 *Hans Lüdemann* was also damaged by shellfire.

The British ships had now turned to escape and were heading westwards for Ofotfjord at 15 knots. As they passed across the entrance to Herjangsfjord they ran into the path of three destroyers from 4. Z-Flottille approaching at high speed, Z 9 *Wolfgang Zenker*, Z 13 *Erich Koellner* and Z 12 *Erich Giese*. A furious running battle ensued in which *Hunter* was seriously damaged and eventually sank after being rammed by *Hotspur*, fifty survivors from her crew being picked up by the three German destroyers. Z 2 *Georg Thiele* and Z 11 *Bernd von Arnim*, which had been in an arm of the fjord to the south-west, near Ballangen, sailed to intercept the British flotilla and opened fire on the leading ship, *Hardy*, at 0657 at a range of 4,500yds. The British destroyer was hit, set ablaze and so seriously damaged that her captain decided to run her ashore, allowing her crew to escape.

The German force had suffered the following battle damage and casualties:

Z 22 *Anton Schmitt*: Sunk; 50 dead.
Z 21 *Wilhelm Heidkamp*: Constructive total loss; 81 dead.

---

* There are a number of questions which remain unanswered here. The Germans had assumed, incorrectly, that there would be a fort overlooking the Ramnes Narrows, which were only 2–2½ miles wide and twenty miles west of Narvik. Although having understood the importance of the position, they failed to post lookouts ashore there equipped with radio. All the destroyers were equipped with hydrophones, but why no hydrophone watch was kept is a mystery.—Tr.

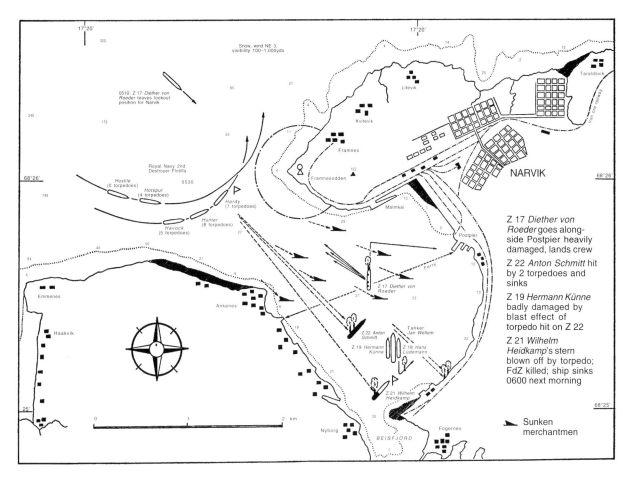

On the map:

Snow, wind NE 3, visibility 100–1,000yds

0510: Z 17 *Diether von Roeder* leaves lookout position for Narvik

Royal Navy 2nd Destroyer Flotilla

Hostile (0 torpedoes)

Hotspur (4 torpedoes)

0530

Hardy (7 torpedoes)

Hunter (8 torpedoes)

Havock (5 torpedoes)

Emmenes

Ankenes

Haakvik

Litevik

Kvitevik

Framnes

Framnesodden

Malmkai

Postpier

Ferry

NARVIK

Taraldsvik

Z 17 *Diether von Roeder*

Z 22 *Anton Schmitt*

Z 19 *Hermann Künne*

Tanker *Jan Wellem*

Z 18 *Hans Lüdemann*

Z 21 *Wilhelm Heidkamp*

Nyborg

Fogernes

BEISFJORD

Z 17 *Diether von Roeder* goes alongside Postpier heavily damaged, lands crew

Z 22 *Anton Schmitt* hit by 2 torpedoes and sinks

Z 19 *Hermann Künne* badly damaged by blast effect of torpedo hit on Z 22

Z 21 *Wilhelm Heidkamp*'s stern blown off by torpedo; FdZ killed; ship sinks 0600 next morning

Sunken merchantmen

Above: The inner harbour at Narvik during the British destroyer attack, 10 April 1940 (after Fechter and Schomakers, *Der Seekrieg 1939/1945 in Karten*, Preetz, 1967).

Z 17 *Diether von Roeder*: Five shell hits; boiler room No 2 unserviceable; heavy damage to hull plating; manoeuvrable but no longer seaworthy; 13 dead.

Z 18 *Hans Lüdemann*: Shell hits on No 1 gun (gun unserviceable) and in compartment III (fire); magazine flooded; 2 dead.

Z 19 *Hermann Künne*: Splinter damage; torpedo blast on Z 22 and shells exploding nearby put out main and auxiliary machinery and electrical plant temporarily; ship not clear to sail until after battle ended; 9 dead.

Z 2 *Georg Thiele*: Seven hits; gunnery data and fire direction centres and No 1 gun unserviceable; magazine flooded; fires forward and astern; 13 dead.

Z 11 *Bernd von Arnim*: Five hits; boiler No 3.2 unserviceable; very limited seaworthiness, with shell holes in side plating and foreship; 2 dead.

Z 9 *Wolfgang Zenker*, Z 12 *Erich Giese* and Z 13 *Erich Koellner* had no battle damage but had used

considerable amounts of fuel and 50 per cent of their ammunition. Especially serious was the loss of the FdZ, who would be replaced later by Fregattenkapitän Bey, commander of 4. Z-Flottille.

Signals indicated the known activity of the enemy and his naval build-up, and, once a reasonably clear view of the situation in Narvik had been obtained, a signal was transmitted to Gruppe West at 1050: 'Surprise attack Narvik 0530 in mist and snow by British destroyers. Sunk Heidkamp, Schmitt. Serious damage Roeder. Thiele, Lüdemann, Künne limited readiness. Kommodore Bonte dead, three British destroyers sunk. At 1406 Gruppe West replied: 'To leader 4. Z-Flottille. Destroyers ready to sail, full load fuel;' and, at 1516, 'To leader 4. Z-Flottille. Personnel and material from unserviceable destroyers for support Army.' Finally, at

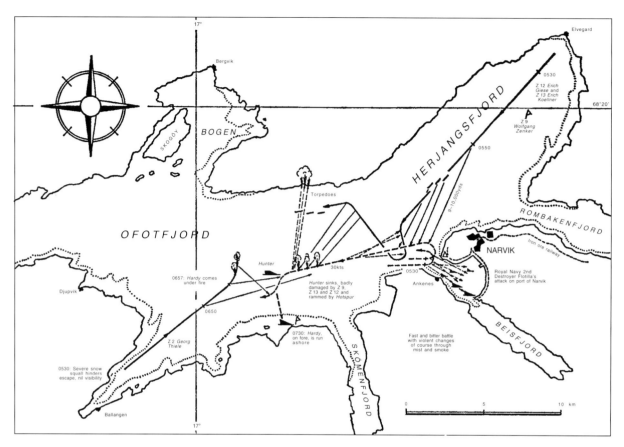

Above: Phase I of the battle following the British destroyer attack, 10 April 1940 (after Fechter and Schomakers, *Der Seekrieg 1939/1945 in Karten*, Preetz, 1967).

1544, came the signal: 'To everybody. All cruisers, destroyers and torpedo boats able to do so sail tonight. Narvik destroyers form on C-in-C Fleet. Will be left up to commander Hipper and three destroyers because of speed limit battleships 25 knots. Break-out if necessary after refuelling at sea or per orders at sea if grouping up. Do not go to Basis Nord.* CinC Cruisers and Hipper report intentions. Gruppe West.'

This order was binding on the Narvik destroyers, and at about 2040 on 10 April Fregattenkapitän Bey ordered *Wolfgang Zenker* and *Erich Giese* to sail for home. They had been under way only for a short time when they ran across patrolling British vessels and turned back. On 11 April a signal instructed the ships to use any subterfuge, including the flying of the White Ensign, to get out.

The day was spent by other units in a frantic effort to get repairs completed. At 1359 Bey signalled that

Zenker, Koellner, Künne and *Lüdemann* were ready for sea and that *Thiele* and *Arnim* were at conditional readiness. The survivors from *Heidkamp* and *Schmitt*, and some from *Roeder*'s complement, had been put ashore to reinforce the Army, he stated. From about 1800 those destroyers that were ready mounted a form of picket duty, the other ships keeping to the fjord inlets. Z 13 *Erich Koellner* ran aground while manoeuvring and stuck fast, suffering such serious damage in the process that she was deleted from the list of four ships ready sail. Z 9 *Wolfgang Zenker* touched bottom but came free.

The routine of 11 April was similar to that of the previous day: everything was now being concentrated with a view to repelling the arrival of enemy naval forces in the harbour with a troop landing, all indications—supported by running situation reports from *Gruppe West*—promising that this was the case. To cope with

---

* Basis Nord was a bay near Murmansk at which, under a secret protocol concluded between the German and Soviet governments, German ships—blockade runners and also U-boats requiring fuel—were allowed to call for short stays before making the run home to Germany.

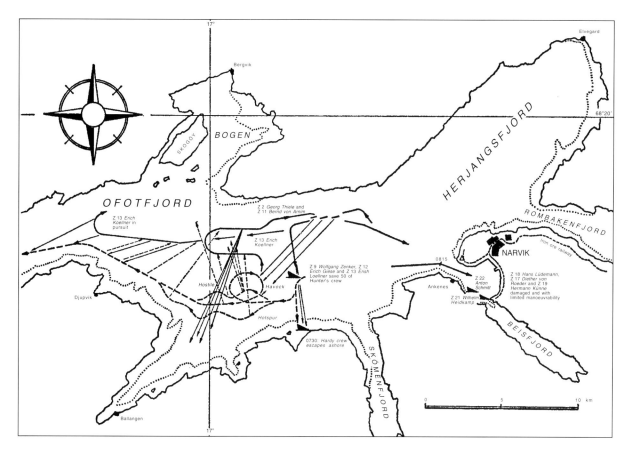

Above: Phase II of the battle following the British destroyer attack, 10 April 1940 (after Fechter and Schomakers, *Der Seekrieg 1939/1945 in Karten*, Preetz, 1967).

that eventuality, it was decided to take the following measures: (i) Position *Koellner* as a defensive battery at Taarstad (he should arrive there by the afternoon); (ii) Order all destroyers able to sail distribute themselves around the fjord inlets from where they could surprise enemy units, as had occurred on 10 April; (iii) order even destroyers not yet able to sail to be at immediate readiness from 1300 (*Erich Giese* on one engine, the other for emergency use only).

Z 19 *Erich Koellner* left for her allotted position at 1030, escorted through the harbour by *Hermann Künne*. Some of her crew had been landed, others put at the disposal of Z 19. *Koellner* did not reach Taarstad, for the British had guessed her intention, and she put into Djupvik Bay instead. Meanwhile *Künne* signalled the enemy presence, reporting nine destroyers and the battleship *Warspite*. Thus began the final battle of the German destroyers at Narvik.

At 1217 on 13 April Z 19 *Hermann Künne* opened fire at a range of 17,000yds and laid a smoke screen. At 1245 and 1259, respectively, Z 18 *Hans Lüdemann* and Z 13 *Erich Koellner* followed suit, but the latter fell almost at once under straddling salvos from *Warspite* and her destroyer escort. Without U-boats the battle was obviously hopeless, and all the German destroyers were either sunk or scuttled after expending all their ammunition during the course of the afternoon. Kapitänleutnant (Ing) Heye, Z 13 *Erich Koellner*'s chief engineer, recalled:

During the morning of 9 April we disembarked our mountain troops and put into the inner harbour at Narvik to repair and refuel for the return voyage. When you think of the sophisticated engine rooms we had to run, and the terrible weather conditions, it was a miracle that all ten destroyers had actually got here. Nevertheless, we chief engineers—with some reservations—thought it was possible to get the ships ready for the voyage home. Our oiler had not arrived; only the U-boat tanker *Jan Wellem* was in the harbour. We could burn the right mix of diesel and heating oil, but she had such relatively small pumping gear that it was bound to be a slow business.

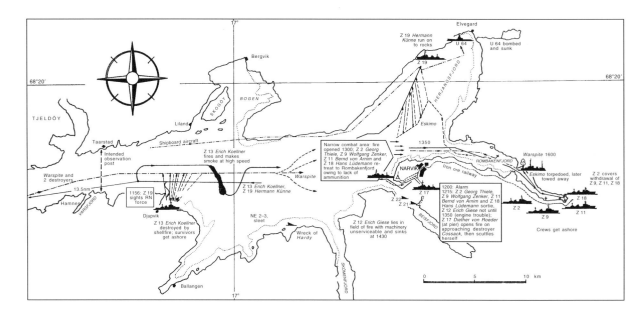

Each destroyer needed about 800 tonnes, which meant that it would take twenty-four hours to refuel two destroyers. Since there were ten destroyers, our stay in Narvik—which we were supposed to leave on 10 April—was going to be longer than expected.

All destroyers were low on fuel, and what was left could not be used because it served as liquid ballast. On board Z 13 we only had 60–70 cubic metres. During the night of 10 April we went alongside *Jan Wellem* to ship fuel just to move about the fjord, but we didn't get any since we had to wait our turn in the queue. That morning we were surprised by the British, who came in and fired blind into the harbour. We were in a fjord inlet, weighed anchor straight away, but then had to turn back because the heating oil pump of the bunker used for combat would not work when the tank was critically low.

During the night of 12 April we were sent to picket and ran aground on an uncharted submerged skerry. This tore open the hull from forward to midships. The rock held us and prevented the ship sinking, which enabled us to plug her up from inside. Once we got free we crept back to Narvik with the spring pumps in the flooded rooms running full out. Z 13 was no longer of much use in a fight. We needed a dockyard for the repairs, and there wasn't one here—and a return to Germany was out of the question. Thus, during the 12th, the commander, the No 1 and I discussed what was to be done. We decided that there was only one solution: dismount the guns and set up the battery ashore together with the ammunition and weapons personnel. Then Z 13 could be towed by a patrol boat over a bar into the southern arm of Ofotfjord. This was Beisfjord. There she could be placed in the farthest extremity out of harm's way, since no warship could cross the bar and Z 13 would be out of gun range.

Hardly had we got to Narvik than the No 1 and I began to put the idea into practice, and we started the job of unshipping. At about 1100 *Fregattenkapitän* Bey appeared and looked with astonishment at what we were doing. The commander was sent for and had to explain. Bey ordered him to put absolutely everything back on board again. All this was incomprehensible to the ship's company. They had been through an indescribably hard voyage in a hurricane and lost two men overboard. And on top of all the physical exhaustion they knew after the first few days at Narvik that they wouldn't be going home—at least, not on this ship. Now this. We started shifting it all back.

We were no longer battleworthy. The gunnery data centre was flooded and we were reduced to firing our guns individually by the backsight. Two of our boiler rooms were unserviceable, the feedwater was completely salinated, there were no mechanical reserves, the forecastle deck only held with props and our top speed was five knots. The task envisaged for us now was 'advanced gunnery observation point'. In the front line with our broken-down gunnery equipment! Nobody had thought of using us as a an advanced torpedo battery. We had given our reserve to other destroyers, but on the 13th we could have made good use of them.

Later I found out the reason for Bey's decision. There had been a lot of signals traffic between Bey and HQ about the fate of the Narvik destroyers. Apparently *Gruppe West* still thought it possible to get the destroyers out of Narvik and bring them down the 'free' North Sea, by using, for example, North Base near Murmansk. Finally it turned out as it had to, and Z 13 went down under the fire of a numerically superior British naval force.*

Throughout the history of naval warfare, in all theatres of war, allegations have been laid from time to time concerning the murder of survivors in the water. The German naval authorities, after evaluating statements from various witnesses, concluded that there was evidence of an atrocity committed by the Royal Navy at Narvik, and on 25 June 1940 a senior civil servant requested the OKM to investigate. For tasks of this nature there existed at the time a legal office known as the Wehrmachtuntersuchungsstelle (WUSt), or Wehrmacht Investigation Bureau, which investigated all allegations of war crimes, even those supposedly committed by German forces. The commission was headed by a serving naval judge, Sieber, whose terms of reference from OKM requested speed and thoroughness.

Before his inquiry began, on 8 August 1940, ten crew members of the sunken Z 22 *Anton Schmitt* had made depositions under oath to a naval officer at Wilhelmshaven. These were repeated to Judge Sieber on 15–16 August together with depositions from four crew members from the sunken Z 12 *Erich Giese*. Subsequently, Sieber had to travel to Paris to take the affidavit of Korvettenkapitän Smidt.

The interim report to the OKM on 27 August 1940 stated:

Up to 6 August 1940, as a result of draftings of, and leave by, Narvik destroyer crews, it had not been possible to secure the names of those allegedly fired on in the water by the British. Before Judge Sieber was appointed to investigate the allegations, only the crews of *Erich Giese* and *Georg Thiele* were said to be involved. Inj the process of the inquiry, it now transpires that crew members from *Anton Schmitt* were fired on in the water on 10 April.

Other witnesses came forward alleging the machine-gunning in the water of crewmen from Z 9, Z 21, Z 19 and Z 2. These men were requested on 22 August to forward their statements to Judge Sieber. On 9 September. in Swinemünde. several officers and men from Z 2 *Georg Thiele* gave affidavit evidence, as did the ship's commander, Korvettenkapitän Wolff, at Kiel the next day. On 16 September the papers were forwarded with a summary to OKM and WUSt.

The painstaking and reserved evaluation of the documentation concluded that only in the case of Z 12 *Erich Giese* was their clear evidence of a war crime having been committed. In all the other cases—Z 2, Z 22, Z 11 and Z 9—crewmen in the water gained the impression of being fired upon when shrapnel and splinters resulting from the battle fell around them. In the case of Z 22 *Anton Schmitt*, for example, the distance between the nearest British destroyer and the men in the water was over three kilometres—far too distant for the act complained about to have taken place—besides which it was snowing hard and misty. However, a rider was added that the men might have been fired on with handguns from British freighters in Narvik harbour. Nevertheless, a control carried out immediately afterwards discovered no supporting evidence.

Wolff, of Z 2 *Georg Thiele*, stated in his sworn deposition:

Throughout the action the British destroyers were at least four kilometres off. It is clear that at this range their shells would not only hit the German destroyer, but would also fall long and short, and one can understand that the men in the water were in danger from these shells. On the contrary, whilst the crew was abandoning ship, the enemy fire on the burning and sinking ship ceased, and was aimed instead on crew men climbing over the rocks near where the ship was grounded and seeking cover there. They were using not only 12cm but also their 4cm pompoms [*sic*], which because of their flat trajectory we could hear whistling over heads. To keep our casualties down we tried to climb up using depressions and fissures in the rock face. A 12cm shell exploded amongst a group, killing six. This proves, however, that the British were not firing on the men in the water, but those who had got ashore. I would add that our men were unarmed and were intent only on saving their own lives, carrying their wounded with them.

WUSt concluded that shooting at the men who had got ashore, although it might not be chivalrous, so to speak, did not constitute a breach of international criminal law.

In his sworn declaration delivered on 23 August 1940, Korvettenkapitän Smidt of Z 12 *Erich Giese* declared:

When the crew were in the water—about 200 of us—the British destroyers opened fire with guns and MGs. Several times I distinctly felt the pressure wave from an exploding shell close to me. From my observations none of our men were hit. We lost many men to MG fire; the bullets could be heard distinctly. Easy to identify were the British

*This force consisted of the 30,600-ton Queen Elizabeth class battleship *Warspite* (8 × 15in, 24 knots), the 1,350-ton 'F' class destroyers *Foxhound* and *Forester* (4 × 4.7in, 8 torpedo tubes): the 1,690-ton 'K' class destroyer *Kimberley* (6 × 4.7in, 10 torpedo tubes): the 1,340-ton 'H' class destroyer *Hero* (4 × 4.7in guns, 8 torpedo tubes), the 1,370-ton 'I' class destroyer *Icarus* (4 × 4.7in, 10 torpedo tubes) and the 1,870-ton 'Tribal' class *Bedouin*, *Punjabi*, *Cossack* and *Eskimo* (8 × 4.7in, 4 torpedo tubes). All these destroyers could make 36 knots.

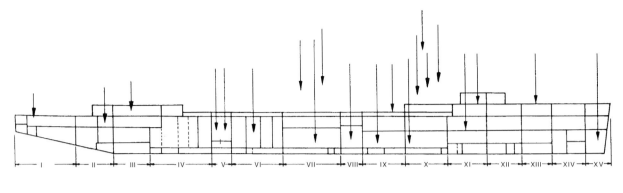

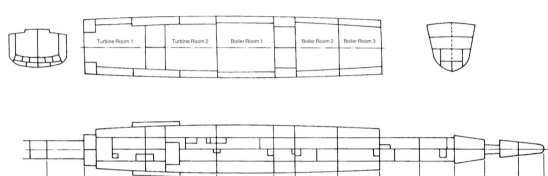

Hits Scored on Z 12 *Erich Giese*, 13 April 1940

Location	Consequences	Remarks
Compartment XV, waterline	–	–
Compartment XIII, forecastle near No 1 gun	Casualties No 1 gun	Hit madetowards end of battle, all ammunition expended, forecastle on fire
Compartment XI, at base of No 2 gun, shell exploded nearby, star-board side	Casualties, 2cm ammunition set alight	Hit made towards end of battle
Compartment XI, near Seaman NCOs' deck	Casualties, fire below forecastle	Gunnery data centre companionway blocked, personnel used emergency exit
Compartment X, on wheelhouse	Helmsman and engine-room telegraphist killed, command equipment destroyed	No further effect as engine room already out of commission
Compartment X, in cipher room	Casualties, radio room out of commission	Hit made early in action
Compartment X, in radio room	Equipment rendered unserviceable	–
Compartment X, on bridge	Casualties, damage to bridge area	–
Compartment X, in boiler room 3	Casualties, serious danger from steam and fire in boiler room 3	Boiler room evacuated
Compartment IX, hit in forecastle down to sick bay	Casualties, fire in compartment IX	–
Compartment IX, in boiler room 2	Casualties, danger from gases and steam, main feedwater pump and lighting fail	Boiler shut down from upper deck, port boiler in boiler room 2 still working, starboard boiler just reached turbine start-up stage
Compartment VIII, hit in auxiliary engine room	Heating oil leaks into electrical plant 3	Room evacuated

Compartment VII, in boiler room 1	–	Room shut down
After funnel	After rangefinder unserviceable because of smoke and oil	After torpedo tubes impeded by smoke
3.7cm flak, starboard side	Casualties, damage, ready ammunition on fire	–
Compartment VI, in turbine room 2	Casualties, chief engineer seriously wounded, serious damage from steam, turbine room and E-plant 2 shut down	Room abandoned
Compartment V, in stabiliser room	Casualties, danger from steam	–
In AA magazine	Casualties, ammunition explosions	–
Compartment III, on after deckhouse	Casualties, ammunition supply for Nos 3 and 4 guns unserviceable	Ammunition already spent
Compartment II, near ammunition ready room	Casualties, No 4 gun and ammunition supply for No 5 gun unserviceable (later repaired, enabling the last ten rounds to be fired)	–
Compartment I, through weather deck abaft bulkhead, Compartment I	Splinter damage to smoke-gernerating room, rendered unserviceable.	–

pompoms. From reports made to me by crewmen immediately after we got ashore, it was obvious that several of our men had been cut down in the water by MG fire. Zivilsteward Masula had a bullet graze. Some days after the battle the body of Obermaschinenmaat Ospelkaus was found. He had a bullet in the back of his head, which he can only have received in the water.

From numerous other reports after the battle I concluded that many men had been fired on in the water and had lost their lives in that manner. It was repeatedly described by comrades close by how they would suddenly cease swimming, their heads streaming blood. Corroborating statements indicated that the British concentrated their fire on the liferafts, one of which had no paddle and was adrift in the fjord. For some reason they took nine prisoners from this raft.

At the time, of course, propaganda was made out of the allegations, and in this way the British Admiralty must have been aware that something improper had occurred. On 16 April 1940 the commander of HMS *Icarus* stated that, contrary to the conduct of the commanders of HMS *Cossack* (already known to WUSt investigators following the *Altmark* incident in February 1940*) and HMS *Bedouin*, he had never taken part in warfare fought in such a manner. *Icarus*'s commander had found it necessary during the battle to signal the commander of the destroyer *Foxhound*: 'If you are not otherwise engaged, pick up any Germans in the water', and it was *Foxhound* that picked up the survivors from the unmanoeuvrable raft.

From Narvik to the Capitulation

In the wake of the disaster at Narvik on 13 April 1940, the four existing Z-Flottillen were disbanded and re-formed under a caretaker FdZ, Fregattenkapitän Alfred Schemmel, between 18 April and 14 May 1940. Kapitän zur See Erich Bey was appointed on the latter date, and he held the post until his death aboard the battleship *Scharnhorst* on 26 December 1943.

The two new flotillas were numbered 5 and 6. 5. Z-Flottille consisted of the former 1. Z-Flottille based at Swinemünde—Z 4 *Richard Beitzen*, Z 14 *Friedrich Ihn*, Z 15 *Erich Steinbrinck* and Z 16 *Friedrich Eckholdt*. 6. Z-Flottille comprised the remaining survivors, Z 5 *Paul Jacobi*, Z 6 *Theodor Riedel*, Z 7 *Hermann Schoemann*, Z 8 *Bruno Heinemann*, Z 10 *Hans Lody*

and Z 20 *Karl Galster*. These flotillas had little real significance because the small number of ships and their lack of operational readiness led to units being sent wherever the necessity for them arose. During 1940 three new destroyers, Z 23, Z 24 and Z 25, entered service, but they were not combat-ready until March 1941.

No destroyer operations were carried out in the Baltic east of the Kattegat in 1940, and there were no further German destroyer losses during 1940.

* During the *Altmark* incident in Jössingfjord on 16 February 1940, crewmen on HMS *Cossack* had shot down eight crew members from *Altmark* who had left their ship and were running across the ice towards the shore.—Tr)

The immediate priority following the occupation of Norway was to close down the Skagerrak, and on 28 April Z 4 *Richard Beitzen* and Z 8 *Bruno Heinemann* took part in the first day's operation to lay the Sperre 17 mine barrage in company with the minelayers *Roland*, *Kaiser*, *Preussen* and *Cobra*. The torpedo boats *Leopard*, *Möwe* and *Kondor* were also present, though *Leopard* was sunk in a collision with *Preussen*. After an improvement in the weather, the work was completed on 17 and 19 May, Z 4 being accompanied by Z 7 *Hermann Schoemann* on these two latter occasions.

At the beginning of June an operation codenamed 'Juno' was begun, the objective of which was to penetrate to the end of Andfjord and attack the town of Harstad, which British forces had invested as a naval base with a view eventually to re-taking Narvik. At 0800 on 4 June a German formation led by the battleship *Gneisenau*, flagship of Admiral Marschall, set out northwards from Kiel. In line astern followed the battleship *Scharnhorst*, the heavy cruiser *Admiral Hipper* and the destroyers *Hans Lody*, *Hermann Schoemann*, *Erich Steinbrinck* and *Karl Galster*. The attack on Harstad was planned for the early hours of 9 June, but once it had been confirmed that the British and French occupation force had abandoned the town, and a full evacuation from Norway was in progress, Gruppe West ordered Marschall to attack a reported convoy instead. A scouting line with 10nm between each ship was formed, and at 0605, in position 67°20'N 04°00'E the sweep encountered a westbound tanker, *Oil Pioneer* (5,666grt), escorted by the 530-ton 'Tree' class corvette *Juniper*—'an unwelcome stop in our search for the valuable convoy with its cruiser and destroyer escort', Marschall recorded. While *Gneisenau* dealt with the tanker, leaving *Hermann Schoemann* to rescue the eleven survivors, *Admiral Hipper* finished off the corvette. *Juniper*'s depth charges exploded as she sank, leaving only one survivor to be picked up by *Hans Lody*.

The search line re-formed, and shortly after 1000 *Lody* reported smoke from several ships to the north which proved to be the hospital ship *Atlantis*, which was allowed to proceed unmolested, and the empty troop transporter *Orama* (19,840grt). The latter was suspected to be an AMC, and when, at 1104, movement on deck was interpreted as an attempt to man her guns, *Hipper* turned broadside-on and opened fire with tail-fused salvos from all her main turrets at a range of 13,000yds. *Lody* began shooting at the same time, and, just as she was being ordered via ultra-short wave radio to cease firing, *Hipper*'s foretop rangefinder operator reported that the *Orama* had struck her flag and was being abandoned by her crew. *Lody* had the *Orama* on a bearing from which it was not possible to see the transport's lifeboats being lowered—and her ultra-short wave radio was not functioning. She therefore received neither the order from *Hipper* to cease firing nor one from the fleet commander not to fire torpedoes. *Hans Lody* unfortunately continued to shell the stricken ship and, to hasten her demise, loosed off two torpedoes. Both of these were rogues, but although one was a surface-runner which hit a loaded lifeboat at 40 knots and failed to explode, the other deviated and detinated prematurely close to *Hipper*. At 1220 the *Orama* sank by the stern, leaving fourteen survivors to be picked up by the heavy cruiser and 98 by the destroyer. An hour later the cruiser and destroyers were sent into Trondheim to refuel.

On 10 June the cruiser sortied in company with the battleship *Gneisenau* and the same four destroyers— Z 7, Z 10, Z 15 and Z 20—to attack British shipping, but as a result of adverse Luftwaffe reconnaissance reports were back at their moorings the next day. Bomber aircraft attacked the German units on several occasions.

Between 14 and 17 June, in an operation codenamed 'Nora', the cruiser *Nürnberg*, Z 15 *Erich Steinbrinck* and a minesweeping flotilla escorted the troopship *Levante* with 3. Gebirgsjager Division from Trondheim to Elvegardsmoen in Narvikfjord, returning with the paratroop force relieved there.

On 20 June the battleship *Scharnhorst*, which had been torpedoed during the action in which she and her sister-ship *Gneisenau* sank the aircraft carrier *Glorious* and three destroyers, left Trondheim for Kiel flanked by Z 7 *Hermann Schoemann*, Z 15 *Erich Steinbrinck*, Z 10 *Hans Lody* and several torpedo boats; that same evening *Admiral Hipper* and *Gneisenau* sailed from Trondheim escorted by Z 20 *Karl Galster* and a seaplane on an operation to 'roll up' the British Northern Patrol, this having the secondary purpose of distracting attention from the departure of *Scharnhorst*. Shortly before midnight, at the entrance to Trondheimfjord, the submarine *Clyde* torpedoed *Gneisenau* forward of 'A' turret and the German force had to turn back.

On 25 July *Hipper* left Trondheim in company with the homebound damaged *Gneisenau* and her escort, consisting of the cruiser *Nürnberg*, Z 5 *Paul Jacobi*, Z 14 *Friedrich Ihn* and Z 20 *Karl Galster*. As arranged, *Hipper* was soon detached and steered north alone for anti-contraband reconnaissance in polar waters, and the force for Kiel was reinforced the next day by the torpedo boats *Seeadler*, *Iltis*, *Jaguar*, *Luchs* and T 5. *Luchs* was sunk when she intercepted a torpedo intended for *Gneisenau* from the British submarine *Swordfish*, but the remainder of the convoy reached Kiel on 28 June.

Between 31 August and 2 September Z 5 *Paul Jacobi*, Z 15 *Erich Steinbrinck*, Z 20 *Karl Galster* and four torpedo boats assisted the minelayers *Tannenberg*, *Roland* and *Cobra* to lay the Sperre 3 barrage in the south-western North Sea.

From 13 September 1940 *Admiral Hipper* was on standby at Kiel for Operation 'Seelöwe' (Sealion), the planned invasion of Britain, for which her task was to make a diversionary break-out to the north of either Scotland or Ireland to lure the Home Fleet out of the English Channel. All operational destroyers were sent to the French Channel ports of Brest and Cherbourg during September and October for 'Seelöwe': Z 6 *Theodor Riedel*, Z 10 *Hans Lody*, Z 14 *Friedrich Ihn*, Z 16 *Friedrich Eckholdt* and Z 20 *Karl Galster* sailed from Germany on 9 September, followed on the 22nd by Z 5 *Paul Jacobi* and Z 15 *Erich Steinbrinck*. Z 6 *Theodor Riedel* was of little use on account of persistent problems with her port engine. Z 4 *Richard Beitzen* arrived on 21 October.

The principal operations carried out against the British south coast occurred on the night of 28 September, when Falmouth Bay was mined by *Paul Jacobi*, *Hans Lody*, *Friedrich Ihn* and *Friedrich Eckholdt*; on 17 October, when *Hans Lody*, *Friedrich Ihn*, *Erich Steinbrinck*, *Karl Galster* and 5. *Torpedobootflottille* skirmished briefly with a mixed force of Royal Navy cruisers and destroyers in the Western Approaches (*Lody* was struck twice by shells); and in the early morning of 19 November when, off Plymouth, *Richard Beitzen*, *Hans Lody* and *Karl Galster* engaged the destroyers *Jupiter*, *Javelin*, *Jackal*, *Jersey* and *Kashmir*, *Galster* suffering light splinter damage and *Javelin* being torpedoed forward and aft.

With the abandonment of 'Seelöwe' in October, German destroyers had begun to trickle away from Brest and Cherbourg to Germany to refit and repair, and by early December Z 4 *Richard Beitzen*, at Brest, was the only German destroyer operational anywhere.

Six new destroyers (Z 23–28) became operational during 1941, and, as no destroyers were lost, the total available for duty at the end of the year rose to sixteen. Z 4 *Richard Beitzen* remained the only destroyer active off the French coast until March. She escorted *Admiral Hipper* out of Brest at the commencement the cruiser's second raiding operation and met her on her return to the French port on 14 February.

Z 4 left for Germany on 16 March and was replaced in early April by Z 8 *Bruno Heinemann*, Z 14 *Friedrich Ihn* and Z 15 *Erich Steinbrinck*, which were based at La Pallice. From 22 to 24 April these destroyers escorted *Thor* across Biscay to Cherbourg on the completion of the raider's successful Atlantic cruise. In May Z 8 and Z 15 repeated the exercise for the naval oiler *Nordmark* after her six-month sojourn in mid-Atlantic replenishing the pocket battleship Admiral Scheer. In the morning of 1 June all three destroyers met the cruiser *Prinz Eugen* as she put in at Brest astern of *Sperrbrecher 13* at 1525 to conclude the disastrous 'Rheinübung' operation (in which the battleship *Bismarck* was sunk).

In mid-June the new destroyers Z 23 and Z 24 arrived at Brest and together with Z 8 and Z 15 ran escort for the battleship *Scharnhorst* on her occasional movements down the Breton coast. On 24 July, while engaged in gunnery practice off La Pallice, *Scharnhorst* was bombed and had to return to Brest for repair. From 21 to 23 August Z 23, Z 24, *Erich Steinbrinck* and *Bruno Heinemann* escorted the raider *Orion* across the Bay of Biscay and into the Gironde estuary after her epic seventeen-month cruise (all incoming prizes and steamers headed for St-Nazaire or the Gironde estuary using the so-called 'Prize Channel'. By the end of October all the destroyers based in France had returned to Germany.

Meanwhile, further north, between 26 and 28 March Z 23 escorted *Admiral Hipper* into Kiel after the latter's break-out from Brest, and the same destroyer met *Admiral Scheer* returning from the Indian Ocean on 30 March, the voyage finishing at Kiel on 1 April. At 1125 on 19 May, off Cape Arcona, Rügen Island, the battleship *Bismarck* and heavy cruiser *Prinz Eugen* moved off astern of a protective screen formed by Z 15 *Erich Steinbrinck*, Z 23 and two *Sperrbrecher* for the southern entrance to the Great Belt, where Z 10 *Hans Lody*, several minesweepers and eight aircraft joined for the crossing of the Skagerrak. At 0900 the next morning *Prinz Eugen* and the destroyers put into Korsfjord and refuelled in Kalvenes Bay. At 2000 the battle group assembled behind the destroyer screen, reaching the open sea by way of Hjeltefjord at 2200 on 21 May. The destroyers were released into Trondheim at 0510 the following morning.

On 11 June 1941 the light cruiser *Leipzig*, the destroyers Z 16 *Friedrich Eckholdt* and Z 20 *Karl Galster*, three torpedo boats, two U-boats and a large air escort set out from Kiel to accompany the heavy cruiser *Lützow* (formerly the pocket battleship *Deutschland*) on the first stage of Operation 'Sommerreise', a raiding cruise to the Indian Ocean. The naval escort terminated at Oslofjord, and *Lützow* continued alone. She got as far as Egersund before being crippled by an RAF torpedobomber. Z 10 *Hans Lody* and Z16 *Friedrich Eckholdt* escorted her back to the yards at Kiel on 14 June.

With the opening of the campaign against the Soviet Union—'Barbarossa'—a two-part Baltic Fleet was formed. On 23 September 1941 the northern group, comprising the battleship *Tirpitz*, the cruisers *Nürnberg* and *Köln* and the new destroyers Z 25, Z 26 and Z 27, left Swinemünde for the Gulf of Finland to intercept Russian warships seeking internment in Sweden. On 27 September the force appeared off the Aba-Aaland skerries, but, as it turned out, the Red Fleet had no intention of leaving Kronstadt.

Shortly after the outbreak of war with the Soviet Union, 6. Z-Flottille (Kapitän zur See Alfred Schulze-Hinrichs), consisting of Z 4 *Richard Beitzen*, Z 7 *Hermann Schoemann*, Z 10 *Hans Lody*, Z 16 *Friedrich Eckholdt* and Z 20 *Karl Galster*, set out for northern Norway, arriving on 10 July at Kirkenes, a port in the Barents Sea close to the Kola peninsula and Murmansk. On 12 July the force split into two groups and on the first foray attacked a small Russian convoy of tugs, sinking the Soviet patrol ship *Passat* and a trawler. In a three-day sortie near the port of Iokanga on the Kola peninsula near the mouth of the White Sea, Z 4, Z 7, Z 16 and Z 20 sank the Soviet survey ship *Meridian*, but a similar raid which set out on 29 July was broken off after the Luftwaffe reportedan approaching British force of two carriers, two cruisers and four destroyers which subsequently attacked Kirkenes.

On 9 and 10 August 1941 *Beitzen*, *Lody* and *Eckholdt* operated in the Kildin–Kola Inlet area, where, in a short engagement, the Soviet patrol vessel *SKR-12* was sunk. *Beitzen* was straddled by enemy fire but not hit. When Z 4 and Z 7 returned to Germany for repairs in August, the remaining three destroyers were limited to escort duties following the British attack on the *Bremse* convoy of 6 September.

By November the Seekriegsleitung had recognised the frequency of the British Murmansk convoys and decided to adopt a far more aggressive policy in the Arctic. For this purpose 8. Z-Flottille (Kapitän zur See Gottfried Pönitz), composed of five new destroyers together with four E-boats and six U-boats, was sent to Kirkenes to relieve 6. Z-Flottille, the heavy ships following shortly afterwards.

From 16 to 18 December Z 23, Z 24, Z 25, and Z 27—Z 26 turned back with engine trouble—sailed to lay a minefield north of Cape Gordodetzky on the Kola peninsula at the entrance to the White Sea but were disturbed by the Murmansk-based *Halcyon* class minesweeping sloops *Speedy* and *Hazard*, which had set out to escort convoy PQ.6. *Speedy* was hit and seriously damaged by four 15cm shells, but the German destroyers broke off the action when two Russian destroyers and the heavy cruiser *Kent* steamed out of the Kola Inlet to engage. On Boxing Day Z 23, Z 24, Z 25 and Z 27 operated off the Lofoten Islands following the British commando raid there at Christmas when an important radio mast had been destroyed and the small German naval base at Vaagso attacked.

During the course of 1942 Z 7 *Hermann Schoemann*, Z 8 *Bruno Heinemann* and Z 16 *Friedrich Eckholdt*, plus Z 26, were lost, and Z 29, Z 30 and Z 31 became operational, as did ZG 3 *Hermes* in the Mediterranean. By the end of the year sixteen destroyers were available—the same number as on 31 December 1941. Throughout 1942 all destroyer operations were concentrated in Norwegian waters: even Operation 'Cerberus'—the 'Channel Dash'—in February having as its primary object the removal of three heavy units from Brest to Norway.

The year opened with the laying of a 100-mine EMC field by the Kirkenes-based destroyers Z 23, Z 24 and Z 25 on 13 January in the western channel of the entrance to the White Sea near Cape Kocovsky. Meanwhile the battleships *Scharnhorst* and *Gneisenau* and the heavy cruiser *Prinz Eugen* had been at Brest for between six and nine months, and it was decided to extricate them by sailing them through the English Channel in broad daylight—the so-called 'Channel Dash'. Final discussions on the planned break-out from Brest were held in Paris on 1 January, those present including *Admiräle* Saalwächter, Schniewind and Ciliax and the commanders of the three heavy units. Hitler gave his consent to the operation on 12 January. Towards the end of the month seven destroyers were despatched to Brest, but on 25 January, off Calais, Z 8 *Bruno Heinemann*, sailing in a group with Z 4, Z 5 and Z 7, struck two mines and sank—the first German destroyer lost since Narvik. Later Z 14, Z 25 and Z 29 arrived at Brest without incident. It was suspected that the principal target during the 'Channel Dash' would be *Prinz Eugen*, because of her part in sinking the battlcruiser *Hood* the previous May, and she was fitted with an extra five quadruple AA guns and allocated Z 14 *Friedrich Ihn*, which carried an unusual amount of sophisticated technology, as escort. Notice for steam was given for 2030 on 11 February. In command of the squadron was Vizeadmiral Ciliax, on board the flagship *Scharnhorst*.

Sailing was delayed by an air raid warning, and when the ships weighed anchor at 2245 their departure went unnoticed, the British submarine keeping watch off the port being engaged in recharging her batteries offshore. Escorting the three heavy ships—steaming in the order *Scharnhorst, Gneisenau, Prinz Eugen*—were the destroyers Z 4 *Richard Beitzen*, Z 5 *Paul Jacobi*, Z 7 *Hermann Schoemann*, Z 14 *Friedrich Ihn*, Z 25 and Z 29; the torpedo boats T 11, T 2, T 5, T 12 and T 4 of the 2nd Flotilla, T 13, T 15, T 16 and T 17 of the 3rd Flotilla and *Seeadler, Falke, Kondor, Iltis* and *Jaguar* of the 5th Flotilla; and the 2nd, 4th and 6th E-boat Flotillas. Luftwaffe air cover comprised 176 Bf 110s and fighters.

The British were not alerted to the passage of the German armada until it was beyond Calais. The wind was south-west force 6 and the sea state 5. The first MTB attacks began at 1320, after the ships were beyond the range of the Dover batteries. Next came a suicidal low-level attack by six Swordfish torpedo bombers, all of which were shot down, one by the Luftwaffe, two by *Friedrich Ihn* and three by *Prinz Eugen* firing in barrage. In the North Sea the German units had the advantages of favourable weather and a heavy air umbrella.

In the entire action, 42 of the 600 British aircraft engaged were destroyed. When *Scharnhorst* was mined off the Scheldt, Ciliax transferred to Z 29, but, finding she had engine and other battle damage, he raised his flag aboard Z 7 *Hermann Schoemann* for the run to port.

At 0245 on 20 February *Prinz Eugen* (flagship of Vizeadmiral Ciliax) and *Admiral Scheer* left Brunsbüttel for Norway accompanied by *Beitzen, Jacobi, Schoe-*

mann and Z 25. When reported by air reconnaissance before midday, the group reversed course for a while to throw the enemy off the scent. An unsuccessful air attack resulted in one aircraft being shot down. The ships put into Grimstadfjord on 22 February and left for Trondheim the same evening, but the escort was reduced by 50 per cent when *Beitzen* and *Jacobi* were forced into Bergen on account of damage cause by the heavy weather.

At 0702 the next morning, *Trident*—one of four British submarines positioned off the coast—hit *Prinz Eugen*'s stern with a torpedo which knocked off her rudder though left her propellers undamaged. The after section was almost severed, and the cruiser was unmanoeuvrable. Defensive measures prevented further attacks, and the unfortunate vessel limped into Lofjord during the night of 24 February. The scale of the damage was such that repairs in a German shipyard was dictated, and emergency work was begun at once alongside the workshop vessel *Huascaran*.

On 5 March German aircraft south of Jan Mayen reported a fifteen-ship convoy sailing on an eastward heading. This proved to be PQ.12, and at the same time convoy QP.8 was sailing westwards for Iceland. The battleship *Tirpitz*, in company with Z 14 *Friedrich Ihn*, Z 7 *Hermann Schoemann* and Z 25, sailed from Trondheim to intercept the merchantmen but missed the convoys in storm and fog, their only victim being the straggling Soviet freighter *Izora*, sunk on 7th March by *Ihn*.

On 19 March *Admiral Hipper* sailed north from Brunsbüttel in company with the destroyers Z 24, Z 26 and Z 30 and the torpedo boats T 15, T 16 and T 17 and on the 21st joined the heavy cruisers *Admiral Scheer* and *Prinz Eugen* in Lofjord near Trondheim. In the evening of 28 March the Kirkenes destroyers Z 24, Z 25 and Z 26 took on the role of light cruisers to attack convoy PQ.13. After having sunk the straggler *Bateau*—which was stopping to rescue her crew and that of the *Empire Ranger* found adrift in lifeboats—the trio were surprised in poor visibility in the morning of 29 March by the cruiser *Trinidad* (8,000 tons, 33 knots, 12 × 6in guns, 2 torpedo tubes) and the destroyer *Fury* (1,350 tons, 36 knots, 4 × 14.7in guns, 8 torpedo tubes). Z 26 was seriously damaged and set on fire after hits from *Trinidad* but found refuge in a snow squall. When contact was renewed, the British cruiser attempted to torpedo Z 26. Her tubes were iced over, however, and the only torpedo to come free was a rogue which circled back and hit the ship which had fired it. Z 24 and Z 25 missed the cruiser with torpedoes. Short exchanges occurred in the poor visibility between snow showers, culminating in a second British destroyer, *Eclipse* (1,375 tons, 4 × 4.7in, 8 torpedo tubes) shooting Z 26 to a standstill. Z 24 and Z 25 rained shells down on to *Eclipse* but eventually allowed her to escape, preferring to save Z 26's crewmen before the destroyer sank in waters which the human body could not survive for more than a minute or so. Even so, the death toll aboard Z 26 was grievous: 283 men failed to return home.

On 9 April 1942 Z 7 *Hermann Schoemann* sailed for Kirkenes as a replacement for the sunken Z 26, and on 1 May she sortied with Z 24 and Z 25 to attack convoy QP.11, which had already been intercepted by U-boats. The convoy was relatively well protected. Close in was the light cruiser *Edinburgh* (10,000 tons, 32 knots, 12 × 6in guns) and the destroyers *Forester* and *Foresight* (1,350 tons, 36 knots, 4 × 4.7in, 8 torpedo tubes), the remaining escort being composed of the destroyers *Bulldog* and *Beagle* (1,360 tons, 35 knots, 4 × 4.7in, 8 torpedo tubes), *Amazon* (1,352 tons, 37 knots, 4 × 4.7in, six torpedo tubes) and *Beverley* (1,190 tons, 25 knots, 3 × 4in, 3 torpedo tubes), plus four corvettes and a trawler. Well to the rear were some Soviet vessels coming up from Murmansk. *Edinburgh* had been torpedoed by U 456 on 30 April.

In thick snowfall and drift ice, the three German destroyers clashed first with the four outer destroyers, damaging *Amazon*. Shortly afterwards they came across the motionless *Edinburgh*. Her guns were still intact, and she soon had *Hermann Schoemann* wallowing, one of the first hits knocking out the destroyer's main steam feed, causing her current and both turbines to fail. Attempts by Z 24 and Z 25 to finish off *Edinburgh* with torpedoes were frustrated by iced-up tubes, only one torpedo getting clear. After laying a smoke screen to protect Z 7, they then took on *Forester* and *Foresight*, inflicting serious damage on both, but Z 25 had four dead in her radio room as a result of a direct hit. *Edinburgh* later sank. After picking up what survivors from *Schoemann* she could find, Z 24 scuttled Z 7 with explosives. U 88 found a number of the destroyer's survivors in boats and on rafts, her final tally of dead being eight.

In Operation 'Walzertraum' (Waltz Dream), the heavy cruiser *Lützow* set out on 15 May with Z 4, Z 10, Z 27, Z 29 and a fleet escort boat to join Kampfgruppe I (Battle Group I) at Trondheim. The voyage was interrupted at Kristiansand to allow the completion of a minelaying operation by Z 4 *Richard Beitzen*, and then the convoy proceeded, arriving at Trondheim to join *Admiral Scheer* on 20 May as Kampfgruppe II. Bogen Bay near Narvik was reached on the 26th.

On 13 June *Admiral Hipper* moved up to Bogen Bay to form part of Kampfgruppe I under the fleet commander Admiral Schniewind aboard his flagship *Tirpitz*. The next stage of the process was Operation 'Musik', the transfer northward to Altaford, and, on arrival in Grimsöytraumen, *Lützow*, *Theodor Riedel*, *Hans Lody* and *Karl Galster* all struck uncharted shallows and were ruled out of the main operation.

On 3 July the two Kampfgruppen joined forces to attack the heavily escorted convoy PQ.17, which consisted of 36 freighters, one tanker and three rescue ships and was heading for Murmansk. The operation was codenamed 'Rösselsprung' (Knight's Move). *Tirpitz*, *Admiral Hipper*, *Admiral Scheer*, six destroyers— Z 14 *Friedrich Ihn*, Z 24, Z 27, Z 28, Z 29 and Z 30— and two torpedo-boats put to sea on 5 July. They were beyond the North Cape steering north-east when the recall order was transmitted at 2200 that evening, and by 7 July the fleet was back at anchor. The Seekriegsleitung and the British Admiralty made a similar decision to withdraw naval surface forces from the area at about the same time. The preparations of the combined German battle group had been observed by British aerial reconnaissance, resulting in the recall of the naval escort and the controversial order to the convoy to disperse, which was to prove its death knell. On the German side, the wireless monitoring service had decoded British signals traffic reporting the German preparations, and SKL ordered the formation at sea to return to harbour on the grounds of the risk incurred. PQ.17 was then savaged by U-boats and the Luftwaffe.

On 17 August *Richard Beitzen*, *Erich Steinbrinck* and *Friedrich Eckholdt* escorted *Admiral Scheer* towards Bear Island for her solitary anti-shipping cruise, Operation 'Wunderland', into the Kara Sea, where she bombarded Port Dickson on the North Siberian mainland. On 29 August she met up with the same three destroyers off Bear Island for the return to Kirkenes. Z 4, Z 15 and Z 16 had escorted the minelayer *Ulm* to Bear Island to sow a field north west of Novaya Zemlya. On the way back *Ulm* fell foul of the British destroyers *Marne*, *Martin* and *Onslaught* and was sunk after a brief engagement.

70

Operation 'Doppelschlag' (Double Blow) was a continuation of 'Wunderland'. It was planned that *Admiral Scheer*, *Admiral Hipper* and three destroyers would operate off the estuaries of the Ob and Yenisei rivers on the north Russian coast before hunting for independent shipping on the Novaya Zemlya–Spitzbergen track. The operation was cancelled because of ice and the state of *Scheer*'s diesels.

On 13 September Hitler issued an order forbidding the employment of surface warships against eastbound convoys. Between 4 and 8 September *Richard Beitzen*, Z 29 and Z 30 had laid mines at the entrance to the Kara Strait. On the 24th of the month, as the flagship of Admiral Kummetz, *Hipper* set out with *Beitzen*, *Steinbrinck*, *Eckholdt* and Z 28 steering north-north-east into the Barents Sea and during the evening of 26 September laid 96 mines off the Matoshkin Strait at the centre of Novaya Zemlya. The purpose of this operation, codenamed 'Czarin' (Empress) was to force enemy convoys closer to the coast of Norway and thus nearer to German naval units. The group dropped anchor in Altafjord on the 28th.

Between 13 and 15 October *Friedrich Eckholdt*, Z 24, Z 27 and Z 30 laid a minefield off the Kanin peninsula at the mouth of the White Sea, and this quickly claimed a victim when the Soviet icebreaker *Mikoyan* blew up. On 5 November *Hipper* sortied from Kaafjord into the Barents Sea in company with *Beitzen*, *Eckholdt*, Z 27 and Z 30 on Operation 'Hoffnung' (Hope) with the idea of criss-crossing the convoy tracks in search of merchant vessels sailing alone. Whilst in pursuit of a tanker sighted by *Hipper*'s shipboard Arado, Z 27 sank the Soviet submarine-chaser *BO-78*, picking up 43 crew members: the same destroyer, at the far end of the patrol line, also sank the Russian tanker *Donbass* (8,000grt) with three torpedoes, the crew being brought aboard. The German ships returned to Altafjord on 9 November.

Following the discovery by U 85 on 28 December of what was reported to be a lightly defended convoy of ten ships 70 miles south of Bear Island, all available surface units in northern Norway were brought to readiness on 29 December, and, in a conference the following day, C-in-C Cruisers, Vizeadmiral Kummetz, explained Operation 'Regenbogen' to the commanders. The first destroyer to detect the convoy would shadow it while the remainder of the destroyer force closed in. The cruisers would stand off until first light. The first objective was to destroy the convoy escort before attacking the merchantmen. A superior enemy was to be avoided.

On 30 December, the German Kampfgruppe, consisting of the flagship *Admiral Hipper*, the heavy cruiser *Lützow* and six destroyers—*Richard Beitzen*, *Theodor Riedel*, *Friedrich Eckholdt*, Z 29, Z 30 and Z 31, headed north on course 60° once clear of the coast. Kummetz ordered a 65-mile scouting line to be formed as from 0830 on 31 December, the six destroyers combing forward in a south-easterly direction 15nm apart. *Hipper* and *Lützow* would keep station astern of and to seaward of the northern and southern ends of the line respectively for an 85-mile width of search, while the destroyers would advance in the order *Eckholdt*–Z 29–*Beitzen*–Z 31–Z 30–*Riedel*. Whilst the warships were forming into their allotted positions in the scouting line, *Hipper* detected by radar two shadows at 60° which could not be German vessels, and *Eckholdt* was detached as contact keeper. Thus at the start of the engagement the German group was effectively divided into two sections, the northern of which consisted of *Hipper* and the destroyers *Beitzen*, Z 24 and *Eckholdt*.

At 0842—daybreak—*Friedrich Eckholdt* reported ten vessels steering 90°, and at 0910, at a range of 18.000yds bearing 140°, *Hipper* sighted a number of vessels, including destroyers, consituting the main convoy escort on its northern flank. The destroyers were *Onslow*, *Obedient*, *Obdurate*, *Orwell* and *Achates*. The fourteen ships of convoy JW.51B were steaming initially on an easterly bearing and bore round south at 1020. At 0930 Z 4, Z 16 and Z 24 fired on *Obdurate*. Spotting and rangefinding were very difficult in the poor light and poor visibility and because of the icing and misting over of instruments.

At 1018 the destroyer *Onslow* was hit by a salvo from *Admiral Hipper* and at 1027 was reported by *Richard Beitzen* as burning fiercely and down by the stern. At 1030 Hipper was about 15nm to the north of the convoy and steering east. The convoy was now on a course to the south towards *Lützow*, but *Hipper* was entrammelled with the escorts and having to concentrate on the destroyer *Achates* and the radar-equipped minesweeper *Bramble*.

At 1135, on ultra-short wave radio, *Friedrich Eckholdt* asked a series of questions to establish the identity of a warship she had just sighted. In a batch of replies at 1136 Kummetz signalled, 'In combat with escort forces—no cruisers', although two minutes earlier *Admiral Hipper* had been surprised by fire from a cruiser with large bridge, a raked forefunnel and turrets fore and aft, making 31 knots and identified as probably a *Southampton* or *Fiji* class cruiser. *Hipper* had been hit and had her speed reduced, so that at 1137 Kummetz, who was in any case in two minds because of an ambiguous signal from ashore, decided to abandon the operation. At 1143 the destroyer *Eckholdt*, ignorant of *Richard Beitzen*'s warning radio message, decided that the cruiser she was facing must be German, and was sunk with all hands by *Sheffield*. The German force returned to Altafjord, where it dropped anchor on 1 January 1943.

The unforeseen outcome of the operation had the most serious consequences for the German surface fleet. Although the Kampfgruppe commander was bound by orders which required him to abandon the mission if heavy enemy forces appeared, the attack had already been reported as a great success, and when news of a fiasco was conveyed to Hitler instead, he reacted by decommissioning all ships of the size of light cruiser and above. Raeder resigned a few days later and was replaced by Grossadmiral Dönitz. The latter obtained some concessions, but on the whole the directive remained in force until the course of the war determined otherwise.

At the end of 1943 the number of operational Kriegsmarine destroyers was twenty, with ZH 1, Z 32, Z 33, Z 34, Z 37 and Z 38 now in commission. ZG 3 *Hermes* was lost off Tunisia in May, while Z 27 became a casualty in December.

On January, in Operation 'Fronttheater', *Scharnhorst* and *Prinz Eugen* were met off Hela by *Paul Jacobi*, *Friedrich Ihn* and Z 24 for the run to Norway, but when the squadron was sighted off the Skaw by RAF Coastal Command on the 11th the operation was broken off; a repeat attempt, code-named 'Domino', on the 25th with the destroyers *Jacobi*, *Erich Steinbrinck*, Z 32 and Z 37 was similarly unsuccessful, the units repairing to Gotenhafen on the 27th.

On 24 January *Richard Beitzen*, Z 29 and Z 30 sailed with *Admiral Hipper* and the light cruiser *Köln* from Altafjord to Bogen Bay and then Trondheim, leaving on 7 February for Kiel. The minelayer *Brummer* and the destroyers Z 6 *Theodor Riedel* and Z 31 laid the only offensive field of 1943 in the roadstead near Kildin Island, Kola Bay, between 4 and 6 February.

On 6 March *Scharnhorst* sailed from the Baltic. Having set out with *Jacobi*, *Steinbrinck*, Z 24, Z 25 and Z 28, plus five torpedo boats as escort, she arrived at Bogen Bay on 9 March with only Z 28 for company, the remainder following eight days later after having had weather damage repaired at Trondheim.

Between 31 March and 2 April *Paul Jacobi*, *Theodor Riedel* and *Karl Galster* waited near Jan Mayen for the blockade-runner *Regensburg* returning from Japan. The meeting never took place, the freighter having been sunk in the North Atlantic by the light cruiser *Glasgow*.

The major offensive of the year was the occupation of Spitzbergen, which was carried out between 6 and 9 September. While *Lützow*, Z 5 *Paul Jacobi* and Z 14 *Friedrich Ihn* remained in the anchorage at Altafjord to cover the numerous absences for the benefit of Allied air reconnaissance, the battleships *Tirpitz* and *Scharnhorst* and nine destroyers—Z 6, Z 10, Z 15, Z 20, Z 27, Z 29, Z 30, Z 31 and Z 33—headed for Barentsburg. During the approach to the town three destroyers were hit by coastal artillery: Z 29 suffered four hits, damage to outer plating, three dead and three wounded, Z 31 received eight hits on the upper deck, with one dead and one wounded, and Z 33 received no fewer than thirty-three hits to her hull and bridgework, resulting in 28 casualties, three of them fatal.

The last anti-convoy sortie by any German heavy warship ended in disaster on 26 December after *Scharnhorst*, accompanied by Z 29, Z 30, Z 33, Z 34 and Z 38 left Kaafjord on Christmas Day. Once the destroyer escort had been released because of the bad weather, the battleship continued alone and ran foul of the convoy escort—of capital-ship strength—off the North Cape. The FdZ, Bey, was commanding the operation aboard *Scharnhorst* and went down with his ship.

During 1943 the Kriegsmarine found it necessary to strengthen the escort force in the Bay of Biscay both for U-boats based there and for inbound merchantmen. Germany was not reliant on imports by sea as was Great Britain, but the occasional blockade-runner making the voyage to France from the Far East with high-value raw materials was of such importance that as many as five destroyers would sail to meet an inbound ship. For example, in July 1943 Z 23, Z 32 and Z 37 came in with *Himalaya*, in early August Z 23 and Z 32 actually entered the Atlantic beyond the longitude of Cape Ortegal to meet up with *Pietro Orsedo*, and on 23 December Z 23, Z 24, Z 27, Z 37 and ZH 1 escorted *Osorno* into the Gironde.

Late on Boxing Day 1943, Z 23, Z 24, Z 27, Z 32 and Z 37 sailed with six torpedo boats of 4. T-Flottille—

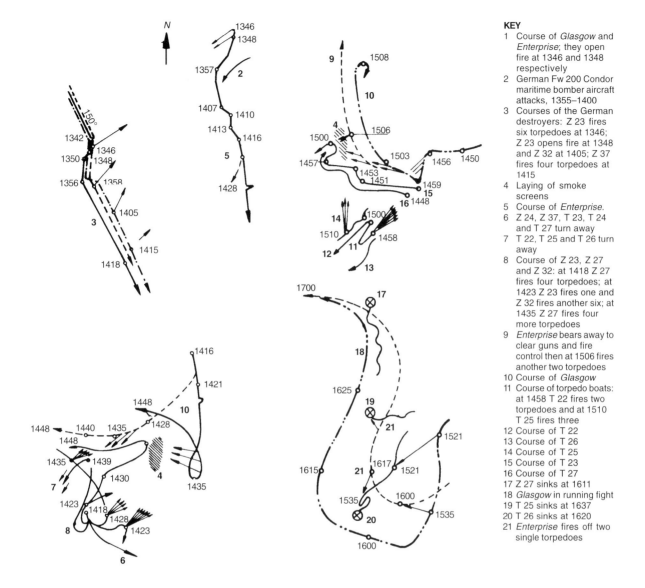

KEY
1 Course of *Glasgow* and *Enterprise*; they open fire at 1346 and 1348 respectively
2 German Fw 200 Condor maritime bomber aircraft attacks, 1355–1400
3 Courses of the German destroyers: Z 23 fires six torpedoes at 1346; Z 23 opens fire at 1348 and Z 32 at 1405; Z 37 fires four torpedoes at 1415
4 Laying of smoke screens
5 Course of *Enterprise*.
6 Z 24, Z 37, T 23, T 24 and T 27 turn away
7 T 22, T 25 and T 26 turn away
8 Course of Z 23, Z 27 and Z 32: at 1418 Z 27 fires four torpedoes; at 1423 Z 23 fires one and Z 32 fires another six; at 1435 Z 27 fires four more torpedoes
9 *Enterprise* bears away to clear guns and fire control then at 1506 fires another two torpedoes
10 Course of *Glasgow*
11 Course of torpedo boats: at 1458 T 22 fires two torpedoes and at 1510 T 25 fires three
12 Course of T 22
13 Course of T 26
14 Course of T 25
15 Course of T 23
16 Course of T 27
17 Z 27 sinks at 1611
18 *Glasgow* in running fight
19 T 25 sinks at 1637
20 T 26 sinks at 1620
21 *Enterprise* fires off two single torpedoes

Above: The Battle of Biscay, 28 December 1943.

T 22, T 23, T 24, T 25, T 26 and T 27—to meet the blockade-runner *Alsterufer*. However, this large freighter had already been sunk by the Royal Navy, and on 28 December the German force encountered the light cruisers *Glasgow* (9,100 tons, 32 knots, 12 × 6in guns) and *Enterprise* (7,580 tons, 33 knots, 7 × 6in guns) in what the Germans refer to as *Das Gefecht in der Biskaya* (The Battle of Biscay). The German vessels had several knots' more speed in ideal sea conditions than the two British cruisers, and also mounted a superior number of guns of the same calibre, but

Glasgow and *Enterprise* were far more seaworthy in heavy weather. The latter factor was decisive. There was a big sea running which slowed the German force considerably, and as gun platforms the German destroyers were inferior on the day because of the wild rolling motion. *Glasgow* and *Enterprise* put their speed and manoeuvrability to better use and sank Z 27 and the torpedo boats T 25 and T 26. Of the 740 men aboard these three ships, only 293 could be saved—21 by U 618, 34 by U 505, six by Spanish destroyers, 64 by British minesweepers and 168 by an Irish freighter.

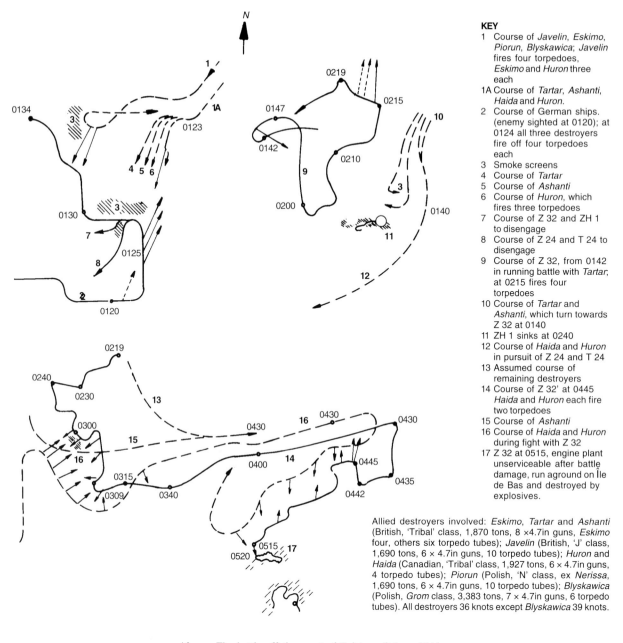

KEY

1 Course of *Javelin*, *Eskimo*, *Piorun*, *Blyskawica*; *Javelin* fires four torpedoes, *Eskimo* and *Huron* three each
1A Course of *Tartar*, *Ashanti*, *Haida* and *Huron*.
2 Course of German ships. (enemy sighted at 0120); at 0124 all three destroyers fire off four torpedoes each
3 Smoke screens
4 Course of *Tartar*
5 Course of *Ashanti*
6 Course of *Huron*, which fires three torpedoes
7 Course of Z 32 and ZH 1 to disengage
8 Course of Z 24 and T 24 to disengage
9 Course of Z 32, from 0142 in running battle with *Tartar*; at 0215 fires four torpedoes
10 Course of *Tartar* and *Ashanti*, which turn towards Z 32 at 0140
11 ZH 1 sinks at 0240
12 Course of *Haida* and *Huron* in pursuit of Z 24 and T 24
13 Assumed course of remaining destroyers
14 Course of Z 32' at 0445 *Haida* and *Huron* each fire two torpedoes
15 Course of *Ashanti*
16 Course of *Haida* and *Huron* during fight with Z 32
17 Z 32 at 0515, engine plant unserviceable after battle damage, run aground on Île de Bas and destroyed by explosives.

Allied destroyers involved: *Eskimo*, *Tartar* and *Ashanti* (British, 'Tribal' class, 1,870 tons, 8 ×4.7in guns, *Eskimo* four, others six torpedo tubes); *Javelin* (British, 'J' class, 1,690 tons, 6 × 4.7in guns, 10 torpedo tubes); *Huron* and *Haida* (Canadian, 'Tribal' class, 1,927 tons, 6 × 4.7in guns, 4 torpedo tubes); *Piorun* (Polish, 'N' class, ex *Nerissa*, 1,690 tons, 6 × 4.7in guns, 10 torpedo tubes); *Blyskawica* (Polish, *Grom* class, 3,383 tons, 7 × 4.7in guns, 6 torpedo tubes). All destroyers 36 knots except *Blyskawica* 39 knots.

Above: The battle off the coast of Brittany, 9 June 1944.

Kapitän zur See Max-Eckart Wolff, who had been deputizing for Konteradmiral Bey as FdZ since 30 October 1943, took over the post in a caretaking capacity on 27 December. On 26 January 1944 Vize-admiral Leo Kreisch was appointed the last FdZ, relinquishing the appointment on 29 May 1945. At the beginning of 1944 the five destroyers of 8. Z-Flottille— Z 23, Z 24, Z 32, Z 37 and ZH 1—were operating out of Biscay ports as U-boat escorts and were frequently under air attack. By the end of August all five were either beyond repair or sunk.

During a flotilla exercise on 30 January Z 32 and Z 37 collided and both ships were badly damaged. Z 32 was laid up for repair until May and Z 37, listing heavily, was towed into Bordeaux, where it was decided not to repair the damage. Her guns were landed and earmarked for coastal defence use, and the ship decommissioned on 24 August.

On D-Day, 6 June, Z 24, Z 32, ZH 1 and the torpedo boat T 24 set out from the Gironde for Brest. After surviving determined air attacks en route, the flotilla headed for Cherbourg, from where mines were to be laid off Brest. The enemy had got wind of this operation, and off Wissant a superior force of British destroyers was waiting for the four German ships. ZH 1 received such heavy damage that she was scuttled that same day, and the other three dispersed and made a run for it. Z 24 and T 24 returned to Bordeaux, but Z 32, after initially making for St-Malo, reversed course and ran once more into the enemy destroyers. She received such serious damage that her commander was forced to sacrifice his ship by running her aground on rocks off the Île de Bas, Roscoff.

On 12 August Z 23, in dock at La Pallice, was bombed beyond repair during an air raid, She was decommissioned on 2 August. On 2 August Z 24 and T 24, anchored in the roadstead at Le Verdon, were attacked by bomb- and rocket-carrying Beaufighters of Nos 236 and 404 Squadrons RAF. T 24 was sunk; Z 24 managed to get alongside the quay at Le Verdon but capsized and sank there next day.

When not in the shipyard, *Richard Beitzen*, *Theodor Riedel*, *Friedrich Ihn* and *Karl Galster*, together with Z 30, worked out of southern Norwegian ports during 1944 on escort and minelaying duties. Mines were shipped at Fredrikshaven in Denmark and brought to Horten in Oslofjord to be distributed amongst the various units. Acting under instructions from the light cruiser *Emden* (flagship, C-in-C Minelayers), on 1 October Z 4, Z 14, Z 20 and Z 30 laid the Skagerrak XXXIIb Caligula field, the group coming under constant air attack while doing so. On 5 October the same ships laid the XXXIIa Vespasia field, also in the Skagerrak. On 20 October Z 30 struck a mine in Oslofjord and was towed to the shipyard by *Ihn*, *Galster* and UJ 1702. The repair work was still incomplete at the time of the capitulation.

Apart from a single sortie from Altafjord as far as Bear Island by Z 29, Z 31, Z 33, Z 34 and Z 38 on 30 May, the destroyers' main task was to defend the battleship *Tirpitz*, principally against air attack. Following her demise in October and the decision to abandon the 'Polar Front', the destroyers escorted troop transports southwards and mined a number of fjords and sounds. No destroyers were lost in this theatre during 1944.

By early March 1944, Z 25, Z 28, Z 35 and Z 39 had all arrived in the eastern Baltic and begun minelaying operations in the Gulf of Finland. A major sortie was carried out there on dates between 13 and 25 April by Z 28, Z 35 and Z 39, the torpedo boat T 30, the minelayers *Brummer*, *Roland* and *Linz* and various minesweepers and R-boats. The new Z 36 joined the flotilla in June, but Z 39 returned to Germany for a long drawn-out repairs to bomb damage.

From 7 to 28 June, in Operation 'Tanne West', the heavy cruiser *Prinz Eugen* patrolled the Finnish coast north of Utö in the Aaland Sea in a show of strength to cover the German withdrawal. She was relieved by the heavy cruiser *Lützow*, escorted by the destroyers Z 25, Z 28, Z 35 and Z 36.

Between 30 July and 1 August 1944, in the Gulf of Riga, the same four destroyers were placed under Army direction for the bombardment of Soviet positions inland. On 5 August all four escorted *Prinz Eugen* from Riga to the island of Oesel to fire inland, and on 19 August, off Kurland in the Gulf of Riga, *Prinz Eugen* rained 265 rounds of 20.3cm on Soviet positions at Tukkum, a road and rail junction 25 kilometres inland, while the four destroyers and two torpedo boats engaged other targets.

During September 1944 Z 25, Z 28 and four boats of 2. T-Flottille covered the withdrawal from Reval, six freighters evacuating over 23,000 people. On 21 September Z 25 and Z 28 brought out 370 evacuees from Baltisch Port to Libau, and on the 22nd they escorted the remaining German ships in the Aaland Sea to Gotenhafen.

On 10 October Kampfgruppe II Thiele—comprising *Prinz Eugen* and the four destroyers—sailed from Gotenhafen. Z 25 had as an additional task the delivery of 200 Army personnel to Memel, returning overnight with 200 female naval auxiliaries. The ship re-joined the group on the 11th, and over the next five days *Prinz Eugen*, *Lützow* and the destroyers attacked 28 land targets in the defence of Memel. On 15 October, off Gotenhafen, Z 35 and Z 36 stood by the cruisers *Prinz Eugen* and *Leipzig* after they had become locked together following a collision in the approach channel. On the 24th of the month Z 28, Z 35 and Z 36, in company with *Lützow* and three torpedo boats, bombarded inshore targets around Memel and on the Sworbe peninsula. They came under attack from Soviet aircraft for the first time on this day: Z 28 was hit by five bombs and suffered nine dead and numerous

75

wounded, while Z 35 received splinter damage from a near miss.

On 22 November 1944, Z 25, Z 43 and 2. T-Flottille, together with the heavy cruiser *Admiral Scheer*, relieved *Prinz Eugen* and 3. T-Flottille off Oesel, covering the withdrawal until its completion on 24 November despite constant Soviet air attacks; 4,700 German soldiers were evacuated.

On 9 December, 6. Z-Flottille, consisting of Z 35 (flag), Z 36, Z 43 and two torpedo boats, left Gotenhafen to lay a mine barrier off the Estonian coast in Operation 'Nil' (Nile). On their arrival in the scheduled area on 12 December there was a thick ground fog, and as a result of poor navigation and the 'confused, inflexible and deficient operational plan' drawn up by Kapitän zur See Kothe (for which he was blamed posthumously), Z 35 and Z 36 entered the German-laid Nashorn minefield, where they were mined, blew up and sank with all hands. The situation offered no prospect for a rescue.

At the beginning of 1945, Z 33 was under repair at Narvik, and after enduring the occasional battering from the air in her attempts to get back to Germany, she sailed on 26 March from Trondheim for Swinemünde—the last German destroyer to leave the northern Norwegian theatre. After laying mines in Laafjord and the Mageröy and Brei Sounds during the latter part of January, Z 31, Z 34 and Z 38 had left Tromsö for German Baltic waters on the 25th. By the 28th they had reached Sognefjord, where they were intercepted by a British squadron which included the light cruisers *Mauritius* (8,000 tons, 12 × 6in guns, 6 torpedo tubes) and *Diadem* 5,770 tons, 8 ×5.25in guns, 6 torpedo tubes). Z 38 broke off the action with a funnel fire and split boiler tubes, and she made Kiel via Aarhus later with Z 34. The latter carried out three torpedo attacks on the British cruisers and received a shell hit on the waterline. Z 31 came off worst in the encounter. She was hit seven times, her 15cm twin turret was totally destroyed and she suffered 55 dead and 24 wounded. She put into Bergen for repair and eventually left the Oslo yard for Germany in mid-March.

Until the capitulation on 8 May 1945, and even afterwards, German units worked on a naval evacuation programme which dwarfed anything ever seen previously. Destroyers were involved in escorting refugee sships and boats of all kinds, and often embarked thousands of refugees themselves. Actual combat in the Baltic in 1945 was limited to gunnery engagements with Soviet troop dispositions and armour and artillery

Above: The end: Z 33 at Wilhelmshaven after the war, flanked by *Otto Wünsche* (right) and the torpedo boat T 17 (left).

inland, the last rounds being fired on 4 May, after which a partial ceasefire came into effect, enabling the evacuation to proceed as agreed.

Between January and May 1945 1,420,000 individuals were evacuated by sea to the west, most of them refugees or Wehrmacht wounded, although fighting troops numbered more prominently amongst those brought out towards the end. On 2 May a report from Hela spoke of 150,000 soldiers and 26,000 refugees awaiting transport, plus 75,000 troops and 9,000 refugees in the Vistula lowlands.In the evening of 5 May numerous vessels arrived in Gotenhafen from Copenhagen and embarked refugees and troops to capacity, setting off westwards in four large convoys. These included the auxiliary *Hansa* (12,000 refugees), the minelayer *Linz* (4,900), the destroyers *Karl Galster*, *Hans Lody*, *Theodor Riedel* and Z 25 (6,000 in all) in Convoy 1; the troopships *Ceuta* (4,500) and *Pompeii* (5,400) with three torpedo boats (1,975 total) as Convoy 2; the destroyer *Friedrich Ihn*, T 28, the depot ship *Isar* and V 2002 (5,500 total) as Convoy 3; and M 453, V 303 and the training ship *Nautik* (2,700 total) as Convoy 4. During the night of 7 May small boats and naval launches brought 14,590 Wehrmacht personnel plus 1,810 wounded and refugees from the Vistula plain to Hela, and the following night the destroyers *Karl Galster*, *Friedrich Ihn*, *Hans Lody*, *Theodor Riedel*, Z 25, Z 38, Z 39 and five torpedo boats embarked another 20,000, the steamers *Weserberg* and *Paloma* carrying 5,730 more. A total of 100,000 persons on Hela and in the Vistula area could not be brought out, and these became prisoners of the Soviets.

By the time the surrender came into effect, a total of 116,692 soldiers and 5,397 refugees were still at sea in German warships, heading for either Copenhagen or Kiel.

Individual Ships' Careers

Z 1 *Leberecht Maass*

Origin of the Name

Konteradmiral Leberecht Maass, FdT (Führer der Torpedoboote) and Admiral II. Aufklärungsstreitkräfte (Scouting Forces), commanded a small German squadron at the Battle of Heligoland Bight on 28 August 1914 aboard the cruiser *Cöln*, which was lost with all hands bar a solitary stoker in a disastrous skirmish with British battlecruisers.

Career

Z 1 *Leberecht Maass* was a Type 1934 destroyer commissioned on 14 January 1937 by Korvettenkapitän Friedrich Traugott Schmidt. On 11 and 12 March 1937 she ran her speed trials over the measured mile off Neukrug, achieving a best speed of 29.4 knots from an output of 54,000shp at 298rpm per shaft.

Z 1 was appointed FdT flag destroyer on 1 May 1937 and served with Fleet, Korvettenkapitän Gerhard Wagner commanding from October 1937. In May 1938 the ship visited Göteborg, and this was followed by a refit to fit a new bow. In December 1938, in company with Z 2, Z 3 and Z 4, she cruised as far as Iceland to prove her seaworthiness in North Atlantic winter conditions.

On 23 March 1939 *Leberecht Maass* formed part of the large naval presence at Memel to mark the re-incorporation of the territory into the Reich.

Her last captain, Korvettenkapitän Fritz Bassenge, assumed command in April 1939. From 18 April to 16 May 1939 she took part in the first and only large-scale German Atlantic naval exercise, with *Gneisenau* (flagship, CinC Admiral Carls), *Deutschland*, Z 14 and Z 15, plus two U-boat flotillas and support vessels.

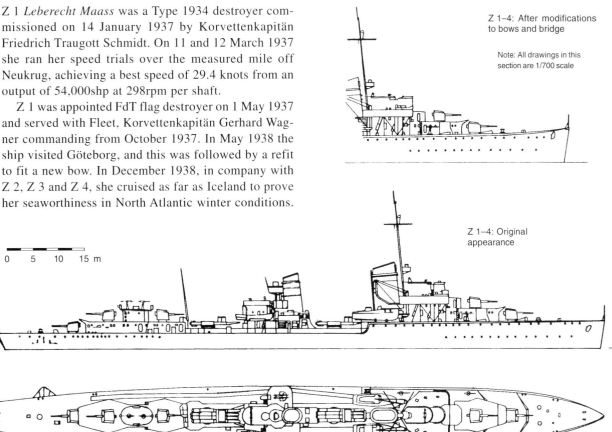

Z 1–4: After modifications to bows and bridge

Note: All drawings in this section are 1/700 scale

Z 1–4: Original appearance

0   5   10   15 m

Visits were made by Z 1 to Ceuta and the Bay of Arosa. After manoeuvres in the Baltic in August 1939, the destroyer—now flag vessel, FdT Vizeadmiral Lütjens—assembled with 1. and 4. Z-Flottillen at Pillau naval base on the eastern side of the Bay of Danzig in the final days of the month in preparation for the attack on Poland

On 1 September 1939 the destroyer squadron formed up off the Gulf of Danzig near Hela to harass shipping off the Polish coast. Z 1 avoided torpedoes fired by the submarine *Wilk*, and early on the morning of 3 September, off Gotenhafen and in company with Z 9 *Wolfgang Zenker*, she fought an engagement with the destroyer *Wicher* and the Polish flagship, the minelayer *Gryf*. She lost four dead—the first shipboard Kriegsmarine deaths of the war—and on 4 September put into Swinemünde for repair.

In late September Z 1 was based in the Jade estuary. She carried out sea rescue patrol duty and escorted Z 8 *Bruno Heinemann* during engine trials. On the 29th of the month she entered the Swinemünde yard for a scheduled refit.

On 30 November 1939 the destroyer flotillas were reorganised under an FdZ, but Z 1, for the time being, remained the flag vessel of the FdT for 1., 2., 5. and 6. Torpedobootflottillen and 1. and 2. Schnellbootflottillen. On 22 December *Leberecht Maass* was attached to 2. Z-Flottille.

On 10 February 1940 she was one of the nine destroyers that laid 360 mines off Happisburgh and Orfordness. On 18 February, in company with the battleships *Scharnhorst* and *Gneisenau*, the heavy cruiser *Admiral Hipper* and the destroyers Z 5, Z 20 and Z 21, she took part in Operation 'Nordmark', an impromptu search for enemy shipping as far as the Bergen–Shetlands Narrows, in an effort to avenge the *Altmark* incident of two days previously. Nothing was achieved, and the following day Z 1 was detached with Z 5 to search for enemy commerce in the Skagerrak, returning to Wilhelmshaven on the 20th. On 22 February, whilst proceeding to the Dogger Bank on an anti-trawler raid in flotilla, *Leberecht Maass* was bombed and damaged by a friendly aircraft in the German Bight, and whilst drifting subsequently near the Westwall minefield she suffered an explosion which sank her; 282 men were lost.

Z 2 *Georg Thiele*

Origin of the Name

In the First World War, Korvettenkapitän Georg Thiele was senior officer of VI. Torpedobootflottille, consisting of T 115, T 117, T 118 and T 119, his flag vessel. On 17 October 1917 the flotilla encountered a numerically superior British force off Texel and was destroyed.

Career

Z 2 was a Type 1934 Type commissioned on 27 February 1937 by Fregattenkapitän Hans Hartmann. The first sea trials proved that the Type was too wet even in light seas and at medium speed, shipping water over the bows as far aft as the bridge. Damage occurred frequently, and the forward guns could not be depended upon for readiness. As a result, Z 2 went back to the yards to have her bow lengthened by 33cm, the deck receiving a profile 0.7m higher at the peak—neither of which measures, it has to be said, helped to solve the problem to any great extent.

On 21 August 1937 *Georg Thiele* ran her speed trials over the measured mile off Neukrug, achieving 36 knots from an output of 63,000 shp at 420rpm per shaft She took part in the fleet exercises of September 1937, and then continued working up. The ship was attached to 1. Z-Division on 1 December.

On 22 August 1938 Z 2 took part in the Naval Review and manoouvres to celebrate the launch of the heavy cruiser *Prinz Eugen* at Kiel in the presence of the Hungarian regent. Korvettenkapitän Rudolf von Pufendorf served as the destroyer's second commander from August to October 1938. On 26 October 1. Z-Division was incorporated into 1. Z-Flottille, based at Swinemünde, when the destroyer's third and last commander, Korvettenkapiptän Max-Eckart Wolff joined her.

On 8 December 1938 Z 2 was present at Kiel for the launching of the aircraft carrier *Graf Zeppelin*, after which she sailed with the three other Type 1934 destroyers on an Atlantic winter proving voyage as far north as Iceland. In March 1939, following fleet manoeuvres, she took part in the Memel operation, and in April and May she joined in Kriegsmarine exercises in the Atlantic and Mediterranean, on 30 May forming part of the escort for the ships bringing the Condor Legion (Spanish Civil War) veterans back to Hamburg.

On 26 August 1939 Z 2 towed Z 3 *Max Schultz* to Swinemünde for repair following a collision between the latter and the torpedo boat *Tiger* while on patrol duty in the Sound with lights extinguished.

On 1 September 1939 *Georg Thiele* was transferred from the Bay of Danzig into the North Sea for patrol duties and a shipyard refit. She ran trials from 2 April 1940, but after damage to the bearings of the main cooling water pump went back to Deschimag for more work to be done. Attached to Kriegsschiffgruppe 1 for the invasion of Norway, destination Narvik, she moored at Bremerhaven on 4 April and embarked mountain troops at the Columbus Quay on the 6th. During the run-in through Narvikfjord near Skomen, she assisted Z 11 *Bernd von Arnim* to overcome the Norwegian coast defence ship *Norge* at about 0600 on 9 April before mooring at the iron-ore pier in the Inner Harbour at Narvik alongside Z 11 *Bernd von Arnim* to disembark her occupation forces. After refuelling from the oiler *Jan Wellem* she took up a position in Ballan-genfjord, from where early next morning, when five British destroyers made their surprise attack, she came out in company with Z 11 to intercept. A fierce battle ensued, the British losing the destroyers *Hardy* and *Hunter*. Z 2 received seven shell hits and put back into Narvik ablaze and with 27 casualties, her pumps having failed. Z 11 assisted in putting out the fires.

During the night of 10 April Georg Thiele picketed Ofotfjord, returning the next day to Narvik to continue with her repairs. On 13 April, when the battleship *Warspite* arrived with nine destroyers, Z 2 withdrew into Rombakenfjord and, in company with Z 18 *Hans Lüdemann* lay broadside across the fjord to bring her torpedoes and full broadside to bear. In the ensuing engagement she succeeded in demolishing the bows of the destroyer *Eskimo* with her last torpedo. Once out of ammunition, she reversed at full speed on to the rocks of the fjord, where she remains, upright and partially projecting out of the water, to this day.

Z 3 *Max Schultz*

Origin of the Name
Korvettenkapitän Max Schultz, commanding V 69, flagvessel of the ill-fated VI. Torpedobootflottille, died on 23 January 1917 in an engagement with British cruisers off the Hoofden while making for Zeebrugge.

Career
Z 3 was a Type 1934 Type ship commissioned on 8 April 1937 by Korvettenkapitän Martin Balzer. During June–August 1937 she ran her speed trials over the measured mile off Neukrug, achieving 36 knots from an output of 64,500shp at 365rpm per shaft. She took part in Fleet exercises with the light cruisers in July and also participated in the autumn manoeuvres. In the spring of 1938 bad-weather trials were carried out in the North Sea, after which she sojourned in May in Hardangerfjord before returning to Kiel for a bow and bridge refit similar to that carried out on Z 1.

On 22 August 1938 Z 3 formed part of the Naval Review and manoeuvres to celebrate the launch of the heavy cruiser Prinz Eugen at Kiel in the presence of the Hungarian regent, Admiral Horthy. Korvettenkapitän Claus Trampedach served as her second and last commander from August 1938.

On 26 October 1938 1. Zerstörerdivision was incorporated into 1. Zerstörerflottille, based at Swine-münde. On 8 December *Maz Schultz* was present at Kiel for the launching of the carrier *Graf Zeppelin*, after which she sailed with the three other Type 1934 destroyers on an Atlantic proving voyage to Iceland. In March 1939, following manoeuvres, she took part in the Memel operation, and in April and May she exercised with the fleet in the Atlantic and Mediterranean.

On 26 August 1939, whilst on patrol in the Sound and in 'darkened-ship' condition, she rammed and sank the torpedo boat *Tiger* off Bornholm. After rescuing the crew, Z 3 was towed by Z 2 into Swinemünde at four knots, from where she docked at the Oderwerke, Stettin, for repair.

Z 3 *Max Schultz* was returned to operational readiness at the end of September 1939 and joined the escort force protecting *Gneisenau* and *Köln* on their antishipping foray to the northern North Sea between 8 and 10 October. During late October she carried out contraband control in the Skagerrak, but while returning on 28 October she suffered a turbine explosion brought about by a fault in the main feed pump; boiler room No 1 flooded, and all boiler fires there had quickly to be extinguished. Without power, Z 3 anchored, but attempts to tow her failed. Eventually she managed to get under way, and, escorted by Z 14 and Z 16, put into dock at Kiel.

Once repaired, she formed part of the sortie which mined the Shipwash on 10 February 1940. Hoeever, on 22 February, while part of Operation 'Wikinger'—the six-ship force sent on an anti-spy trawler mission north of the Dogger Bank—she was mined and sunk while attempting to assist in the rescue of survivors from Z 1. Her entire complement of 308 perished.

Z 4 *Richard Beitzen*

Origin of the Name

Kapitänleutnant Richard Beitzen was CO of XIV. Torpedobootflottille, and on 30 March 1918, off Heligoland, he entered a minefield in his boat G 87 in an attempt to save survivors from the sunken G 93 and G 94. His own boat was then mined and sunk.

Career

Z 4 *Richard Beitzen* was a Type 1934 destroyer commissioned on 13 May 1937 by Korvettenkapitän Hans Joachim Gadow. On 19–20 July and 25 August 1937 she ran her speed trials over the measured mile at Neukrug, achieving 36.0 knots from an output of 63,000shp at 350rpm per shaft. Immediately after entering service in July 1937 she took part in exercises with the light cruisers.

In May 1938, under a new commander, Korvettenkapitän Moritz Schmidt, she visited the Norwegian fjords, after which she went for refit at Deutsche Werke Kiel to have her bows and bridge modified. She took part in the Horthy Naval Review of 22 August, and on 26 October was attached to 1. Z-Flottille at Swinemünde under her third commander, Korvettenkapitän Hans von Davidson. In December, accompanied by her three sister-ships Z 1, Z 2 and Z 3, she carried out Atlantic bad-weather trials as far north as Iceland in order to prove the type's seaworthiness.

In early 1939, following fleet manoeuvres, she formed part of the force reoccupying Memel, the ex-German territory which had been allocated to Lithuania under the terms of the Treaty of Versailles. In April and May 1939, together with Z 17 and other units, she exercised in the Atlantic and off the Spanish Mediterranean coast. On her return in the Jade estuary she was rammed in the stern by the fleet escort F 7.

From the end of August 1939 *Richard Beitzen* patrolled the western Baltic, and in September she was involved in anti-contraband control duties in the Kattegat. She formed part of a squadron visiting the British East Coast to lay mines on four occasions—on 12 December 1939 (to the Tyne; the sortie that resulted in Z 4 and Z 8 escorting the crippled *Leipzig* back to port); on 6 January 1940 (Thames estuary); on 10 January 1940 (Tyne); and on 10 February (Happisburgh Sands and Shipwash). On 19–20 February Z 4 acted as escort for a limited part of the excursion by *Scharnhorst*, *Gneisenau* and *Admiral Hipper* to the Shetland Narrows, and on 22nd of the month was part of Operation 'Wikinger', the intended trawler round-up in which Z 1 and Z 3 were lost.

For the occupation of Norway, Z 4 was placed in reserve with Z 7 in the German Bight on escort standby. On 11 April she arrived with Z 7 off Maurangerfjord near Bergen and met up with the torpedo boats *Leopard* and *Wolf* escorting the cruiser *Köln* to Wilhelmshaven. From 28 April to 20 May 1940 she was involved in the Sperre 17 minelaying operation in the Skagerrak, following which she went to Deutsche Werke, Kiel, for a refit which lasted until September.

Fully operational once more, *Beitzen* sailed alone down-Channel to Brest and worked in the Bay of Biscay. In the morning of 19 November, and in company with Z 10 and Z 20, she was laying mines off Plymouth when five British destroyers came up. A brief action ensued in which *Javelin* was hit by two torpedoes. In December *Richard Beitzen* was the Kriegsmarine's only operational destroyer.

In January 1941 Z 4 carried out a minelaying operation code-named 'Weber' off the south-east coast of Britain with the torpedo boats *Seeadler* and *Iltis*. On 1 February, together with *Seeadler* and *Kondor*, she escorted *Admiral Hipper* to sea from Brest on the latter's second raiding cruise, meeting her on her return on 14 February. On 16 March *Beitzen* left Brest for a refit at Kiel.

She was transferred from Kiel to Kirkenes on 1 July 1941, where she took part in various minelaying and offensive operations along the Kola peninsula and in the White Sea. She was straddled but not hit during the action on 9 August 1941 off the Kola Inlet when the Soviet warship *Tuman/SKR-12* was sunk.

On 25 August she sailed with Z 7 *Hermann Schoemann* from Narvik for a refit. She carried out trials and worked up in the Baltic in December 1941, and between

14 and 17 January 1942 she sailed as escort with Z 5 and Z 8 for the battleship *Tirpitz* transferring from the Jade to Trondheim (Operation 'Polarnacht'), returning to Kiel on the 20th. On the 24th the three units, now with Z 7 attached, passed through the Kiel Canal and headed for France to take part in Operation 'Cerberus'— the break-out of the German heavy ships from Brest. Off Calais *Bruno Heinemann* struck two mines and sank, Z 4 picking up 188 and Z5 34 survivors while under enemy aircraft fire. 'Cerberus' got under way during the night of 11 February, and the three heavy units at Brest sailed for the English Channel with a large sea and air escort including Z 4, all German vessels arriving in Dutch or German waters by the 13th.

Early on 20 February *Beitzen*, with Z 5, Z 7, Z 14 and Z 25 escorted *Prinz Eugen* and *Admiral Scheer* from Brunsbüttel northwards for Trondheim (Operation 'Sportpalast'), but Z 4, Z 5 and Z 14 were sent into Bergen after reporting that they could not keep up in the heavy seas. They reached Trondheim on the 24th, by which time *Prinz Eugen* had been torpedoed and damaged, the opportunity for the submarine commander having undoubtedly been enhanced by the lack of escorts. By this time the condition of Z 4's turbines—

the ship experienced three breakdowns in a year— dictated the need for a thorough overhaul, and on 14 March she put into Deschimag at Bremen.

In May, together with Z 10, Z 27, Z 29 and the fleet escort F 1, *Richard Beitzen* escorted the heavy cruiser *Lützow* to Bogen Bay to join Kampfgruppe I. On 17 May she laid mines in the Skagerrak, and once fully operational joined Kampfgruppe I, on 2–3 July escorting the naval oiler *Nordmark* and the tanker *Tiger* into Gimsöy and then accompanying the Group to Altafjord, from where Operation 'Rösselsprung' against convoy PQ.17 commenced on 5 July.

From 17 to 19 August *Beitzen* attended *Admiral Scheer* at the outset of Operation 'Wunderland' and then took part in minelaying operations in Arctic waters (24 August), the Kara Strait (5–8 September) and Kanin Nos in the White Sea (13–15 October), in Operation 'Hoffnung' between 5 and 9t November and in the ill-starred Operation 'Regenbogen' between 30 December and 1 January 1943.

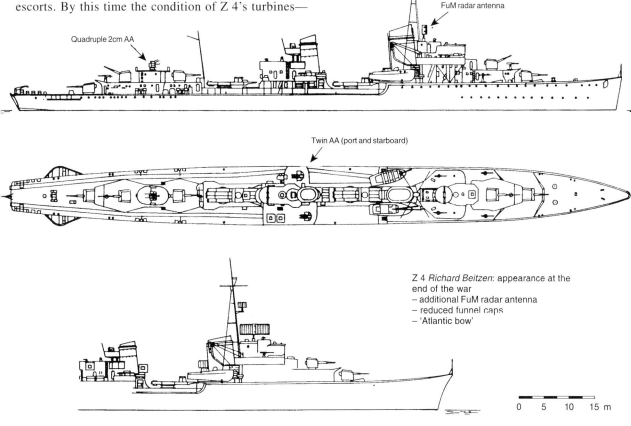

Z 4 *Richard Beitzen*: appearance in 1942

FuM radar antenna

Quadruple 2cm AA

Twin AA (port and starboard)

Z 4 *Richard Beitzen*: appearance at the end of the war
– additional FuM radar antenna
– reduced funnel caps
– 'Atlantic bow'

0 5 10 15 m

On 24 January 1943, under new commander *Fregattenkapitän* Hans Dominik, Z 4, in company with Z 29 and Z 30, offered protection to *Admiral Hipper* and *Köln* during their protracted return voyage to Kiel from Altafjord via Trondheim, and in April the destroyer escorted *Nürnberg* back to her cadet training duties Germany. She called in at Swinemünde subsequently in order to refit and was operational again in October.

On the 27th of that month, on her return to northern waters, she ran aground in the Karmsund and was not refloated until 5 November. She made Bergen via Haugesund for emergency repairs and, after a stay in the yards at Stettin, had a new bow section fitted at Gotenhafen. Kapitänleutnant Walter Lüdde-Neurath was appointed commander in April 1944, and he was succeeded by Korvettenkapitän Rudolf Gade in June.

Z 4 resumed operations from Horten on 5 August 1944—under her last commander Korvettenkapitän Helmut Neuss, appointed in September—carrying out escort work and minelaying in the Skagerrak, including, in early October, the Klaudius and Caligula XXXIIa and XXXIIb fields. On 5th November, after grounding at Horten she proceeded to Oslo for repair.

Z 4 was still not fully operational on 20 December when she returned to escort duty. On 28 December she sailed to Aarhus to collect a new drive shaft, and this was fitted in Oslo during work commencing on 16 January 1945. On 15 February she emerged from the shipyard and resumed her escort duties. During an air attack on 24 April the destroyer was damaged by a near miss and limped back to the Oslo yard at 15 knots. She was still there at the capitulation and decommissioned on 14 May 1945.

Following temporary repairs, Z 4 *Richard Beitzen* was towed by the British tug *Enchanter* to Rosyth for breaking-up.

Z 5 *Paul Jacobi*

Origin of the Name

Korvettenkapitän Paul Jacobi, CO XVII. Torpedobootflottille, was lost with his crew when his flag vessel V 25 was mined and sunk on the Amrum Bank on 2 December 1915.

Career

Z 5 *Paul Jacobi* was a Type 1934A destroyer commissioned on 29 June 1937 by Korvettenkapitän Rudolf Peters. Between 8 and 13 September 1937, and on 14–15 February 1938, she ran her speed trials over the measured mile at Neukrug, achieving 34.8 knots from 60,000shp at 340rpm per shaft. She took part in the annual autumn manoeuvres of 1937. In April 1938, together with Z 8 *Bruno Heinemann*, she practised gunnery in Norwegian waters, then took part in exercises with the light cruisers. Z 5 remained in Norwegian waters during August 1938, with a visit to Kiel on the 22nd of the month for the Naval Review to mark the launching of the heavy cruiser *Prinz Eugen*.

On 6 October Z 5 sailed with her sister-ships of 2. Z-Division—Z 6 *Theodor Riedel* and Z 7 *Hermann Schoemann*—for exercises in the Irish Sea and Eastern Atlantic with the pocket battleship *Admiral Graf Spee*, after which the squadron cruised to Spain and North Africa, visiting Vigo, Tangiers and Ceuta. The voyage ended at Wilhelmshaven on 23 October. On 26 October 1938 Z 5 was attached to 2. Z-Division based at Wilhelmshaven, her new commander being Korvettenkapitän Hans Georg Zimmer. From February 1939 until 29 September 1939 Z5 was in the Wilhelmshaven yards for refit.

Paul Jacobi was operational once more from 11 October 1939 and participated in several of the 'stop and search' patrols in the Skagerrak up till February 1940, although visits to the shipyards restricted her activities. She took part in none of the minelaying sorties to the East Coast of England. Attached to Kriegsschiffgruppe 2 bound for Trondheim for the Norwegian operation, she embarked 200 mountain troops at Cuxhaven and reached her destination on 9 April, having suffered storm damage and engine breakdowns, and was short of fuel on arrival. What bunkerage she had was transferred to Z 16 and she underwent repairs at the quayside. Once limited readiness was restored, she completed her voyage, landing her Gebirgsjäger upfjord. On 8 May she sailed for home, putting into Wilhelmshaven shipyard for repair on the 10th.

Jacobi was operational once more on 11 June, and she sailed with Z 10 for Trondheim on the 30th. She formed part of the escort for the crippled *Gneisenau* returning to Kiel on 25 July. Between 14 August and 2 September, working out of Cuxhaven, she helped lay the Sperre SW 3 minefield.

On 22 September Z 5 sailed with Z 15 *Erich Steinbrinck* for French bases at the western end of the

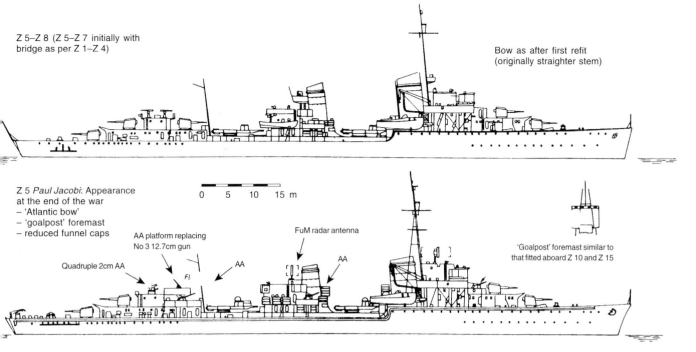

Z 5–Z 8 (Z 5–Z 7 initially with bridge as per Z 1–Z 4)

Bow as after first refit (originally straighter stem)

Z 5 *Paul Jacobi*: Appearance at the end of the war
– 'Atlantic bow'
– 'goalpost' foremast
– reduced funnel caps

0   5   10   15 m

AA platform replacing No 3 12.7cm gun

FuM radar antenna

'Goalpost' foremast similar to that fitted aboard Z 10 and Z 15

Quadruple 2cm AA

AA

AA

Fl

Channel as part of Operation 'Seelöwe' and was part of the destroyer squadron which laid mines off Falmouth on 28 September. On 8 November she returned to Wilhelmshaven for a major refit.

Jacobi returned to operational readiness in October 1941, her third commander, Korvettenkapitän Hermann Schlieper, having been appointed in February. She sailed in company with Z 24 and Z 26 from Aarhus for Norway but her port propeller became entangled with a channel buoy and she was forced to return to Kiel. She left the yard on 24 November but, having loaded mines at Aarhus, suffered a boiler breakdown, necessitating her return to Kiel and then to the yards at Wilhelmshaven, where, in an air attack on 29 December, she had three crew killed and suffered damage from bomb splinters.

The ship was operational again on 13 January 1942, and between 14 and 17 January Z 5 sailed as escort with Z 4 and Z 8 for the battleship *Tirpitz* transferring from the Jade to Trondheim (Operation 'Polarnacht'), returning to Kiel on the 20th. On 24 January these units, now with Z 7 attached, passed through the Kiel Canal and headed for France to take part in Operation 'Cerberus', the break-out of the heavy ships from Brest. Off Calais *Bruno Heinemann* struck two mines and sank; 93 crewmen were lost, Z 4 picking up 188 and Z 5 34 survivors under enemy aircraft fire. 'Cerberus' got under way during the night of 11 February, and the

three heavy units at Brest sailed for the English Channel with a large sea and air escort (including Z 5), all the German vessels arriving in Dutch or German ports by the 13th.

Early on 20 February, and in company with Z 4, Z 7, Z 14 and Z 25, Z 5 escorted *Prinz Eugen* and *Admiral Scheer* from Brunsbüttel northwards for Trondheim (Operation 'Sportpalast'), but Z 4, Z 5 and Z 14 were sent into Bergen when they could not keep up owing to the heavy sea running. They reached Trondheim on the 24th, but in the meantime *Prinz Eugen* had been torpedoed and damaged.

On 6 March *Paul Jacobi* sailed into the Barents Sea with *Tirpitz*, Z 14 and Z 7 to intercept convoys PQ.12 and QP.8 but failed to find them, Z 14 sinking a Soviet freighter as a consolation. Between 16 and 18 May 1942, in Operation 'Zauberflöte' (Magic Flute) destined for Kiel, *Paul Jacobi*, together with Z 25 and two torpedo boats, acted as close escort to the crippled cruiser *Prinz Eugen*, cooperating with the heavy ship in a flak barrage which led to a number of enemy aircraft being shot down during the continual air attacks on the small convoy. On arrival, Z 5 was laid up for refit at Deutsche Werke, Kiel, from 20 May to December 1942.

On 6–7 January the following year Z 5 exercised with *Scharnhorst*, *Prinz Eugen*, *Emden*, other destroyers and torpedo boats and took part in the two failed operations, 'Fronttheater' and 'Domino' later in the month. On 3 February she made her own way to Norway via Bergen and Trondheim and between 31 March and 2 April, together with *Theodor Riedel* and *Karl Galster*, waited in vain off Jan Mayen for *Regensburg*. She exercised with the *Kampfgruppe* in Arctic waters between 5 and 7 July but remained at her moorings in Altafjord with *Lützow* in a deception role during the Spitzbergen raid. On 23 September Z 5, Z 14, Z 15 and Z 27 escorted *Lützow* to Kiel in Operation 'Hermelin', Z 5 then entering Deutsche Werke for a major refit on 30 September 1943.

During an air raid on 4 January 1944 fire broke out in connection with welding work. This was extinguished after three hours, but during a raid the following day Z 5 was hit by incendiaries and a shipyard chimney fell across the deck, destroying a 2cm quadruple mounting. During this lay-up *Jacobi* was fitted with a new bow section, a 'goalpost' foremast, new radar aerials and the 'Barbara' AA suite. Following further air raid damage on 18 July, the destroyer was towed to Swinemünde on 9 August. Her last commander, Korvettenkapitän Max Bülter, was appointed in July 1944.

Z 5 commenced trials on 31 October 1944. On 5 November she was declared fit for limited operations, and two days later she arrived at Gotenhafen for final trials, being signed off fully operational on the 13th. Her first task was to escort the hospital ship *Steuben* to Swinemünde, where new 3.7cm guns were fitted on 20 December.

During torpedo practice off Bornholm on 14 January 1945, *Jacobi* was hit and damaged by her own surface-running 'rogue'. From 19 January to 4 February she ran escort and patrol duties to and from Gotenhafen, Libau and Swinemünde, however, while entering the latter port on 4 February she was rammed astern by the freighter *Helga Schröder*. While the destroyer was under repair, the opportunity was taken to equip her with additional anti-aircraft guns.

She was operational again from 27 February, and off Dievenow on 6 March bombarded Soviet land posi-

tions, Further bombardment was carried out off Fritzow and Kammin on 8 and 9 March, respectively, before she joined *Prinz Eugen* at Elbing on the 11th and 12th. On 14 March, in the roadstead at Gotenhafen, she came under fire from inland and moved to Zoppot; on the 15th she ran escort for *Prinz Eugen* and troopships; and she again escorted *Prinz Eugen* whilst in the Gulf of Danzig on the 18/19th.

On 21–22 March 1945 *Paul Jacobi* fired on Soviet psoitions at Gross-Katz and Lensitz, returning on the 23rd to Gotenhafen to shepherd *Prinz Eugen* and *Lützow*. That evening she steamed to Copenhagen as escort for the hospital ship *Pretoria* and gunnery training ship *Mars*, returning from there to Hela on 25 March with the liner *Potsdam*. She made another round trip (Hela–Copenhagen–Hela) between the 27th and 30th, collecting *Pretoria* and the liner *Deutschland* for the return leg.

From 1 to 4 April, Z 5 engaged Soviet positions in the Gotenhafen/Neufahrwasser region, and on 8–9 April she escorted *Prinz Eugen* and *Lützow* into the Kaiserfahrt channel at *Swinemünde*. On 18 April she shifted to Rostock for land bombardment, to be carried out on 30 April and 1 May. On 2 May she put into Kiel but moved to moorings in Flensburger Förde next day. That night, in order to prevent the destroyer putting to sea for the round trip with the last huge refugee convoy, a number of crewmen sabotaged the gyro compass. After a drumhead court-martial three men were sentenced to death.

Paul Jacobi was decommissioned at Flensburg-Mürwik on 7 May 1945. Some of the German crewmen remained aboard until 21 May, when the destroyer was transferred from Kiel to Wilhelmshaven as a British prize. She sailed on 16 January 1946, but was given over to France on 2 February, entering service under the *tricolore* as *Desaix*. She was finally decommissioned on 17 February 1954 and, though retained as a hulk under the designation Q 02, she was eventually scrapped.

Z 6 *Theodor Riedel*

Origin of the Name
Korvettenkapitän Theodor Riedel, CO 6. T-Boot Halb-flottille (Half-Flotilla), fell with all but three of the crew aboard his flag vessel V 48 between the battle lines in the early stages of the Battle of Jutland on 31 May 1916.

Career
Z 6 *Theodor Riedel* was a Type 1934A destroyer commissioned on 2 July 1937 by Korvettenkapitän Max Fechner. She ran her speed trials over the measured mile at Neukrug between 23 and 26 August 1937 and 26 and 30 April 1938, achieving 36.4 knots from 72,100shp

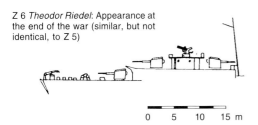

Z 6 *Theodor Riedel*: Appearance at the end of the war (similar, but not identical, to Z 5)

0   5   10   15 m

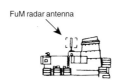

FuM radar antenna

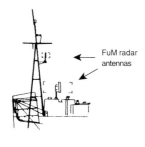

FuM radar antennas

at 430rpm per shaft and 35.8 knots without the wooden wedge keel.

She participated in the autumn 1937 fleet manoeuvres and cruiser exercises as part of her working-up programme. She was towed to Wilhelmshaven yard following a grounding on 8 June 1938 off Heligoland, a survey showing that the port engine was out of alignment; this was a problem which led to trouble with the pressure bearings in the early war years, and not until the major scheduled 1942 refit were the foundations renovated and the handicap overcome.

Z 6 visited Norwegian waters during August 1938 but was at Kiel on the 22nd of the month for the Naval Review to mark the launching of the heavy cruiser *Prinz Eugen*. On 6 October she sailed with her sister ships of 2. Zerstörerdivision, Z 5 *Paul Jacobi* and Z 7 *Hermann Schoemann*, for exercises in the Irish Sea—from where Z 6 made an unscheduled call at Lough Swilly for attention to an engine—and eastern Atlantic with the pocket battleship *Admiral Graf Spee*, after which the squadron cruised to Spain and North Africa, visiting Vigo, Tangiers and Ceuta. The voyage ended at Wilhelmshaven on 23 October. On 26 October 1938 Z 6 was attached to 2. *Z-Division*, based at Wilhelmshaven, her new commander being *Korvettenkapitän* Gerhardt Böhmig. Between February and August 1939 *Riedel* was refitting at Wilhelmshaven.

On the outbreak of war Z 6 took part in the extension of the Westwall minefield and during October 1939 undertook anti-contraband patrols in the Skagerrak. On 12 November, owing to a hot-running drive shaft, she was forced to return prematurely from a minelaying sortie in the Thames estuary. On 9 February 1940 she joined the squadron laying mines off Cromer; from the 18th to the 21st of that month she stopped and searched neutral shipping for contraband in the Skagerrak; and on the 22nd she formed part of the ill-fated 'Wikinger' anti-spy trawler operation to the Dogger Bank in which Z 1 and Z 3 were lost.

In 'Weserübung' (the invasion of Norway) she was assigned to Kriegsschiffgruppe 2 for Trondheim and landed her occupation troops despite the failure of the port engine en route. On arrival she grounded and was beached in the Strömmen Bay shallows as a floating battery to repel the expected British counter-attack. Having survived a number of air raids, on 20 April she was refloated and towed to Trondheim for repairs and became the first German destroyer to be fitted with radar.

On 7 June 1940 she made the trip to Wilhelmshaven shipyard for overhaul and was sufficiently operational to voyage with Z 10, Z 14, Z 16 and Z 20 to the western end of the English Channel, but with her port engine continuing to be a handicap she served no useful purpose there and on 5 November sailed from Brest for Kiel shipyard, where she remained until the end of March 1941. Whilst laid up she had a fire in the boiler room and during working-up was hit and damaged by a practice torpedo. A new commander, *Korvettenkapitän* Walter Riede, was appointed in April 1941.

On 9 August Z 6 was operational once more and sailed for Norway, but on the 12th she struck an uncharted reef in the dangerous Skatesströmmen skerries and required tug assistance to get her to Bergen for temporary repairs before returning to Kiel shipyard, where she remained until 10 May 1942.

On 11 June 1942 she sailed for Norway and took part in Operation 'Musik', the Fleet's transfer to Altafjord, but, like Z 10 and Z 20, she grounded in Grimsöystraumen and had to return to Trondheim for survey, two tugs being necessary to assist Z 6 and Z 10 from Trondheim to Kiel on 25 May. *Riedel* was operational again in December and returned to Altafjord to take part in the ill-fated Operation 'Regenbogen' on the last two days of the year.

Between 4 and 6 February 1943 *Theodor Riedel* laid the only offensive minefield of the year in the Barents Sea area when, with the minelayer *Brummer* and Z 31, she visited the Kildin roadstead off Kola Bay. From 31 March to 2 April she waited in vain with *Paul Jacobi* and *Karl Galster* off Jan Mayen for the blockade-runner *Regensburg* and received storm damage while doing so, necessitating her return to Trondheim for repairs. On 18 June she arrived at Kaafjord, from where she participated in the Spitzbergen operation from 6 to 9 September. Korvettenkapitän Freiherr Lothar von Hausen was appointed commander in September until January 1944, when Korvettenkapitän Rudolf Menge took over. For the remainder of 1943 the ship worked out of Stavanger and Kristiansand.

In June 1944, following a long refit for his ship at Kiel, Menge was succeeded by Korvettenkapitän Hans Blöse and Z 6 was attached to 5. Z-Flottille, exercising in the Skagerrak and carrying out various minelaying and, from November, escort duties. On 18 November she collided with the outer mole at Frederikshavn;

repairs took place at Oslo, and she was operational for minelaying and escort from 7 January 1945.

In the evening of 5 May Riedel sailed from Copenhagen for Hela to embark refugees, returning on the 7th and, together with Z 10, putting into Kiel on the 9th, to be decommissioned the following day.

After the capitulation *Theodor Riedel* was sailed by a mixed British-German crew to Wilhelmshaven, where, after repairs, she was awarded as spoils to Britain and towed there in January 1946. As with Z 5, however, she passed into French hands and entered service as *Kléber*, being finally decommissioned on 21 April 1954. Designated Q 86, she was laid up as a hulk before being scrapped.

Z 7 *Hermann Schoemann*

Origin of the Name

Kapitänleutnant Hermann Schoemann, cavalier CO of the Flanders Torpedo Boat Flotilla, was lost aboard his flag vessel A 2 when surprised by a superior British destroyer force in the English Channel on 1 May 1915.

Career

Z 7 was a Type 1934A ship commissioned on 15 September 1937 by her commander, Korvettenkapitän Erich Schulte-Mönting. She ran speed trials over the measured mile at Neukrug on six occasions between November 1937 and May 1938, experimenting with six varieties of propeller, the marginally best speed of 36.8 knots from 66,000shp (380rpm per shaft) being obtained from the Germania 'mussel' type. After completing her trials and working up, she joined the light cruiser squadron, taking part in the usual manoeuvres.

On 22 July 1938, Hitler, Göring, Keitel and senior officers embarked in order to observe torpedo practice in Eckernförder Bay. In August 1938, with her sister vessels of 2. Zerstörerdivision, Z 5 and Z 6, *Hermann Schoemann* cruised in Norwegian waters, and on the 16th of the month Admirals Raeder and Carls, Vizeadmiral Densch and Konteradmiral Lütjens (FdT) came aboard to observe a gunnery exercise in the central Baltic. On the 19th Carls, C-in-C Fleet, took the salute at a Fleet Review. Z 7 formed part of the Horthy Review of 22 August for the launch of the cruiser *Prinz Eugen*.

The destroyer's second commander, Korvettenkapitän Theodor Detmers, was appointed in October 1938. Fleet manoeuvres were followed by a voyage with Z 5, Z 6 and the pocket battleship *Admiral Graf Spee*

to Spain and North Africa, where Vigo, Ceuta and Tangiers were visited, Z 7 and Z 6 both needing assistance at Lough Swilly with machinery repairs. On 1 November 1938 Z 7 was attached to 2. *Z-Flottille* based at Wilhelmshaven, where she docked in February 1939 and remained unavailable for operations until early October.

On 3 October 1939, together with Z 14, Z 15 and the torpedo boats *Greif*, *Falke* and *Albatros*, *Schoemann* carried out commerce inspection duty in the Skagerrak and Kattegat, returning to the shipyard for ten days from the 5th; she was back in the Skagerrak by the 17th for three days. On 12 November she was forced to pull out of the Thames estuary minelaying sortie with engine problems, but she sailed directly from the repair yard at Wilhelmshaven on 13 December to escort the torpedoed cruisers to port. On the 18th of that month Z 7 helped mine the Humber, but while in the Jade estuary on 23 December on coastal protection duty she collided with Z 15 *Erich Steinbrinck* in thick fog.

Interspersed with North Sea patrols in the New Year, *Schoemann* was attached to destroyer squadrons which mined the Thames estuary on 6 January and the Suffolk coast on 9 February and made various minor escort runs until her machinery caused fresh problems on 2 March.

Attached to *Kriegsschiffgruppe 2* (Trondheim) for the invasion of Norway, Z 7 was at Cuxhaven to embark troops on 6 April but had to be replaced by Z 16 *Friedrich Eckholdt* on account of yet further engine breakdowns. She remained in German waters as a reserve, based at Wilhelmshaven shipyard, where she spent the period until 10 April undergoing repair. Before dawn on 11 April, however, she arrived off Maurangerfjord near Bergen in company with Z 4 *Richard Beitzen* to escort the cruiser *Köln*, sailing with the torpedo boats *Leopard* and *Wolf*, to Wilhelmshaven. Between 17 and 20 May she and, again, *Richard Beitzen*, in company with torpedo boats, covered ships laying the Sperre 17 minefield in the Skagerrak, and in early June she joined the Fleet at Trondheim for 'Juno', assisting in the sinking of the tanker *Oil Pioneer* and taking aboard the latter's eleven survivors.

On 20 June 1940 Z 7 was part of the escort for the crippled battleship *Scharnhorst* on her return to Kiel, afterwards entering the yards at Wilhelmshaven on 25 June for a refit. Korvettenkapitän Detmers left to command the raider *Kormoran*, and was replaced by First Officer Korvettenkapitän Konrad Loerke on a care-taking basis until Korvettenkapitän Heinrich Wittig, her last commander, was appointed in October 1940.

After leaving the yards on 15 February 1941, *Schoemann* worked up in the Baltic, but continued to be plagued by engine problems and was not operational until 19 June. Now attached to 6. Z-Flottille, she tranferred to Kirkenes in July for various escort and anti-shipping duties, but persistent engine problems forced an early return to the German yards and she sailed for home from Narvik on 25 August 1941 for a lay-up which lasted into the new year.

On 24 January 1942, fully operational again, she joined up with Z 4, Z 5 and Z 8 and headed for France to take part in Operation 'Cerberus', the break-out of the heavy ships from Brest. Because of the severe weather she lost contact with the group and sought refuge at Flushing, where she waited until 7 February to resume the voyage to Brest in company with Z 25, which had left Kirkenes on the 27th to replace the sunken *Bruno Heinemann*. On the night of 11 February

'Cerberus' got under way and the three heavy units at Brest sailed for the English Channel with a large sea and air escort, including Z 7. On the 12th *Schoemann* became flagship of the whole armada when Vizeadmiral Ciliax transferred aboard after *Scharnhorst* hit a mine. All the German vessels arrived safely at Dutch or German ports by 13 February.

Early on 20 February, with Z 4, Z 5, Z 14 and Z 25 in Operation 'Sportpalast', *Schoemann* escorted *Prinz Eugen* and *Admiral Scheer* from Brunsbüttel north-wards for Trondheim. Z 4, Z 5 and Z 14 were sent into Bergen when they could not keep up owing to the heavy sea running, and in their absence *Prinz Eugen* was torpedoed and lost her steering gear.

On 6 March *Hermann Schoemann* sailed into the Barents Sea with *Tirpitz*, Z 14 and Z 5 to intercept convoys PQ.12 and QP.8 but failed to find them, although Z 14 sank a Soviet straggler.

On 9 April Z 7 was attached to 8. Z-Flottille at Kirk-enes as the replacement for Z 26 sunk on 29 March. On 1 May she sailed with Z 24 and Z 25 against the well-defended westbound convoy QP.11. The next morning, in heavy snow and pack ice, the three destroyers came across the four British destroyers of the outer escort and in a skirmish damaged *Amazon*. During the con-fused chase, Z 7 suddenly found herself confronted by the light cruiser *Edinburgh*, which had been tor-pedoed by U 456 and lay immobile in the water but with her armament intact. In the ensuing close-range encounter the first shells destroyed the German's main steam feed, leaving *Schoemann* without current or any means of propulsion. Z 24 and Z 25 laid a veil of smoke to protect the stricken Z 7, and after a brief engagement with two destroyers of the close escort returned to pick up the survivors and scuttle Z 7 with explosives. U 88 found other survivors in boats and on liferafts later.

Z 8 *Bruno Heinemann*

Origin of the Name

Korvettenkapitän Bruno Heinemann was the First Officer of the battleship *König* and was murdered by revolutionaries on 5 November 1918 while attempting to prevent the raising of the red flag.

Career

Z 8 *Bruno Heinemann* was a Type 1934A ship com-missioned on 18 January 1938 by her commander,

Korvettenkapitän Fritz Berger. As an experiment she was fitted with four First World War-vintage 15cm guns in single gunhouses, but these were replaced in May 1938 by the standard 12.7cm weapons. Between 12–14 March and 14–17 May 1938 she ran speed trials over the measured mile off Neukrug, achieving 36 knots from an output of 69,000shp at 400 rpm per shaft.

Z 8 took part in the Naval Review of 22 August 1938 and then in manoeuvres in the Skagerrak and North

Sea. The routine of exercises in the North Sea and Baltic was continued after she was attached to *4. Z-Flottille* on 1 November. Most of pre-war 1939 was spent in the shipyard.

On 30 August 1939 Z 8 shadowed the Polish destroyers *Grom*, *Burza* and *Blyskawica* on their flight across the Baltic. After participating in the blockade of Hela at the outbreak of war, she drydocked at Wilhelmshaven until 29 September. On leaving the yard she was machine-gunned by a Blenheim aircraft and was slightly damage. During November, as part of 4. Z-Flottille, Z 8 inspected neutral ships for contraband in the Skagerrak and Kattegat. In the early morning of 13 December, after laying mines off Newcastle, she drifted for ninety minutes within sight of the English coast with fire in one of her turbine rooms. Z 15 *Erich Steinbrinck* stood by. When finally clear she set off for home on one engine, beating off several air attacks. From the German Bight she escorted the torpedoed cruiser *Leipzig* to port before entering the yards herself for repair. Her second commander, Korvettenkapitän Georg Langheld, was appointed in December.

Heinemann sailed carried out two further minelaying sorties to the British East Coast—on 10 January 1940 to the Tyne and on 9 February off Cromer and Happisburgh. On 12 February she was attached to 2. Z-Flottille. For the Norwegian operation, *Heinemann* was assigned to Kriegsschiffgruppe 2 bound for Trondheim. After disembarking her troops, she sailed on 14 April with Z 16 Eckholdt and arrived at Wilhelmshaven without mishap. Korvettenkapitän Hermann Alberts took over as acting commander for a month in April, and was appointed the ship's third and last commander in May 1940.

Between 28 April and 1 May the destroyer worked with Z 4 laying the Sperre 17 minefield in the Skagerrak, and on 21 May she entered the yards at Wesermünde for a tripod mast and radar to be fitted. On 19 October she was transferred to Deschimag, where she remained until March 1941.

On 4 th April 1941 Z 8 left Wilhelmshaven with Z 14 and Z 15, docking at La Pallice on the 19th. She took part in all the major escort duties of the period—*Thor* (April), *Nordmark* (May), *Prinz Eugen* (June) *Scharnhorst* (July) and *Orion* (August). Between June and the end of August she was based at Bordeaux, from where she sailed for Deschimag, Bremen, on 6 September for a refit. In December 1941 she took part in intensive manoeuvres in the Baltic.

Between 14 and 17 January 1942 Z 8 sailed escort with Z 4 and Z 5 for the battleship *Tirpitz* transferring from the Jade to Trondheim (Operation 'Polarnacht'), returning to Kiel on 20th. On 24th the destroyers, now with Z 7 attached, passed through the Kiel Canal and headed for France to take part in Operation 'Cerberus', the break-out of the heavy ships from Brest. Off Calais *Heinemann* struck two mines and sank, losing 93 crew members, Z 4 piced up 188 and Z 5 34 survivors under enemy aircraft fire.

Z 9 *Wolfgang Zenker*

Origin of the Name

Leutnant zur See Wolfgang Zenker was shot to death by revolutionaries aboard the battleship *König* on 5 November 1918 whilst attempting to prevent the raising of the red flag.

Career

Z 9 was a Type 1934A ship commissioned on 2 July 1938 by Korvettenkapitän Gottfried Pönitz, her only commander. She was attached to 6. Z-Division, and her initial work-up was interrupted to enable her to take part in the August 1938 Naval Review to mark the launch of the heavy cruiser *Prinz Eugen* at Kiel. In early September 1938 she ran her speed trials over the measured mile off Neukrug, 36.4 knots being achieved from an output of 61,500shp at 340rpm per shaft.

At the end of August she transferred to the Baltic to join the force blockading the Gulf of Danzig, and on 3 September, together with Z 1, fought an engagement with two Polish naval units, the action being discontinued once within range of the coastal batteries. On 10 January 1940, in company with Z 8 and Z 13, *Zenker* laid mines off Cromer, but a second operation on the 17th with Z 13 was abandoned after the old battleship *Schlesien* had forced a path through the frozen sea: offshore, heavy seas caused the loss of 32 mines overboard. After a short lay-up for repair, Z 9 took part in the minelaying operation off Happisburgh on 10 February. That month she was attached to 4. Z-Flottille based at Wesermünde but required further attention from the 18th as a result of storm damage and flooding in the forecastle.

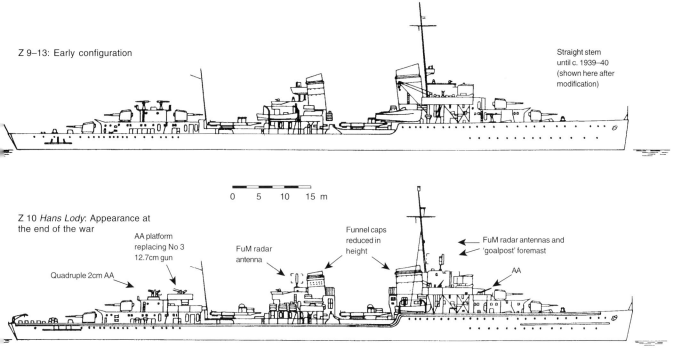

Z 9–13: Early configuration

Straight stem until c. 1939–40 (shown here after modification)

0 5 10 15 m

Z 10 *Hans Lody*: Appearance at the end of the war

AA platform replacing No 3 12.7cm gun

Quadruple 2cm AA

FuM radar antenna

Funnel caps reduced in height

FuM radar antennas and 'goalpost' foremast

AA

With Kriegsschiffgruppe 1 bound for Narvik, *Zenker* landed her troops at Elvegard, refuelled and, once repaired, returned to Herjangsfjord. Together with Z 12 and Z 13, she gave chase to the five British destroyers attempting to escape after bombarding the inner harbour at Narvik in the early hours of 10 April. After a bitter engagement, the three German destroyers over- whelmed and sank *Hunter*, returning to Narvik with her fifty survivors. That evening Z 9 attempted a break- out from the fjord with Z 12, but this was frustrated by enemy shadowers. On returning to Elvegard, Z 9 ran aground, damaging her port propeller. During the battle of 13 April, she withdrew into Rombakenfjord after firing off all her ammunition, and the crew scuttled her.

Z 10 *Hans Lody*

Origin of the Name

On the outbreak of the First World War, *Oberleutnant zur See (Reserve)* Hans Lody, who had been declared medically unfit for military service, immediately volun- teered for espionage duty. He arrived in England posing as an American, but he was soon arrested: the network of German secret agents in Britain had already been betrayed and eliminated. Lody was executed by firing squad for espionage at the Tower of London on 6 November 1914. Until 1945 a plaque in his honour was to be found at the gate of Lübeck fortress.

Career

Z 10 was a Type 1934A ship commissioned on 17 March 1938 by her commander, *Korvettenkapitän* Karl Jesko von Puttkamer. She ran her speed trials over the mea- sured mile off Neukrug between 30 November and 3 December 1938, achieving 37.8 knots from an output of 65,000shp at 370rpm per shaft.

Attached to 8. Zerstörerdivision, she joined the Fleet after working up and formed part of the escort and homecoming celebrations for the Condor Legion (Spanish Civil War) veterans on 30 May 1939. In August 1939, *Korvettenkapitän* Puttkamer was appointed Hitler's Naval ADC and replaced by *Korvettenkapitän Freiherr* Hubert von Wangenheim.

After three day's blockade duty off Danzig at the outbreak of war, Z 10 transferred into the North Sea to help lay the Westwall defensive minefield. While she was loading, a mine exploded, killing two and wounding six of her crew. During October, in company with Z 15 *Erich Steinbrinck* and 6. Torpedobootflottille, Z 10 inspected neutral commerce in the Skagerrak and Kattegat, often in severe weather. In the operation of 27–29 October she suffered storm damage and lost one man overboard with three injured.

Hans Lody sailed on two offensive minelaying oper- ations against the British coast, on 18 November to the Thames estuary and on 6 December off Cromer, where, with Z 12 *Erich Giese*, she fought a torpedo action against two British destroyers, one of these, *Jersey*, being hit and damaged. On 9 December Z 10 sailed to Wesermünde for a refit and did not emerge until 22 May 1940. Once operational she returned to Trondheim, and on 3 June was attached to the Fleet for 'Juno'. During the sortie she torpedoed and sank the troop transport *Orama* (19,840grt), the largest ship to be sunk by a German destroyer. With *Admiral Hipper*, she returned to Trondheim on 8 June with survivors from the British vessels sunk.

On 13 June 1940 *Lody* was damaged in an air raid aimed at *Scharnhorst* and returned to Kiel for repair, but she was back on the 20th in time to join Z 7, Z 15 and the torpedo boats *Greif* and *Kondor*, escorting *Scharnhorst* to Deutsche Werke. After a call at Wilhelmshaven, she returned to Trondheim in company with Z 5 *Paul Jacobi* to escort home, on 25 July, the damaged battleship *Gneisenau*. During a course change in the Kattegat on the 27th there was a minor collision between *Gneisenau* and Z 10. After completion of the escort, Z 10 transferred to Wilhelmshaven, from where, on 9 September she steamed to the western end of the English Channel with Z 6, Z 14, Z 16 and Z 20 preparatory to Operation 'Seelöwe'.

Z 10 took part in the minelaying operation off Falmouth on 28 September 1940, and on 10 October, during an air raid at Brest, she received shrapnel damage and lost two crew dead and seven wounded to strafing. On 17 October she sortied into the Bristol Channel and received two shell hits from the enemy cruiser and destroyer force. Korvettenkapitän Werner Pfeiffer was appointed *Lody*'s third commander in November 1940.

In the skirmish with five British destroyers off Plymouth on 29 November, Z 10 suffered splinter damage and was raked by anti-aircraft fire. On 5 December she left Brest in company with Z 20 *Karl Galster* for a refit at Wesermünde.

After leaving the yards in April 1941, *Lody* joined the Bismarck escort in the Great Belt on 19 May and was released into Trondheim on the 22nd, returning from there to Wesermünde. Between 11 and 14 June she helped to escort the torpedoed heavy cruiser *Lützow* from Egersund to the repair yard. On 1 July she sailed with 6. Z-Flottille to Kirkenes and carried out various escort duties, reconnaissance sorties and anti-shipping operations with the her sister ships before

returning to Wesermünde at the end of September with boiler damage.

On 15 May 1942, together with Z 4, Z 27 and Z 29, *Hans Lody* escorted *Lützow* to Trondheim in Operation 'Walzertraum', arriving on the 20th and transferring with her northward to Altafjord on 2 July. While anchoring in Gimsöystraumen with *Theodor Riedel* and *Karl Galster* she grounded in uncharted shallows, as a result of which her double bottom was ripped open, the port shaft seized and both propellers received damage. After refloating, the two destroyers returned to Trondheim for survey and emergency repair, and on the 27th both were towed to Deutsche Werke, Kiel. The damage to Z 10 was so extensive that her decommissioning was seriously considered. Korvettenkapitän Karl Adolf Zenker was appointed commander in August 1942.

A boiler room fire broke out during engine trials on 15 February 1943, and not until 22 April was *Lody* sufficiently battleworthy to return to operations in Norway. Meanwhile Kapitän zur See Hans Marks had been appointed her fifth commander.

Lody was part of the force which dispossessed the Soviets of Spitzbergen between 6 and 9 September. While leaving Altafjord on 21 November, she collided with *Erich Steinbrinck*. Korvettenkapitän Kurt Haun was appointed commander in November 1943.

The period until April 1944 was spent on escort and minelaying missions out of southern Norwegian ports, and on 3 May that year Z 10 was laid up at Germania Werft, Kiel, for a refit that lasted until 18 February 1945. While working up in the Baltic afterwards she was attached temporarily to Admiral K-Verbände, the command organisation for the various one- or two-man midget submarines. Once more or less operational again on 5 April, *Lody* ran escort duties from Copenhagen to the Skagerrak, and on 5 May she sailed from Copenhagen to the Hela peninsula to embark refugees, returning in the huge convoy of 7 May with about 1,500 aboard. On the 9th, in company with Z 6, she was removed to Kiel, where she decommissioned the following day.

On 10 May 1945, under Royal Navy command but with German engine-room personnel, *Hans Lody* proceeded to Wilhelmshaven. On 6 January 1946 she arrived at Portsmouth as experimental vessel R 38, German engine room staff being requested of the Naval Officer Commanding, Wilhelmshaven, on the 19th, presumably to help operate the complicated machinery. The ship was scrapped at Sunderland three years later.

Z 11 *Bernd von Arnim*

Origin of the Name

Kapitänleutnant Bernd von Arnim, commander of torpedo boat G 42, fell on 24 April 1917 in an action with the British 3rd Destroyer Flotilla off the Flanders coast.

Career

Z 11 was a Type 1934A ship commissioned on 6 December 1938 by *Korvettenkapitän* Curt Rechel, her only commander. She took part in the autumn manoeuvres that year. In February and early March 1939 the destroyer ran her speed trials over the measured mile off Neukrug, achieving 37 knots from an output of 69,100shp at 400rpm per shaft.

At the outbreak of war Z 11 was part of the force blockading the Gulf of Danzig, after which she was transferred to the North Sea for anti-contraband duties. On 17 November 1939 she laid mines off the Thames estuary with Z 19 and Z 21; four days later, in company with Z 12, Z 20 and the cruisers *Leipzig* and *Köln*, she escorted *Scharnhorst* and *Gneisenau* as far as the Skagerrak on their mission to wind up the Northern Patrol, during which the battleships sank an AMC.

Attached to *Gruppe 1* for Operation 'Weserübung, *Bernd von Arnim* left Wesermünde on 6 April with 200 mountain troops and joined up with the main convoy, heading northwards throughout the 7th in steadily deteriorating conditions. On each of the next three mornings Z 11 fought a naval action. On 8 April, the convoy being widely dispersed, she engaged in a duel with the British destroyer *Glowworm*, scoring hits despite the near-hurricane conditions; early on 9 April, in the approaches to Narvik harbour, she sank the coastal armoured vessel *Norge* with a torpedo after the Norwegian had opened fire on her; and after disembarking her troops and refuelling from the oiler *Jan Wellem*, she took up a position with Z 2 in Ballangenfjord, from where on the 10th she engaged the British destroyer force which had just attacked German shipping in Narvik harbour. In this action she scored hits on *Hotspur* and *Hardy*, the latter being so badly damaged that she had to be run ashore. Z 11 received five hits, suffered two dead and was no longer fully operational. Temporary repairs were put in hand, but the end came in Rombakenfjord on 13 April after she had exhausted her ammunition.

Z 12 *Erich Giese*

Origin of the Name

Kapitänleutnant Erich Giese was commander of the Flandernflottille (Flanders Flotilla) torpedo boat S 20. He was killed in an action with British naval units which, included the cruiser *Centaur*, on 5 June 1917.

Career

Z 12, a Type 1934A ship, commissioned on 4 March 1939. Korvettenkapitän Karl Smidt was to be her only commander.

On 9 and 10 May 1939 she ran her speed trials over the measured mile at Neukrug, making 36.1 knots for an output of 62,800shp at 355rpm per shaft. On 30 May 1939 she helped escort the Condor Legion convoy into Hamburg.

From the outbreak of war until mid-September 1939 Z 12 was engaged in extending the Westwall defensive minefield northwards from the Dutch coast to the Skagerrak. During September and October she carried out anti-contraband patrols in the Skagerrak and Kattegat. She formed part of the squadron involved in mining the Thames estuary (12 November 1939) but returned early, escorting Z 7 *Hermann Schoemann*, which had suffered an engine breakdown.

On 21 November, in company with Z 11, Z 20 and the cruisers *Leipzig* and *Köln*, *Erich Giese* acted as escort as far as the Skagerrak for the battleships *Scharnhorst* and *Gneisenau* on their foray against the Northern Patrol. After a day spent on anti-contraband duty she returned to Kiel. Operating from Wilhelmshaven on 6 December with Z 10 *Hans Lody*, she laid mines off Cromer and fought a brief engagement with the British destroyers *Juno* and *Jersey*, the latter being torpedoed and seriously damaged. On her return on 8 December she entered Germania Werft at Kiel for a refit.

Giese was attached to Kriegsschiffgruppe 1 for 'Weserübung', but during the voyage through the North Sea she lagged ever further behind as the result of oil leaks, pump breakdowns and, finally, water in the fuel, all attributable to the near-hurricane conditions. A sea-sick Gebirgsjäger NCO who came up on deck without permission and failed to harness himself to the superstructure was washed overboard. This was reported at once by a lookout, and despite the dangerous seas Korvettenkapitän Smidt immediately turned the ship through 180 degrees, risking capsize, and, steering alongside the exhausted man in the water, succeeded in having him pulled aboard over the propeller guard—a great feat of seamanship.

After landing her troops at Elvegard, Z 12 refuelled and returned to Herjangsfjord. The next morning, together with Z 9 and Z 13, she gave chase to the five British destroyers attempting to escape after bombarding the inner harbour at Narvik in the early hours of 10 April. After a bitter fight, the three German destroyers overwhelmed and sank *Hunter*, returning to Narvik with her survivors. Z 12 was undamaged but had expended 50 per cent of her ammunition. That evening she tried to break-out from the fjord with Z 9, but this was frustrated by the enemy covering force. *Giese* returned to Elvegardsmoen, effecting repairs at Narvik later.

On 13 April, after the alarm had been sounded, the destroyer raised steam in one boiler, threw off the connections to *Jan Wellem* and gave battle. She was confronted by six enemy warships and battered to a sinking wreck. The British rescued nine men from a float, and the remainder of the survivors got ashore, but 87 men perished.

Z 13 *Erich Koellner*

Origin of the Name

During an operation involving four torpedo boats and six minesweepers of 8. Minensuch-Halbflottille off the Flanders coast on 20 April 1918, M 95 sank in a British minefield. While M 39 was rescuing the crew, this boat was also mined and sunk. M 64 entered the minefield, picked up the survivors of M 95 and M 39, but was then also mined and sunk. Kapitänleutnant Erich Koellner, the CO of the half-flotilla and on board M 64, died with his vessel.

Career

Z 13 was a Type 1934A destroyer. She commissioned on 28 August 1939 and her only commander was Fregattenkapitän Alfred Schulze-Hinrichs. Between 8 and 1 October 1939 she ran her speed trials over the measured mile off Neukrug, achieving a maximum 36.2 knots for an output of 72,000shp at 420rpm per shaft.

She joined 8. Zerstörerdivision in early January 1940 and was part of the force which mined Cromer on 11 January and Happisburgh on 9 February. As one of the destroyers attempting to save the survivors of Z 1 and Z 3 on 22 February near the Heligoland swept channel in the Westwall minefield, she lost one man overboard.

She was attached to Kriegsschiffgruppe 1 for Narvik, but suffered storm damage and machinery breakdown on the voyage and lost two men overboard. On 9 January she disembarked her Gebirgsjäger at Elvegardsmoen, where she grounded for a few hours. She refuelled from *Jan Wellem* at Narvik and returned to anchor in Herjangsfjord. In the morning of 10 April, together with Z 9 and Z 12 she gave chase to the five British destroyers running for the open sea after bombarding the inner harbour at Narvik, scoring hits on *Hunter* which led to this destroyer sinking. She stayed to help pick up *Hunter*'s fifty survivors.

Whilst on patrol later in Ballangenfjord, *Koellner* was held fast for an hour and a half on an uncharted reef but later managed to reach the Postpier at Narvik, albeit with serious damage to her hull. After a cursory survey it was decided to use her as a floating battery across the Ramnes Narrows, and her torpedoes were transferred out and unnecessary crewmen landed. She was making for her appointed position on 13 April when the overwhelming British force was reported present in the fjord. She anchored in Djupvik Bay and at 1259 opened fire on the first vessel she saw, the destroyer *Icarus*. The battleship *Warspite* and the destroyers *Punjabi*, *Bedouin*, *Eskimo* and *Icarus* all replied, and eleven minutes after the action began *Erich Koellner* was abandoned and the ship blew up. There were 39 dead.

Z 14 *Friedrich Ihn*

Origin of the Name

Kapitänleutnant Friedrich Ihn was commander of torpedo boat S 35 and fell at the Battle of Jutland on 31 May 1916. Despite being under very heavy fire the IX. Flottille boat stayed behind to rescue survivors of V 29 (whose commander was Erich Steinbrinck—see Z 15). However, S 35 was so badly damaged that she later sank.

Career

Z 14 *Friedrich Ihn* was a Type 1934A destroyer commissioned on 9 April 1938 by Korvettenkapitän Claus Trampedach. The results of her speed trials are not recorded. During work-up she took part in the Naval Review of 22 August 1938 and was escort vessel to the state yacht *Grille* bearing Hitler, von Horthy and entourage through the Kiel Canal to Brunsbüttel next day. Fregattenkapitän Erich Bey became the ship's second commander in October 1938.

On 23 March 1939 *Ihn* formed part of the show of strength for the reoccupation of the Memel. In April Korvettenkapitän von Pufendorf was appointed commander, and from mid-April to 16 May the ship cruised with the Fleet to the eastern Atlantic and Mediterranean, carrying out there a special mission in company with Z 15 *Erich Steinbrinck*. Based at Swinemünde and attached to 1. Zerstörerflottille, she spent the intervening period until the outbreak of war in the eastern Baltic.

Following patrol duty in the eastern Baltic at the end of August, including the shadowing of Polish destroyers through the Sound, Z 14 was then transferred to the North Sea, where she helped lay the Westwall minefield, performed coastal protection duties and made occasional inspections of neutral shipping in the Skagerrak between the end of September and the end of November. During this period Korvettenkapitän Günther Wachsmuth was appointed commander.

On 8 October *Ihn* was part of the escort for *Gneisenau* and *Köln* for their fruitless anti-shipping foray to Bergen. On 13 December 1939 she returned from the minelaying sortie to the Tyne with boiler trouble and was sent in ahead of the squadron instead of having to find the cruiser escort; she was recalled shortly afterwards to escort *Köln* into port after *Leipzig* and *Nürnberg* had been torpedoed.

On 8 December Z 14 collided with the mine transport *Lauting* while coming alongside, receiving a four-metre long gash in her plating and sustaining damage to a number of fuel bunkers. Repairs took three days. A minclaying sortie to the Thames estuary was successfully accomplished on 6 January, but whilst proceeding to the Tyne five days later she was forced to pull out of the mission with engine trouble, *Richard Beitzen* providing the escort to Wilhelmshaven, where Z 14 was placed at the disposal of the Torpedo Trials Branch.

Friedrich Ihn was operational again at the end of June, and after briefly working up she joined the escort

for the torpedoed *Gneisenau* leaving Trondheim on 25 July for Kiel, and then entered the Blohm & Voss yard at Hamburg for a refit. In September she sailed down-Channel with Z 6, Z 10, Z 16 and Z 20 to Brest and Cherbourg preparatory to Operation 'Seelöwe'. She sailed on the minelaying missions to Falmouth Bay and into the Bristol Channel, but once 'Seelöwe' had been called off she returned to Germany for another refit.

Z 14 left the yards in January 1941, but her work-up in the Baltic was protracted owing to the very severe winter conditions—the coastal seas froze that year—and engine problems. She became operational once more on 29 March and sailed for France on 4 April with Z 8 and Z 15 and took part in the various major escorts for inbound warships across the Bay of Biscay. On 26 July she left Brest for a refit at the Stettin Oderwerke and was laid up until January 1942.

On 29 January she sailed for Brest to take part in Operation 'Cerberus'. During the night of 11 February the three heavy units sailed towards the English Channel with a large escort which included Z 14. North of Calais the force was shelled by British coastal batteries; Z 14 fired in barrage with *Prinz Eugen* and shot down two of the six torpedo-bombers which attacked the cruiser and also helped beat off MTB attack. On the 13th *Ihn* put into the Hook of Holland with twelve split boiler tubes.

On 21 February Z 14 escorted *Admiral Scheer* and *Prinz Eugen* to Norway, heavy seas curtailing her speed to the extent that she was sent into Bergen with other destroyers to await fairer weather next day. On 6 March she joined Kampfgruppe I as escort for the battleship *Tirpitz* with the destroyers Z 7 and Z 25 in the sortie against PQ.12 and QP.8, and, although neither convoy was discovered, Z 14 sank the Soviet straggler *Izora*. At the end of May she put into Trondheim for repairs to a propeller shaft bearing.

Between 2 and 4 July *Ihn* moved northwards to Altafjord with the Kampfgruppe for the short-lived Operation 'Rösselsprung' commencing next day. On the conclusion of this mission she carried out a minelaying sortie in the Skagerrak, and on 7 July entered the yards at Swinemünde. A shortage of materials and shipyard labour delayed the overhaul, with the result that Z 14 was not operational again until the beginning of 1943. Korvettenkapitän Gerhard Frommewas appointed commander in November 1942.

On 9 January 1943 *Friedrich Ihn* was one of the three destroyers escorting *Scharnhorst* and *Prinz*

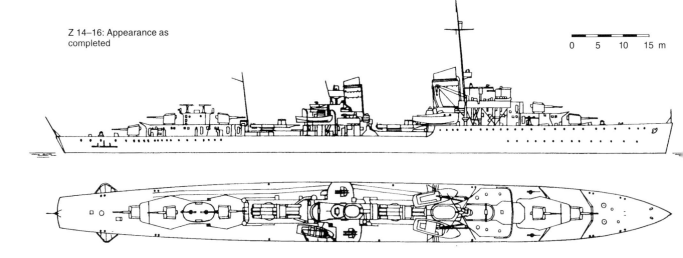

Z 14–16: Appearance as completed

0 5 10 15 m

Eugen as far as the Skaw in 'Fronttheater', following which she ran security patrols and escorts through the Skagerrak while operating out of southern Norwegian bases. In April she returned to northern Norway by way of Trondheim and spent the three days of the Spitzbergen operation in early September occupying net defences in Altafjord with *Lützow* and *Paul Jacobi* in attempt to put the enemy off the scent.

Beginning on 23 September 1943, *Ihn* escorted *Lützow* in company with Z 5, Z 15 and Z 27 towards Kiel (Operation 'Hermelin') but was released off Kristiansand to return northwards to Narvik. On 6 November she headed for Hamburg for a refit at Blohm & Voss which kept her out of commission until June 1944. Korvettenkapitän Carl August Richter-Oldekop was appointed commander in April 1944.

From August 1944 Z 14 worked out of Horten on escort and minelaying duties in the Skagerrak, helping to lay the Klaudius and Vespasia fields on 1 and 5 October with Z 4, Z 20 and the light cruiser *Emden*. On 20 October, when Z 30 was mined, Z 14, Z 20 and the submarine-chaser UJ 1702 towed the disabled destroyer into the yards at Oslo.

Z 14 was at Swinemünde refitting between 21 November and 9 December. Then, after a call at Aarhus,

she returned to southern Norway, from where, on 13–14 January 1945, she helped lay the Titus I minefield in company with the light cruiser *Nürnberg* and other ships. On 5 February she moved down to Copenhagen, and on the 16th, working with the minelayers *Ostmark*, *Lothringen* and *Linz* and the torpedo boats T 12 and T 20, she sailed to lay the Titus II field in the Skagerrak. Escort duties were combined with one final minelaying operation on 17 March with *Ostmark*, *Lothringen*, T 12, T 19 and T 20.

On 5 May 1945 Admiral Dönitz's order to cease naval hostilities with the western Allies came into force. This did not specifically prohibit German units from undertaking missions to evacuate refugees from the eastern territories, and Z 14 made two round trips to Hela for this purpose, the last quota of refugees being landed in Kiel Bay on 10 May, whereupon *Friedrich Ihn* was decommissioned.

In June 1945 Z 14 was sailed by a mixed British-German crew to Wilhelmshaven for overhaul prior to her delivery to the Soviets. She left the German port on 6 February 1946 and was commissioned into the Baltic Red Banner Fleet on 5 November that year as *Prytkiy*. She was deleted on 22 March 1952 and handed over to the shipbreakers in 1955.

Z 15 *Erich Steinbrinck*

Origin of the Name

Kapitänleutnant Erich Steinbrinck fell at the Battle of Jutland on 31 May 1916 after the torpedo boat which he commanded—V 29—was torpedoed and sunk by the British cruiser *Petard*.

Career

Z 15 *Erich Steinbrinck* was a Type 1934A vessel commissioned on 8 June 1938 by Korvettenkapitän Rolf Johannesson. She ran her speed trials over the measured mile at Neukrug on 4 August 1938, achieving a maximum speed of 35.9 knots from 66,000shp at 370rpm per shaft. Like her sister ships, she formed part of the Naval Parade on the 22nd of that month. Following manoeuvres in November she carried out severe-weather trials in the Atlantic in December, after which she entered the yards for repairs to storm damage and outstanding completion work.

Between 18 April and 16 May 1939 *Steinbrinck* cruised with *Gneisenau*, *Deutschland*, Z 1 and other destroyers of *1. Z-Flottille*, two U-boat flotillas and various support vessels in the Atlantic and Mediterranean, with visits to Ceuta and Lisbon. Later she was detached with Z 14 *Friedrich Ihn* to Italy in order to escort the oiler *Altmark* and repair ship *Huascaran*, with Göring aboard, from San Remo to Castellon in Spain, where Göring was to meet with a representative of General Franco. The convoy returned to Livorno over the period 12–17 May before sailing for home, with a call at Caraminal. In the Bay of Biscay the destroyers met passenger vessels of the German fleet heading for Spain to bring home the Condor Legion veterans.

On 25 August *Erich Steinbrinck* sailed from Swinemünde to the western Baltic to take up a position at the exit to the North Sea, but could only shadow the escaping Polish destroyer fleet passing through there on 30 August, any kind of hostilities being forbidden two days before the German attack.

Z 15 was destined to spend two-thirds of the coming war in the shipyard, and in the following paragraphs all her periods of lay-up are described, with the causes, in order to illustrate the kinds of problems which dogged Germany's destroyers at war.

Following the blockade of Hela in the first few days of the Polish war, Z 15 shifted to Wilhelmshaven, where she was required to help lay the Westwall minefield from 7 September onwards. In November she worked in the Skagerrak and Kattegat. On 18 November she formed part of the squadron which mined the Humber. On a second such foray—the 'Torpedoed Cruiser Fiasco' of 12 December—she stood by Z 8 *Bruno Heinemann* while her engine-room hands extinguished a fire in the turbine room, in full view of the Tyne coast. It was discovered shortly afterwards that Z 15 had water in her fuel, and she was sent into port without waiting for the cruiser escort. The lay-up lasted five days, from 12 to 18 December. On 23 December she collided with Z 7 *Hermann Schoemann* in the Jade, resulting in an eight-day lay-up lasting until 1 January 1940.

Z 15 participated in the Thames estuary minelaying sortie on 6 January and then went into the yards for refit from 27 January to 5 May—96 days. The days from 5 to 26 May 1940 were occupied with trials, training, working-up, after which she sailed with Z 20 to Trondheim for Operation 'Juno' beginning on 4 June but was sent into Trondheim on the 8th on one engine and making only 8 knots. She was laid up from 8 to 10 June undergoing engoinme repairs.

She was sufficiently combat-worthy on 14 June for an operation codenamed 'Nora', acting as escort for the troop transporter *Levante* between Trondheim and Narvik and the return (17 June), and on the 20th of the month sailed with the battleship *Scharnhorst*, escorting her to Kiel. Z 15 was in the yards at Blohm & Voss, Hamburg, from 23 June until 14 August (52 days), her subsequent trials and work-up lasting until 29 August a further fourteen days). Working from Cuxhaven, she assisted in laying the Sperre SW 3 minefield between 31 August and 2 September, but a turbine failure resulted in another lay-up, from 5 to 17 September.

On 22 September Z 15 sailed with Z 5 *Paul Jacobi* to Brest and took part in the minelaying offensives against Falmouth on 28 September and in the Bristol Channel on 17 October, where she received splinter damage. Further engine problems forced a return to home shipyards yet again, the lay-up this time at Blohm & Voss, Hamburg, but her ensuing trials only resulted in further engine breakdown, and she spent the following five months, 26 October 1940–29 March 1941 (150 days) undergoing repairs.

On 4 April 1941 *Erich Steinbrinck* sailed for Brest with Z 8 and Z 14, berthing at La Pallice on the 19th. She participated in the inbound escort missions for *Thor* (April) and *Nordmark* (May) but then required a ten-day boiler overhaul at La Pallice, from 25 May to 4 June 1941.

On 24 July she proceded to Brest in company with Z 8, Z 14, Z 23 and Z 24 to escort *Scharnhorst* for gunnery practice off La Pallice, but the battleship was bombed and damaged and had return to Brest for repair. Between 21 and 23 August Z 15 escorted *Orion* into the Gironde. On the 25th of the month she set out for Germany but collided with an uncharted wreck and eventually sailed on 6 September. The damage, dealt with at Blohm & Voss, Hamburg, took her out of service for five days short of a year—from 25 August 1941 until 22 March 1942, with post-repair trials and working up lasting from 23 March until 12 May, and then,

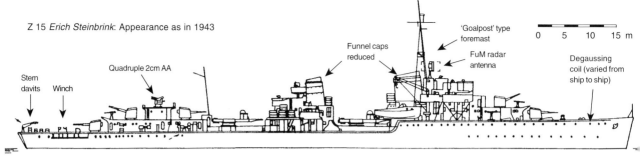

Stem davits

Winch

Quadruple 2cm AA

Funnel caps reduced

'Goalpost' type foremast

FuM radar antenna

Degaussing coil (varied from ship to ship)

0   5   10   15 m

following immediate engine failure (requiring the installation of new turbines), until 5 August.

Korvettenkapitän Freiherr Heinrich Freytag von Loringhausen was appointed commander in January 1942. On 5 August Z 15 made Bogen Bay with the cruiser *Köln*, and on the 17th and 24th, together with Z 4 and Z 16, she escorted *Admiral Scheer* and the minelayer *Ulm* to Bear Island for their respective operations, the same three destroyers meeting *Scheer* off Bear Island on 29 August following the successful completion of Operation 'Wunderland'. However, on leaving Kirkenes on 3 September, *Steinbrinck* grounded and was forced to return to Deschimag, Bremen, for repairs after a stop at Trondheim. This kept her out of the Fleet for another 90 days, from 27 September 1942 until January 1943, during which time Korvettenkapitän Otto Teichmann was appointed her new commander. While the destroyer was in dock, additional anti-aircraft guns were installed and the funnels were shortened and given flatter caps. Post-repair trials resulted in further engine trouble, requiring another ten days' attention in dock.

On her return to Norway Z 15 experienced continued engine trouble and had to put into Bergen for attention. Repairs to the shaft installation meant that it was not until 7 March that the destroyer could embark on her next sortie, forming part of the large escort of five destroyers and five torpedo-boats for the northbound *Scharnhorst*, although the weather was so atrocious that only Z 28 was able to complete the voyage with the battleship to Bogen Bay, the others all putting into ports of refuge for repair. On her arrival Z 15 spent the

next six months taking part in limited exercises and moving around the various anchorages.

From 6 September 1943 *Steinbrinck* participated in the Spitzbergen raid and on 23 September, in company with Z 5, Z 14 and Z 27, returned *Lützow* to Kiel. On 1 November she left Kiel for Kaafjord, where she arrived six days later. On the 21st of the month, in Altafjord, she was on the receiving end of *Hans Lody*'s stem, and, following another collision on 26 November with a Norwegian freighter south of Narvik, emergency repairs were required at Trondheim followed by more permanent repairs at Oslo lasting from 2 December 1943 until 17 January 1944—another 50 days out of service.

Between February and April 1944 *Steinbrinck* took part in escort and minelaying duties in the Skagerrak. In May 1944 she refitted at Blohm & Voss, Hamburg, receiving a 'goalpost' foremast, additional 'Barbara' armament and more radar. Fregattenkapitän Werner Röver was appointed commander in November 1944.

On 4 November Z 15 was badly damaged in an air raid and on 6 December she was towed to the yard at Wesermünde for repair. She never re-entered service: she was to be found at the Steubenhöft quay, Cuxhaven, in April 1945 with only one functioning engine and in any case immobile owing to lack of fuel. She was decommissioned on 7 May 1945.

On completion of her repairs at Wilhelmshaven she sailed for Libau on 2 January 1946 and, allocated to the Soviet Union, entered service under the red flag as *Pylkiy*. She was relegated to the role of accommodation ship under the designation PKZ 2 on 30 April 1949 and was scrapped in 1960.

Z 16 *Friedrich Eckholdt*

Origin of the Name

Kapitänleutnant Friedrich Eckholdt fell at Jutland on 31 May 1916 as commander of the torpedo boat V 48, the flag vessel of 6. Torpedoboot Halbflottille (Half-Flotilla).

Career

Z 16 *Friedrich Eckholdt*, a Type 1934A destroyer, was commissioned on 2 August 1938, just in time for the Naval Review at Kiel. Her first commander was Korvettenkapitän Alfred Schemmel.

In speed trials over the measured mile off Neukrug between 1–9 November 1938 and 25–26 January 1939 a speed of 38.9 knots was achieved from an output of 69,000shp at 400rpm per shaft. On 23 March 1939 Z 16 sailed with the force to reoccupy the Memel, and then joined the Fleet for the April–May cruise to the Mediterranean, attached to 1. Zerstörerflottille based at Swinemünde.

Following blockade duty off Danzig at the start of hostilities with Poland, Z 16 transferred to the North Sea station for patrol work. On 8 October she formed part of the escort for *Gneisenau* and *Köln* on the brief foray as far as Bergen, then detached into the Skagerrak for stop-and-search duty. She took part in four mine-laying operations off the coast of Britain—17 October and 18 November (Humber), 6 January (Thames) and 9 February (Orfordness). On 22 February 1940 she was the flotilla leader of the ill-fated 'Wikinger' anti-spy trawler operation in which Z 1 and Z 3 were lost.

For the Norwegian operation Z 16 was scheduled as escort standby but joined Kriegsschiffgruppe 2 bound for Trondheim when Z 7 *Hermann Schoemann* suffered an engine breakdown on 4 April. Two hundred Gebirgs-jäger were embarked at Cuxhaven on 6 April and were landed at Trondheim on the 9th. The following day Z 16 escorted *Admiral Hipper* for the run home as far as the exit of Ramsöyfjord but was sent back because of heavy weather, finally sailing for Wilhelmshaven on 14 April with Z 8 *Bruno Heinemann*.

Friedrich Eckholdt emerged from the Blohm & Voss yard at Hamburg in early September 1940 and sailed down-Channel with four other destroyers, putting into Le Havre and then Cherbourg, where she was attacked by aircraft on 18 September. After making two mine-laying sorties on the 19th and 29th of the month to Falmouth Bay, she was attacked by aircraft again on 10 October, sustaining serious damage with one crewman dead. On 5 November she put back to Blohm & Voss, where she remained until the end of December.

The period from December to April 1941 was spent working up in the Baltic. On 19 May, in company with Z 23, she formed the advance protective screen off Cape Arcona for *Bismarck* and *Prinz Eugen* and was

released into Trondheim on the 22nd, from where she returned to Wilhelmshaven. On 10 June, sailing from Kiel, she assisted in the escort for the heavy cruiser *Lützow* making for the Indian Ocean, though after the escort was dismissed into Oslofjord the cruiser was torpedoed by aircraft and was forced to return to Kiel. On 21 June Z 16 sailed for Bergen, and from there as part of 6. Z-Flottille to Kirkenes, where she took part in all four anti-shipping missions around the Kola peninsula and various patrol and escort duties. After a short overhaul at Narvik, on 12 October she collided with a Norwegian freighter, resulting in a large gash in the hull port side. Following emergency repairs on the 19th she made Trondheim on one engine, arriving at Germaniawerft, Kiel, on 9 November and remaining until 15 April 1942.

On 11 June 1942 *Eckholdt* returned to Norway in company with Z 6 and Z 20, but further engine problems compelled her to return to the yards. On 9 July she returned to Trondheim with the light cruiser *Köln*, both units carrying mines which they laid at the western entrance to the Skagerrak. On 18 July she arrived at Bogen Bay. *Korvettenkapitän* Friedrich Gerstung was appointed commander in August.

On 17 and 24 August, together with Z 4 and Z 15 and working from Bogen Bay, *Eckholdt* escorted *Admiral Scheer* and the minelayer *Ulm* to Bear Island for their respective operations, the same three destroyers meeting *Scheer* off Bear Island on 29 August following her successful completion of Operation 'Wunderland'. On 13 October, with Z 4, Z 27 and Z 30, she laid a minefield off the Kanin peninsula at the mouth of the White Sea and between 5 and 9 November accompanied *Admiral Hipper* on Operation 'Hoffnung'.

Her fifth and last commander, Kapitänleutnant Günther Bachmann was appointed in December 1942 and, together with the entire crew of Z 16, fell on the 31st of the month during Operation 'Regenbogen' in the Barents Sea following the misidentification of the British cruiser *Sheffield* as a German vessel. All hands—some 340 men—perished.

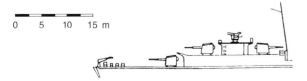

0   5   10   15 m

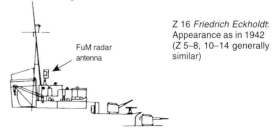

FuM radar antenna

Z 16 *Friedrich Eckholdt*. Appearance as in 1942 (Z 5–8, 10–14 generally similar)

Z 17 *Diether von Roeder*

Origin of the Name

Kapitänleutnant Diether Freiherr Roeder von Diersburg was CO of 13. T-Boot Halbflottille towards the end of the First World War. He dies aboard S 62 in a minefield on 11 June 1918.

Career

Z 17 was a Type 1936, commissioned on 28 August 1938. Her only commander was Korvettenkapitän Erich Holtorf. In her speed trials at Neukrug on 27–28 October and 9–11 November 1938 she required only 1,300shp (121rpm per shaft) for 12.35 knots, 4,189shp (175rpm) for 18 knots and 37,700shp (344rpm) for 32.4 knots. Over the measured mile the highest speed attained was 41.45 knots for 72,500shp at 42rpm per shaft.

On joining the Fleet she formed part of the large force which reoccupied the Memel, and from 18 April to 16 May she took part in the Atlantic and Mediterranean cruises, with calls at various Spanish ports. In July 1939 she cruised with Z 18 and Z 19 to Loenfjord and Sognefjord in Norway.

When war came in September 1939 she helped lay the Westwall mine barrier and carried out anti-contraband patrols in the North Sea. She sailed on one minelaying operation, that in the Humber sstuary on 17 October. On 1 December she joined 5. Z-Flottille based at Swinemünde.

For 'Weserübung' she was attached to Kriegsschiffgruppe 1 for Narvik, disembarked her 200 mountain troops at 2000 on 9 April 1940 and maintained a patrol across the harbour approaches. She had just been relieved by Z 22 *Anton Schmitt* early on 10 April when the British 2nd Destroyer Flotilla made its surprise attack. Z 17 fired a fan of eight torpedoes without success and was hit in her bunkers and below No 1 gun. No 3 gun and her rudder gear were soon unserviceable, and she manoeuvred to the Postpier using only her propellers. There she made fast, facing towards the sea. Depth charges and other explosives were packed into her interior with the intention that she should be blown up remotely if and when a British destroyer came alongside to investigate. This indeed occurred on 13 April, but fire was opened in error from the hills behind the town and the British ship withdrew. Z 17 was then scuttled.

Z 18 *Hans Lüdemann*

Origin of the Name

Hans Lüdemann was an engineer-midshipman aboard the World War I torpedo boat S 148. On 14 May 1913, during manoeuvres, the high-pressure cylinder of the boat's steam reciprocating machinery exploded. Despite his terrible burns, Lüdemann dragged himself into the boiler room and gave orders for it to be shut down, thus saving the remaining personnel. Although conveyed as quickly as possible to a Heligoland hospital, he died shortly afterwards.

Career

Z 18 was a Type 1936 ship and was commissioned on 8 October 1938 by Korvettenkapitän Herbert Friedrichs, her only commander. After completing her trials she voyaged with Z 19 in Norwegian waters during July 1939, visiting Moldefjord and later, with Z 17, Loenfjord and Sognefjord. She took part in torpedo exercises with the Fleet in August.

On the outbreak of war Z 18 helped lay the Westwall minefield and carried out anti-contraband patrols in the Skagerrak and Kattegat. She formed part of the force which mined the Humber and Thames estuaries during the nights of 17 October and 12 November respectively. On 1 December 1939 she was attached to 3. Z-Flottille at Swinemünde and spent the next three months at Stettiner Oderwerke for more shipyard work. Speed trials run at Neukrug on 9 January 1940 showed that 3,01shp (144rpm per shaft) produced a speed of 14.7 knots and 40,400 shp (343rpm) 32 knots. Her best speed over the measured mile was 39.8 knots, for an output of 74,500 shp at 435rpm per shaft.

Assigned to Kriegsschiffgruppe 1 for Narvik, *Lüdemann* took on board her quota of 200 mountain troops at Wesermünde. The detachment was landed at Tjeldöy in Westfjord early on 9 April to take the presumed batteries overlooking the Ramnes Narrows, but as none was found the men were re-embarked for the Narvik Postpier.

Z 18 was refuelling on the town side of the *Jan Wellem* early next morning when the British destroyer force arrived. She was hit and lost the use of No 2 gun and her rudder gear. Two crewmen were killed. She was repaired at the Postpier and on 13 April, when the battleship *Warspite* arrived with nine destroyers, Z 18 sailed with Z 9, Z 11 and Z 2 into Rombakenfjord, where she positioned herself with Z 2 across the Strömmen Narrows as a floating battery. After expending all her ammunition, she raised anchor and ran to the upper end of the fjord, where her commander proposed to run her on to the rocks and destroy the ship with explosives once the crew had got ashore. However, apart from causing a small fire aft the explosion was a failure, and boarding parties from the British destroyers *Icarus* and *Hero* were later able to search the wreck, although they found nothing of military value.

Z 19 *Hermann Künne*

Origin of the Name
Hermann Künne was a torpedo gunner aboard the torpedo boat S 53 at the time of the British raid on Zeebrugge on 23 April 1918. The boat was in harbour, but Künne did not hesitate to join in the hand-to-hand fighting and fell with a bayonet wound.

Career
Korvettenkapitän Friedrich Kothe commissioned Z 19, a Type 1936 destroyer, on 12 January 1939; he was to be her only commander. Speed trials in 65 metres at Neukrug on 21–22 March 1939 showed that the vessel made 20 knots with 7,665 shp (203rpm per shaft) and 29.7 knots at 29,410 shp (310rpm), her best speed over the measured mile bring 39 knots at an output of 72,100shp (420rpm). These trials were interrupted so that Z 19 could take part in the Memel operation.

On 30 June 1939, in company with Z 18, *Hermann Künne* visited Norwegian waters, where she rammed the pier in Moldefjord following rudder failure. Once Z 17, the third destroyer of 5. Zerstörerdivision, had joined the group, calls were made to Loenfjord and Sognefjord. Z 19 returned to Swinemünde on 20 July and took part in the Fleet torpedo exercises the following month.

On the outbreak of war Z 19 was stationed on the North Sea coast and, with Z 20 and the state yacht *Grille*, helped lay the Westwall mine barrier. She stopped and searched neutrals in the Skagerrak between 28 and 30 September and sailed on four minelaying missions against the East Coast—17 Oct-ober (Humber estuary), 12 and 17 November (Thames estuary) and 12 December (Tyne), this last culminating in the 'Torpedoed Cruiser Fiasco' next day in which Z 19 escorted the crippled *Nürnberg* to port. Z 19 was scheduled for another minelaying mission on 17 December but pulled out because of boiler contamination, requiring a lay-up in the yards at Stettin until 14 March 1940.

Trials and working up had to be cut short on notice of attachment to Kriegsschiffgruppe 1 for Narvik. On 6 April she embarked 200 mountain troops at Weser-münde and survived the voyage comfortably. After landing her Gebirgsjäger at Elvegaard, she started to take on sufficient fuel from *Jan Wellem* to enable her to patrol Ofotfjord. She was on the seaward side of the tanker refuelling, her flank being protected by Z 22 *Anton Schmitt*, when the British surprise attack came in the early morning of 10 April. Z 22 was torpedoed and sank. Z 19 threw off the oil hose and lines but was unmanoeuvrable for an hour, and a survey at the Post-pier revealed that her engines had suffered damage from the torpedo blast to Z 22. Repaired by afternoon, she sailed to examine the wreck of the British destroyer *Hardy* on the cape between Skomenfjord and Bollan-genfjord and recovered secret papers.

On 11 and 12 April Z 19 carried out patrol duty. On 13 April she was escorting Z 13 to Taarstad, where the latter was to anchor as a floating battery, when the British task force arrived. After firing off all her ammunition, *Künne* put back into Herjangsfjord, where she was scuttled.

Z 20 *Karl Galster*

Origin of the Name
Kapitänleutnant Karl Galster was lost when his tor-pedo boat S 22 was mined and sunk while engaging the British cruiser *Cleopatra* and two destroyers in the North Sea on 21 March 1916.

Career
Z 20 *Karl Galster* was a Type 1936 ship commissioned on 21 March 1939 by her commander, Korvettenkapitän Freiherr Theodor von Bechtolsheim. She ran speed trials over the measured mile between 16 and 19 May

1939 off Neukrug, reaching 39 knots from 76,500shp at 450rpm per shaft. 1,888shp was found sufficient for 12 knots, 8,473shp for 20 knots and 40,750shp for 31.5 knots. In July she cruised in Norwegian waters, visiting Andalsnes, and the following month took part in the Fleet torpedo practice.

At the outbreak of war *Karl Galster* was part of the force commanded by Vizeadmiral Densch laying the Westwall minefield in the German Bight. At the end of September she patrolled the Skagerrak and on 8 October was an escorting destroyer to *Gneisenau* and *Köln* on their unrewarding raid as far as Bergen. In October and November Skagerrak patrol work alternated with mine-laying sorties to the British East Coast—17 October (Humber) and 12 and 17 November (Thames estuary). On 21 November, in company with *Leipzig*, *Köln*, Z 11 and Z 12, she escorted *Scharnhorst* and *Gneisenau* as far as the Skagerrak for their attack on the Northern Patrol. On 1 December she was attached to 3 .Z-Flottille and until 6 January carried out coastal protection duties in the German Bight. Two minelaying operations followed, on 6 January to the Thames estuary and on 10 February to the Tyne, followed by Operation 'Nordmark' from 18 to 21 February together with Z 1 and Z 21, escorting *Scharnhorst*, *Gneisenau* and *Admiral Hipper* on an abortive anti-shipping raid as far as the Shetland Narrows. On her return she was docked for a refit.

Karl Galster was not operational again until 27 May 1940, when she was dispatched very smartly to Trondheim to take part in Operation 'Juno' in early June. She assisted Z 10 in the rescue of the *Orama* survivors and on 14 June was the only destroyer in the escort for the ambitious sortie by *Gneisenau* and *Admiral Hipper* to knock out the Northern Patrol in the month without darkness in the Arctic. *Gneisenau* was torpedoed by the submarine *Clyde* on leaving Trondheim and the operation was cancelled. On 25 July Z 20 sailed in the large escort accompanying *Gneisenau* to Kiel.

After a brief refit Z 20 was involved in laying the Sperre SW 3 minefield at the southern end of the North Sea between 14 August and 7 September 1940, and on 9 September sailed with Z 6, Z 10, Z 14 and Z 16 down-Channel for Cherbourg and Brest for the preparatory phase of Operation 'Seelöwe'. She engaged in a number of sorties, including the foray in the Bristol Channel with Z 10, Z 14, Z 15 and 5. Torpedobootflottille against a British cruiser and destroyer force and a minelaying

mission off Plymouth code-named 'Seydlitz' in which she received slight damage during an encounter with five British destroyers, one of which was torpedoed. She left Brest on 5 December in company with Z 10 *Hans Lody* and on 9 December arrived at Wilhelms-haven for turbine overhaul.

Z 20 was operational once more by 9 June 1941 and was a member of the escort for *Lützow* both ways, returning with the torpedoed cruiser to Kiel. On 20 June she left for Norway, eventually arriving at the Barents Sea port of Kirkenes on 11 July. After taking part in three of the four main anti-shipping operations carried out by 6. Z-Flottille, she suffered an engine breakdown and sailed for Kiel from Trondheim on 23 November. The repair lasted until 5 May 1942.

After trials and work-up in the Baltic, Z 20 wenrt back to Norway on 11 June to join Kampfgruppe I at Trondheim. On 2 July she sailed as escort for the battleship *Tirpitz* to Altafjord, where she ran aground in uncharted shallows in Grimsöystraumen. Her port engine was unserviceable and the port shaft buckled, requiring emergency repair at Trondheim followed by a return to Kiel, where she entered the yards on 15 July. The repairs were completed at Deschimag by mid-November, by which time a new commander, Korvetten-kapitän Fro Harmsen had been appointed.

Operational again on 8 December 1942, *Galster* escorted *Lützow* to Norway in company with Z 6 and Z 31 but was forced to put into Trondheim with storm damage; this kept her out of Operation 'Regenbogen' on New Year's Eve. She was operational again on 9 January 1943, but boiler damage forced another spell in the shipyard at Trondheim until 27 February.

On 11 March *Galster* accompanied *Tirpitz* to Bogen Bay, from where a number of exercises were carried out, but during the long wait for the blockade-runner *Regensburg*, hove-to off Jan Mayen in rough weather, she received damage and put into Lanfjord alongside the maintenance ship *Neumark* for repair. She took part in the Spitzbergen raid of 6–9 September, and in November she returned to Deschimag, Bremen, for an overhaul.

Although declared operational once more in April 1944, she soon experienced a renewed problem with the starboard engine, which had to be attended to at Kiel before she took up station at Horten for escort and minelaying duties, including the Klaudius and Vespasia fields in the Skagerrak on 1 and 5 October, respectively. Following another spell in the shipyard,

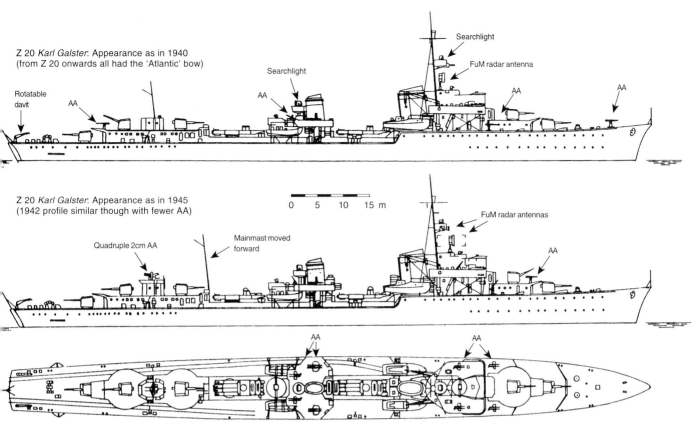

Z 20 *Karl Galster*. Appearance as in 1940
(from Z 20 onwards all had the 'Atlantic' bow)

Searchlight

FuM radar antenna

Rotatable davit

AA

Searchlight

AA

AA

AA

AA

Z 20 *Karl Galster*. Appearance as in 1945
(1942 profile similar though with fewer AA)

0   5   10   15 m

Quadruple 2cm AA

Mainmast moved forward

FuM radar antennas

AA

AA

AA

AA

AA

at Oslo between 20 December 1944 and 13 January 1945—Fregattenkapitän Kuno Schmidt being appointed her last commander in January—*Galster* was transferred from Copenhagen to Gotenhafen in the Baltic for escort and patrol duties, especially on behalf of Kampfgruppe Thiele. Z 20 took part in the massive refugee armadas in early May 1945, making two round trips from Copenhagen to Hela and back on 5 and 8 May. She was decommissioned on 10 May.

Upon the cessation of hostilities a mixed German-British crew sailed her to Wilhelmshaven, where she was allocated to the Soviets as a war prize. On 6 February 1946 she became a Soviet possession at Libau, entering service with the Baltic Red Banner Fleet on 5 November that year as destroyer *Prochnyy*. She was relegated to a role as an accommodation ship, designated PKZ 99, on 28 November 1954 and remained in commission until scrapped in 1958.

Z 21 *Wilhelm Heidkamp*

Origin of the Name
Obermaschinist Wilhelm Heidkamp was pumpmaster aboard the battlecruiser *Seydlitz* at the Battle of the Dogger Bank on 24 January 1915. Within seconds of a hit on C turret, six tons of powder were burning but, despite the noxious gases and intolerable heat, Heidkamp managed to flood the magazine, thereby saving the ship. He died from the effects of his burns in 1918.

Career
Z 21 was a Type 1936 ship commissioned on 20 June 1939 by Korvettenkapitän Hans Erdmenger, her only

commander. Engine trials showed that she was capable of 37 knots at 69,950 shp (440rpm per shaft), but the run over the measured mile was never carried out. At the outbreak of war she was reconditioning engines at Deutsche Werke, Kiel.

Between 28 and 30 September 1939, in company with Z 11, Z 12, Z 17, Z 18, Z 19 and Z 20, she carried out a large-scale anti-contraband patrol in the Skagerrak and between 8 and 10 October formed part of the escort for the battleship *Gneisenau* and light cruiser *Köln* on the unrewarding anti-shipping raid as far north as Bergen. On 17 October she formed part of the minelaying force to the Humber. On 26 October she was detached from her flotilla and appointed FdZ flag vessel. Two further minelaying sorties following, on 12 and 17 November to the Thames estuary.

After a refit at Stettin between 27 November and 24 December, *Heidkamp* helped lay minefields off Newcastle on 10 January 1940 and sailed as offshore escort on the Cromer mission of 10 February. With Z 1 and Z 20, she escorted *Scharnhorst*, *Gneisenau* and the heavy cruiser *Admiral Hipper* on Operation 'Nordmark', an impromptu but fruitless foray to the Shetland Narrows to avenge the *Altmark* incident two days previously.

For the Norwegian campaign, Z 21 was flag vessel of Kampfsschiffgruppe 1 bound for Narvik. Besides the FdZ, Kommodore Bonte, she took on board Generalmajor Dietl, commander of 3. Gebirgsjägerdivision, and the two staffs. Troops were embarked at Wesermünde on 6 April. In the morning of 9 April, off Narvik, she torpedoed and sank the Norwegian coast defence ship *Eidsvold*, whose commander had declined to parley.

After disembarking her occupation troops and refuelling, Z 21 moored astern of the *Jan Wellem* at the head of Beisfjord but, targeted by the British destroyers in their surprise raid early the next morning, was torpedoed aft. The after magazine blew up, killing Bonte and all his staff and also 81 crewmen. The destroyer remained afloat for 24 hours, then turned turtle and sank.

Z 22 *Anton Schmitt*

Origin of the Name

Anton Schmitt was a Bootsmannsmaat (boatswain's mate) aboard the light cruiser *Frauenlob* at the Battle of Jutland on 31 May 1916. When his ship was badly damaged and began to founder, Schmitt found himself the last man at the last intact gun, and he continued to fire it until the cruiser sank, taking him with her. (This heroic sacrifice was exactly paralleled the same day and in the same battle by Jack 'Boy' Cornwall VC of the light cruiser HMS *Chester*.)

Career

Z 22 was a Type 1936 destroyer commissioned on 24 September 1939 by Korvettenkapitän Friedrich Böhme, her only commander. From 7 to 11 November she ran her speed trials off Neukrug, achieving 36.9 knots from an output of 69,000shp at 400rpm per shaft.

Operational in January 1940, she was part of the flotilla which sowed mines off Newcastle on the 10th of that month, and she spent the period from 26 January to March in the shipyard following a boiler-room fire. Attached to Kriegsschiffgruppe 1 for Narvik, Z 22 was next in line to refuel and to seaward of the *Jan Wellem* when the British destroyer force launched its surprise attack in the early hours of 10 April. She was hit by two torpedoes, broke up and immediately sank, sufering 52 dead.

Z 23

Career

Z 23 was a Type 1936A ship and was commissioned on 15 September 1940 by Korvettenkapitän Friedrich Böhme. Following trials and work-up, she joined the Fleet in March 1941 and carried out escort duties in the Baltic and southern Norwegian waters, her charges including *Admiral Hipper* (26–28 March), *Admiral Scheer* (30 March–1 April), *Bismarck* (19–22 May) and *Lützow* (10–14 June).

On 16 June, in company with Z 24, she transferred from Kiel to Brest. Here she ran escort for *Scharnhorst* (20–24 July) and the incoming raider *Orion* to the Gironde estuary (21–28 August). She left France on 23 October, and on the 24th of the following month loaded mines and sailed to join 8. Z-Flottille at Kirkenes. From here she took part in operations until 20 January 1942, when she rammed Z 24 while manoeuvring in thick fog preparatory to leaving Kirkenes for Tromsö, Z 24 having encountered a problem while weighing anchor. Repairs to the damaged bows were put in hand at Trondheim, where Z 23 became the first Type 1936A destroyer to be fitted with a 15cm twin turret on the forecastle deck in place of the single mounting. Fregattenkapitän Heinrich Wittig took over as commander in May 1942.

Z 23 was operational again in August 1942, and between 15 and 19 of the month joined the minelayer *Ulm* coming up from Swinemünde and escorted her to

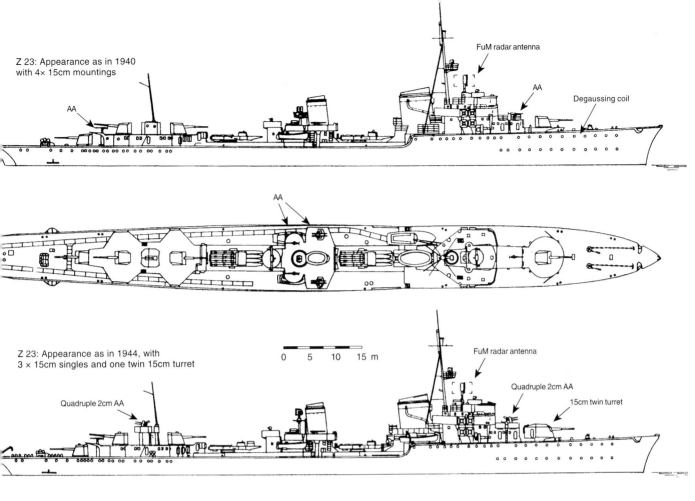

Z 23: Appearance as in 1940
with 4× 15cm mountings

AA

FuM radar antenna

AA

Degaussing coil

AA

Z 23: Appearance as in 1944, with
3 × 15cm singles and one twin 15cm turret

0   5   10   15 m

Quadruple 2cm AA

FuM radar antenna

Quadruple 2cm AA

15cm twin turret

Narvik. On a sortie with *Admiral Hipper* commencing from the iron ore port on 24 September, Z 23, Z 28, Z 29 and Z 30 laid the Zarin minefield across the Matoshkin Strait which separates the two islands of Novaya Zemlya.

On 1 October Z 23 escorted *Admiral Hipper* from Altafjord to Bogen Bay, and *Tirpitz* and *Admiral Scheer* with Z 29 from Bogen Bay to Trondheim between the 23rd and the 24th. On 6 November she, with Z 29 and Z 28, proceeded with *Admiral Scheer* into the Baltic; released off Copenhagen, she returned to Trondheim on 12 November with Z 25, Z 29 and the light cruiser *Nürnberg* (whose seaworthiness was so doubtful that her purpose was simply to make up the numbers).

On 8 February 1943 Z 23 rejoined 8. Zerstörerflottille at Bordeaux for escort duties. While shepherding home the blockade-runners *Himalaya* and *Pietro Orsedo* five crewmen were lost and 31 wounded in an air attack, and she received slight damage in an air raid while drudocked at La Pallice. She escorted the blockade-runner *Osorno* on 23 December and ger forecastle flooded in heavy seas; she lost four men overboard and was released from the escort. She took part in the Battle of Biscay on 28 December and fired seven torpedoes without result.

After Z 32 and Z 37 had collided during offshore manoeuvres on 30 January 1944, Z 23 towed Z 37 into the Gironde. Korvettenkapitän Helmut von Mantey was appointed commander in March.

In the following weeks and months Z 23 escorted U-boats in and out of the Biscay ports, usually under constant air attack. On 12 August, while laid up in the shipyard at La Pallice, the destroyer was badly damaged during an air raid. The necessary repair work appeared so extensive that she was decommissioned instead. For some time the naval authorities toyed with the idea of sinking the destroyer across the harbour entrance as a blockship but nothing came of this and Z 23 languished *in situ*.

In October 1945 the French Navy towed Z 23 to Brest for scrapping.

Z 24

Career

Z 24, a Type 1936A, was commissioned on 23 October 1940 by Korvettenkapitän Martin Saltzwedel. Operational from March 1941, she spent several months running escort duties between the Baltic and Norway. She sailed for Brest on 16 June with Z 23 and worked in Biscay briefly until recalled to Kiel for the 8. Z-Flottille assignment to northern Norway in October 1941.

On Boxing Day 1941, working with Z 23, Z 25 and Z 27, she was involved in securing the Lofotens, and on 3–4 January 1942 escorted the depot ship *Adolf Lüderitz* from Tromsö to Kirkenes. Whilst weighing anchor at Kirkenes for the return, she was rammed in thick fog by Z 23. Taking water, and with her forecastle damaged, she put back to Wesermünde for repairs, which were completed in time for her to escort *Admiral Hipper* to Norway on 18 March.

On 28 March Z 24 sortied with Z 25 and Z 26 from Kirkenes in an attempt to intercept convoy PQ.13 . After sinking the straggler *Bateau*, picking up her crew and then men from the *Empire Ranger* (found adrift in lifeboats after their ship had been sunk by aircraft), the three German ships were surprised next morning by the convoy escorts, including the cruiser *Trinidad*. Z 26 was soon reduced to a wreck. A fan of seven torpedoes fired at the cruiser by Z 24 all missed, but a rogue fired by the cruiser circled and hit her. A brief pursuit resulted in the destroyer *Eclipse* being damaged before Z 24 and Z 25 returned to take off Z 26's survivors. On 1 May Z 24, Z 25 and Z 7 *Hermann Schoemann* sailed to attack convoy QP.11, and in confused fighting Z 7 and the cruiser *Edinburgh* were sunk.

From May to July Z 24 and Z 28 were attached to Kampfgruppe II at Trondheim. On 12 July Z 24 returned to Wesermünde for a refit in which a 15cm twin turret replaced the 15cm single gunhouse on the forecastle deck. She returned to operational status in January 1943.

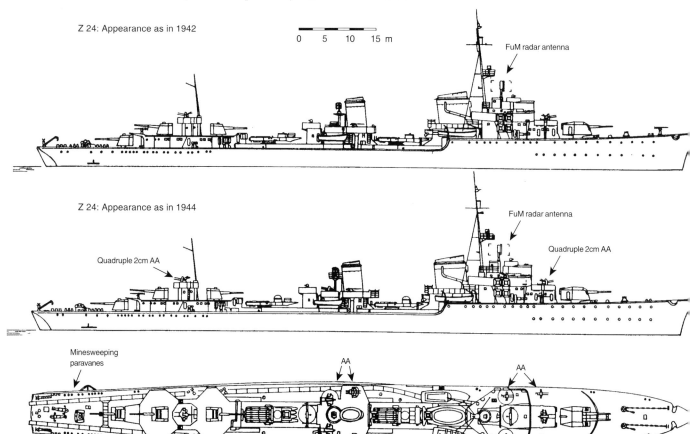

Z 24: Appearance as in 1942

0 5 10 15 m

FuM radar antenna

Z 24: Appearance as in 1944

FuM radar antenna

Quadruple 2cm AA

Quadruple 2cm AA

Minesweeping paravanes

AA

AA

After carrying out various minor escort missions between the Baltic and Norway, on 3rd March 1943 Z 24 joined 8. Z-Flottille. On 14 June she left Royan to meet with U 185 and relieve her of the survivors of U 564. Korvettenkapitän Heinz Birnbacher was appointed commander in August.

Between 23 and 26 December Z 24 formed part of the escort for the blockade-runner *Osorno* and participated in the Battle of Biscay on the 28th. On 14 January 1944 Z 24 entered the yards at La Pallice for a refit.

On 6 June, sailing with T 24, she headed for Brest with the intention of carrying out a mining operation to hinder the Allied landings. On 9 June, together with Z 32 and ZH 1, she was involved in a fight off Roscoff against a superior enemy destroyer force but managed to escape southwards with T 24 to Brest and then

Bordeaux after receiving hits on the bridge, a 15cm gunhouse and the after funnel. She had her machinery overhauled between 13 July and 5 August, and on 14 August, in the roadstead at Royan, she was damaged and suffered casualties in an air raid. although she shot down four of the attacking aircraft.

On 24 August 1944 Z 24 left Bordeaux in company with T 24. In the roadstead at Le Verdon eighteen Beaufighter aircraft of Nos 236 and 404 Squadrons RAF attacked the two German ships with 25lb AP rockets and cannon fire. T 24 was sunk and Z 24 was hit aft threee times, suffering one dead and one wounded. Next day she got alongside the quay, but she later capsized and sank. The crew were remustered ashore as the Narvik Naval Battalion defending Festung Gironde and eventually surrendered there in 1945.

Z 25

Career

Z 25 was a Type 1936A ship and was commissioned on 30 November 1940 with Korvettenkapitän Heinrich Gerlach as her commander. Once operational on 26 June 1941 she made for Bergen but grounded off Haugesund, damaging both propellers and the stabiliser keel on the port side. Repairs at Deschimag took until September.

Z 25 formed part of the German Baltic Fleet in the Aaland Sea from 22 to 29 September 1941. On 28 November she loaded mines at Aarhus and, with Z 23, Z 27, Z 5 *Paul Jacobi* (which dropped out after tangling with a buoy) and the depot ship *Tanga*, headed for Trondheim and then Kirkenes, and took part in the operation off Cape Gordodetsky from 16 to 18 December. After laying mines in the White Sea off Cape Kacovsky on 13 January 1942, Z 25 sailed from Kirkenes for Flushing, where she met up with Z 7, the two destroyers continuing to Brest on 7 February for Operation 'Cerberus'. During the night of 11 February the three heavy units at Brest sailed through the English Channel with a large air and sea escort which included Z 25. All the German vessels arrived at German or Dutch North Sea ports on the 13th.

The following week Z 25 formed part of the 'Sportpalast' escort for the transfer of *Prinz Eugen* and *Admiral Scheer* to Trondheim, during which Z 4, Z 5 and Z 7 were all sent into Bergen because of their inability to cope with the sea conditions. However, one

escort vessel proved to be insufficient protection and *Prinz Eugen* was torpedoed and seriously damaged.

On 5 March Z 25 sailed with *Tirpitz*, Z 7 and Z 14 against convoys PQ.12 and QP.8 but failed to establish contact with either; she escorted the battleship to Trondheim on the return. On 28 March she sortied with Z 24 and Z 26 in search of convoy PQ.13 from Kirkenes, but the three German ships were surprised in poor visibility the next morning by the convoy escorts and Z 26 was soon reduced to a wreck. The pressure was relieved when the British light cruiser *Trinidad* torpedoed herself, and after driving off the destroyer *Eclipse* with damage Z 24 and Z 25 returned to take off the survivors from their sister-ship.

On 1 May 1942 Z 24, Z 25 and Z 7 *Hermann Schoemann* sailed to attack convoy QP.11, and in confused fighting Z 7 and the cruiser *Edinburgh* were sunk the next day. In a sharp engagement with the destroyers *Forester* and *Foresight*, Z 25 suffered four dead and seven wounded after a hit in the radio room. She protected Z 24 while picking up the survivors from *Hermann Schoemann*. On 16 May Z 25 sailed for Germany with Z 5 *Paul Jacobi*, two torpedo boats and the crippled *Prinz Eugen*, arriving at Kiel on the 18th after furious air attacks along the way. In the subsequent refit at Wesermünde a 15cm twin turret replaced the single 15cm gunhouse on the forecastle.

On 11 November Z 25 escorted the cruiser *Nürnberg* from Swinemünde, meeting up with Z 23 and Z 29 for

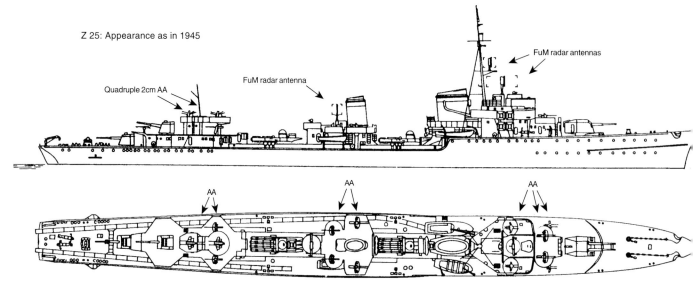

Z 25: Appearance as in 1945

Quadruple 2cm AA

FuM radar antenna

FuM radar antennas

AA   AA   AA   AA

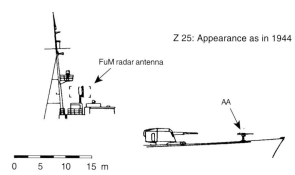

Z 25: Appearance as in 1944

FuM radar antenna

AA

0   5   10   15 m

Trondheim the next day. Z 25 remained in Norwegian waters into 1943, and her intended transfer to France in the spring was called off in March when she developed engine problems: she went into the yard at Wesermünde instead.

She arrived back in Norway on 22 April but the trouble had not been properly cured and a further overhaul was found necessary in August. Korvettenkapitän Heinz Birnbacher, who had been appointed commander in July, left the ship in August.

During trials in Danzig Bay the port engine failed after a ground mine explosion, and ultimately Z 25 remained until the war's end in the Baltic. Korvettenkapitän Alfred Gohrbandt became the destroyer's fourth commander in December 1943.

On 13 February 1944 Z 25 arrived at Reval, Estonia, with Z 35 and T 30 and on 10 March carried out a minelaying operation in the Gulf of Finland with Z 28, Z 35 and Z 39. On 28 June, in company with Z 28, Z 35 and Z 36, she patrolled the Finnish coast around Utö, and from 30 July to 1 August, together with Z 28, Z 35 and Z 36 bombarded Soviet positions inland from the Gulf of Riga under Army direction. The same group escorted *Prinz Eugen* to her fire support position off Oesel on 5 August and Kurland on the 19th of the month. Between 15 and 20 September, with Z 28, Z 25 helped in the evacuation of Reval, sailing escort for refugee ships from Baltisch Port to Libau on the 21st and from the Aaland Sea to Gotenhafen on the 22nd. On 10 October she transported 200 German soldiers to Memel, returning the next day with the same number

of female naval auxiliaries. After landing these she rejoined the Kampfgruppe to attack land targets in the defence of Memel. A presumed near-miss from a torpedo damaged her propellers and the reverberations of her own guns split fuel bunkers, causing an oil leak.

On 4 November 1944 Z 25 joined the newly reorganised 8. Zerstörerflottille. From 19 to 21 November she operated with *Prinz Eugen* and *Lützow* off the Sworbe peninsula in support of the Army, remaining there with *Admiral Scheer*, Z 24 and 2. T-Flottille until the 24th, when the evacuation was completed.

By 29 January 1945 the Soviet 43rd Army at Königsberg had broken through to the Frische Haff west of the city and cut the land connection to Pillau. In order to cover XXVIII Corps' break-out at Cranz, the Kampfgruppe—*Prinz Eugen*, Z 25 and two torpedo boats—bombarded the Russian positions to the east and south of Königsberg. Between 2 and 5 February a narrow corridor was opened to Königsberg and, with support from the naval guns the Corps managed to extricate itself and re-join the 3rd Panzer Army.

106

Later in February Z 25 ran escort for the numerous refugee transports between Gotenhafen and Sassnitz, and on the 20th Soviet positions around Gotenhafen were bombarded. On 26 March, in company with Z 5 *Paul Jacobi*, she escorted the liner *Potsdam*, the troop transport *Goya* and the target ship *Kanonier* with a total of 22,000 refugees aboard, into Copenhagen, thence returning to Swinemünde. On 12 April she accompanied *Kampfgruppe Thiele* from Rögen to Kiel. Despite the acute fuel shortage, she made two further round trips to Hela to collect refugees.

She was decommissioned in Kiel Bay on 10 May and, under British command but with a German engine-room crew, she proceded to Wilhelmshaven for overhaul. On 6 January 1946 she was sailed to Rosyth and on 2 February transferred to France at Cherbourg. She entered service with the French Navy as *Hoche*. After a period in reserve, the destroyer was converted to an escort vessel in 1951–53 and recommissioned on 16 October 1953. She was relegated to a hulk (Q 102) on 28 August 1956, deleted from the register on 2 February 1958 and scrapped in 1961.

Z 26

Career

Z 26, a Type 1936A, was commissioned on 9 January 1941 with Korvettenkapitän Ritter George von Berger as her (only) commander. She was operational from autumn 1941, and between 23 and 29 September was attached to the Baltic Fleet for the mission to the Aaland Sea. On 9 November she headed for Tromsö to load mines and reached Kirkenes in company with Z 23, Z 24, Z 25, Z 27 and the depot ship *Tanga*. In the period 16–18 December 1941 she engaged the British minesweepers *Speedy* and *Hazard* off Murmansk, the former sustaining serious damage. On 5 January 1942, in company with Z 27 she returned to Germany for refit.

On 18 March 1942, with Z 24 and Z 30, she covered *Admiral Hipper* on the run from Wesermünde to Norway. Z 26 reached Kirkenes on 27 March. The next day she sailed with Z 24 and Z 25 to attack convoy PQ.13

in the northern Arctic, the German ships sinking a straggler, *Bateau*, and rescuing 61 men from her crew and also crewmen from another freighter, the *Empire Ranger*, sunk earlier by German aircraft.

The next morning, in snow and poor visibility, Z 26 ran into the path of the cruiser *Trinidad*, was straddled with her first salvo and very quickly had two guns knocked out, the port engine rendered unserviceable and some cartridge propellant ablaze. In further brief exchanges with the destroyers Fury and Eclipse her bridge was destroyed, flames ravaged the foreship and all guns except No 4 1-cm and one 3.7cm AA were put out of action. She began to sink at 1100. Z 24 and Z 25 scored sufficient hits on *Eclipse* to effect her withdrawal and then returned to take off the 88 survivors. Z 26 went down with 240 of her crew; later in the day U 378 found eight more survivors in a boat.

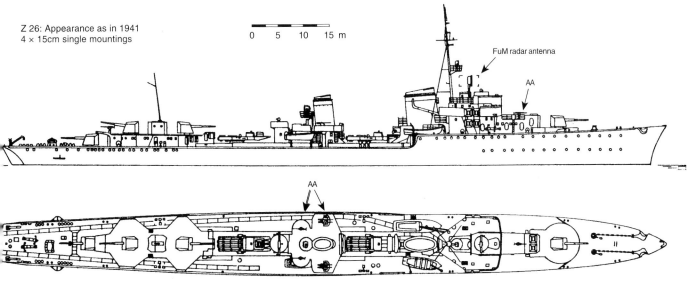

Z 26: Appearance as in 1941
4 × 15cm single mountings

0   5   10   15 m

FuM radar antenna

AA

AA

Z 27

Career

Z 27 was a Type 1936A destroyer and was commissioned on 26 February 1941 with Korvettenkapitän Karl Smidt in command. Although not fully operational, she was attached to the Baltic Fleet in September 1941 and sailed on the mission to the Aaland Sea. On 24 November 1941 she sailed with Z 5 *Paul Jacobi* and Z 23 from Kiel to Aarhus to load mines and on the 29th proceeded to Norway with Z 25. From Trondheim she escorted the depot ship *Tanga*, putting into Tromsö on 6 December. As part of 8. Zerstörerflottille, she operated from Kirkenes until 5 January 1942, when she returned to Germany for a refit.

Z 27 sailed for the northern theatre once more in May 1942, joining Kampfgruppe II. On 5 July she took part in the abortive 'Rösselsprung' adventure. In August Korvettenkapitän Günther Schulz was appointed commander.

Between 13 and 15 October she came up to Kirkenes from Altafjord with Z 4 *Richard Beitzen*, Z 16 *Friedrich Eckholdt* and Z 30, all loaded with mines, for the Kanin Nos offensive at the entrance to the White Sea. On 5

Z 27: Appearance as in 1942
showing differences from Z 26

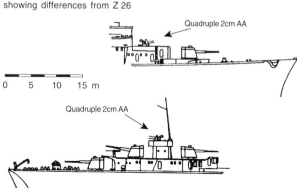

November she sailed from Kaafjord with *Admiral Hipper* and the same three destroyers for the anti-shipping operation 'Hoffnung' along the Murmansk coast. At the end of the patrol line Z 27 had the only success of the outing—disposing of the Soviet submarine-chaser BO 78 and the tanker *Donbass* (8,000 tons) and taking the crews aboard.

On 2 December 1942 Z 27 went to Deschimag, Bremen, for a refit. She was operational again on 15 June 1943 and sailed with Z 30 first to southern Norway, where minelaying was carried out on 19, 25 and 27 June, and then to re-join the Kampfgruppe in Altafjord. On 6 September she took part in the occupation of Spitzbergen and on the 24th formed up with Z 5 *Paul Jacobi*, Z 14 *Friedrich Ihn* and Z 15 *Erich Steinbrinck* to escort *Lützow* to Kiel. On 31 October, in company with ZH 1, she sailed for France, with stops at Rotterdam and Dunkirk. She received light splinter damage from English coastal artillery while negotiating the Straits of Dover and was engaged in a skirmish with British MTBs off Cape Antifer on 4 November, but she anchored safely at Le Verdon the next day. Between 23 and 26 December Z 27 was part of the escort for the *Osorno* into Bordeaux.

On the 26 December, as flag vessel of Flottillenchef (flotilla commander) Kapitän zur See Hans Erdmenger, she sailed with four other destroyers and six torpedo boats of 4. Torpedobootflottille for a rendezvous with the incoming supply ship *Alsterufer*. However, this freighter had already been sunk, and the force was intercepted by the light cruisers *Glasgow* and *Enterprise* instead. In the fierce ensuing Battle of Biscay—which lasted three hours—Z 27 twice fired a fan of four torpedoes but neither was successful. After being heavily hit by enemy fire she sank at 1641, taking with her about 300 dead, including Erdmenger.

Z 28

Career

Z 28 was commissioned on 9 August 1941 by *Korvettenkapitän* Hans Erdmenger. She was a Type 1936A destroyer. She carried out patrol and coastal protection duties in the Skagerrak and Kattegat out of Aarhus in Denmark from late 1941 until the spring of 1942 as part of her work-up. In April and May she did escort duty in the Norwegian theatre and on 9 May, with Z 30, T 5

and T 7, accompanied *Admiral Scheer* and the oiler *Dithmarschen* to Narvik to join up with Kampfgruppe II.

On 5 July she took part in the 'Rösselsprung' operation, then in the 'Zarin' minelaying operation across the Matoshkin Strait with *Admiral Hipper*, Z 4, Z 15 and Z 16. On 1 October she was transferred with the cruiser from Altafjord to Bogen Bay, and on the 24th

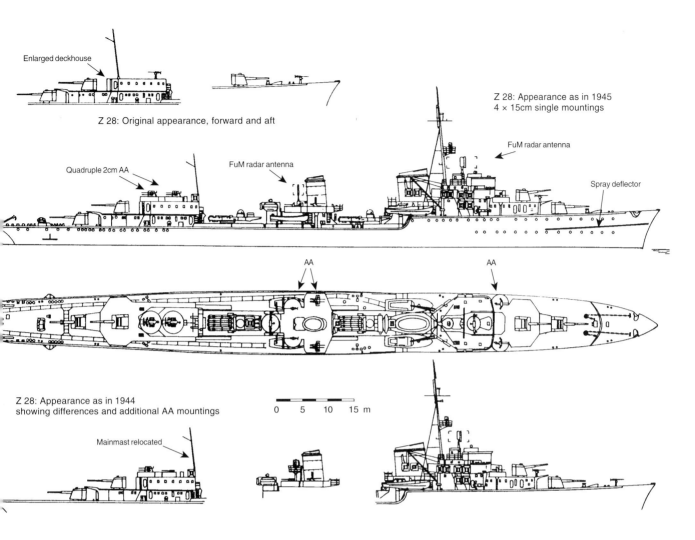

Enlarged deckhouse

Z 28: Original appearance, forward and aft

Z 28: Appearance as in 1945
4 × 15cm single mountings

FuM radar antenna

Spray deflector

Quadruple 2cm AA

FuM radar antenna

AA

AA

Z 28: Appearance as in 1944
showing differences and additional AA mountings

0   5   10   15 m

Mainmast relocated

she sailed with *Tirpitz* and *Admiral Scheer* in the opposite direction to Trondheim, continuing with the latter to Kiel for refit. In the period February–March 1943 Fregattenkapitän Hansjürgen Reinicke and then Korvettenkapitän Karl Adolf Zenker were appointed commanders.

On completion of the shipyard work, Z 28, in company with Z 5, Z 15, Z 24, Z 25 and five torpedo boats, escorted the battleship *Scharnhorst* the full distance to Bogen Bay to join the Kampfgruppe, all other vessels of the formation havinf to seek shelter from the heavy weather encountered on the way up. While proceeding in company with *Richard Beitzen* from Altafjord to Harstad on 2 April, Z 28 grounded in the Gisundet and had to move to Trondheim for repairs. On 24 July she was slightly damaged in an air raid on Trondheim docks, which themselves were badly hit, and sailed to Deschimag for repairs.

From 7 January 1944, under her new commander Fregattenkapitän Heinrich Gerlach, Z 28, assisted by Z 30, operated anti-contraband patrols out of Kristian-sand. On 13 February she sailed for Reval via Copenhagen, Gotenhafen and Libau. On 10 March, in company with Z 25, Z 35 and Z 39, she carried out a minelaying mission in the Gulf of Finland; the next day she penetrated into the Gulf as far east as the Bay of Narwa to bomnbard a land target at Hungerburg; and on 15 March she laid mines in the Gulf. In April she formed part of the major operation involving three minelaying ships, Z 35, Z 39 and T 30.

On 28 June, together with Z 35 and Z 36 she escorted *Lützow* north of Utö in the Aaland Sea and on 30 July and 1 August, with Z 25, Z 35 and Z 36 bombarded Soviet inland positions from the Gulf of Riga under Army direction. The same group escorted *Prinz Eugen* to fire on inland targets at Oesel on 5 August, at Kurland on the 19th and at Tukkum the next day. On 16 September Z 28 and Z 36 escorted the passenger ship *Monte Rosa* with refugees from Baltisch Port to Gotenhafen and four days later assisted with the evacuation of Reval when, with Z 25, four torpedo boats and six merchantmen, she help evacuate 23,172 people, including 2080 stretcher cases. On 21 September, working with Z 25, she helped evacuate another 370 people from Baltisch Port to Libau.

On 22 September 1944 Z 28 re-joined the Kampfgruppe to escort the last ships remaining in the Aaland Sea to Gotenhafen. Soviet land targets were taken under fire at Memel on 10 and 23 October and at Sworbe on the 22nd and 24th; in an air attack during the latter

operation Z 28 was hit by a stick of five bombs (casualties amounting to nine dead and numerous wounded) and returned to Swinemünde via Gotenhafen for repairs which lasted into the new year. On 4 November she was attached to the newly reorganised 8. *Zerstörerflottille* and in December 1944 *Fregattenkapitän* Karl-Heinrich Lampe was appointed commander.

Operational again from 25 February 1945, Z 28 escorted the liner *Deutschland* from Gotenhafen to Sassnitz on 27 February. After a second escort over the same route, on 4 March she was hit amidships by two bombs during a Soviet air raid at Sassnitz and sank with heavy loss of life.

Z 29

Career

Z 29 was a Type 1936A destroyer and was commissioned on 25 June 1941 with Korvettenkapitän Curt Rechel in command. She became operational in January 1942, and between 14th and 17th of that month, together with Z 4 *Richard Beitzen*, Z 5 *Paul Jacobi* and Z 8 *Bruno Heinemann*, she escorted the battleship *Tirpitz* from the Jade to Trondheim in Operation 'Polarnacht'.

After returning to Kiel, she sailed for Brest on the 27th to take part in Operation 'Cerberus', and during the night of 11 February the three heavy units at Brest sailed for Germany via the English Channel with a large escort which included Z 29. After *Scharnhorst* was mined in the North Sea, the commanding admiral, Vize-admiral Ciliax, signalled that Z 29 should come alongside to take him aboard. However, during the manoeuvre Z 29 collided with the stern of the battleship in the heavy swell, damaging her forecastle. Whilst fighting off an aircraft attack, a shell exploded in the barrel of a 15cm gun, killing one man, ripping oilfeed lines and putting the port engine out of commission. Ciliax transferred his flag to *Hermann Schoemann*, allowing Z 29 to continue alone to Wesermünde for repairs.

On her return to operations on 15 May 1942, Z 29 formed part of the 'Walzertraum' escort with Z 4, Z 10, Z 27 and F 1 for *Lützow*, arriving unscathed at Trondheim on the 20th, and moving from there to Bogen Bay with Kriegsgruppe II on the 26th. She idled at her various anchorages until 3 September, when, with Z 4 and Z 30, she sortied to mine the Kara Strait.

On 23–24 October she escorted *Tirpitz* and *Admiral Scheer* from Bogen Bay to Trondheim with Z 28, continuing to Copenhagen with *Scheer* and returning to Altafjord with the virtually useless *Nürnberg* to occupy the empty anchorage. On New Year's Eve she took part in the ill-fated 'Regenbogen' operation in the Barents Sea, and on 24 January 1943 Z 4, Z 29 and Z 30 undertook the long drawn-out escort from Altafjord to Kiel with *Admiral Hipper* and *Köln*. She was then taken in hand for a refit at Wesermünde. Korvettenkapitän Theodor von Mutius was appointed commander in April.

After the usual trials in the Baltic following her discharge from the yards on 22 July, Z 29 joined up with the newly commissioned Z 33 off Swinemünde, and the pair sailed to join the Kriegsgruppe in northern Norway. After repairs to boiler damage received on this voyage, on 3 August Z 29 acted as an AA battery guarding the maintenance ship *Huascaran* in Altafjord.

In the approaches to Barentsburg during the seizure of Spitzbergen in early September, Z 29 took four hits from land-based guns. She had three crew killed, three wounded and hull damage as a result. On Christmas Day 1943 she was part of the destroyer escort for the battleship *Scharnhorst* on the latter's luckless final voyage.

After boiler repairs at the beginning of 1944, on 30 May Z 29 took part in the sortie from Altafjord to Bear Island. On 17 July, in one of the numerous air attacks on *Tirpitz*, Z 29 was damaged by cannon-fire. Between October and December, after *Tirpitz* had been sunk, Z 29 escorted troop transports during the withdrawal from Vardö and Honnigsvaag and patrolled Tanafjord while the Polar Front was being evacuated from there.

Later she laid mines at Honnigsvaag. On 23 December she set off from Laafjord for Wesermünde to refit, during which she received a 15cm twin turret on the forecastle deck and additional 2cm and 4cm Bofors under the 'Barbara' scheme, but the ship was not ready for operations before the capitulation and the *Kriegsmarine* decommissioned her on 7 May 1945.

After the war Z 29 was assigned to the US Navy, but the Americans had no interest in her and on 7 July 1946 she was towed to the western Baltic with other expendable vessels. Having survived the scuttling charges, she was finally despatched with ten rounds of 10.5cm fired by T 19.

Z 30

Career

Commissioned on 15 November 1941, Z 30 was a Type 1936A ship. Her first commander was Fregattenkapitän Heinrich Kaiser. On 14 January 1942, during work-up and trials, she collided with U 216 and damaged her stem. Her first operational duty was on 18 March when she acted as escort for *Admiral Hipper*, sailing from Brunsbüttel to Trondheim with *Theodor Riedel*, Z 24 and three torpedo boats, continuing northwards with *Admiral Scheer* to Narvik for fleet duties with *Tirpitz* and the Kriegsgruppe.

On 24 September 1942, with *Admiral Hipper*, Z 4, Z 15 and Z 16, she helped lay the Zarin minefield in the Matoshkin Strait and with Z 4, Z1 6 and Z 30 another mine barrage off the Kanin peninsula. From 5 to 9 November the same four destroyers formed part of the Operation 'Hoffnung' patrol with *Admiral Hipper*, an anti-submarine vessel and an 8,000-ton tanker, both Soviet, being their reward. At the year's end Z 30 sailed on 'Regenbogen', the ill-starred anti-convoy operation.

On 24 January 1943, in company with *Richard Beitzen* and Z 29, she formed the escort for the protracted

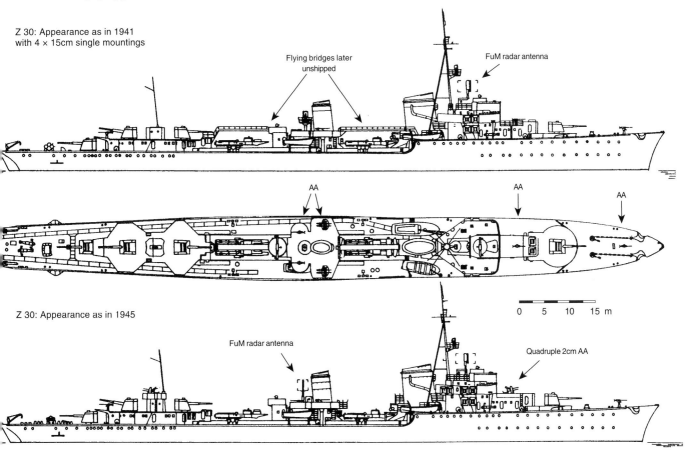

Z 30: Appearance as in 1941
with 4 × 15cm single mountings

Flying bridges later unshipped

FuM radar antenna

AA

AA

AA

Z 30: Appearance as in 1945

FuM radar antenna

Quadruple 2cm AA

0 5 10 15 m

return of *Admiral Hipper* and *Köln* to Kiel. Fregatten-kapitän Karl Heinz Lampe was appointed commander in March.

Z 30 returned to Norwegian waters after a refit, carrying out mining operations with Z 27 between 19 and 28 June, before re-joining the Kriegsgruppe for the Spitzbergen operation in early September and as one of the five escorts in the opening phase of *Scharnhorst*'s final voyage off the North Cape.

The destroyer was transferred to southern Norway and performed escort and minelaying duties from 8 May 1944. She refitted at Swinemünde from 31st August and began operations in the western Baltic and Skagerrak

on completion. On 20 October, after hitting a mine in Oslofjord (nine dead, five missing, twelve injured) she was towed to Oslo shipyard by *Friedrich Ihn*, *Karl Galster* and UJ 1702. The repairs were still incomplete at the capitulation, and Z 30 was decommissioned on 14 May.

On 6 February 1946 the destroyer was towed by the tug *Enforcer* to Rosyth and eventually put to use during 1948 as a trials ship. One-ton amounts of explosive were detonated at various depth and distance settings. A survey revealed poor seam welding in the area of the double bottom after two one-ton charges were exploded simultaneously. The ship was later sunk.

Z 31

Career

Z 31 was a Type 1936A (Mob) ship. She was commissioned on 11 April 1942 by *Korvettenkapitän* Hermann Alberts. On 6 November 1942, during her work-up, she was rammed by the motor schooner *Wilfried*, requiring three weeks to repair her plating. On 8 December she proceded from Gotenhafen to Altafjord with *Lützow*, Z 20 *Karl Galster* and Z 6 *Theodor Riedel* and on 31 December took part in Operation 'Regenbogen'.

Between 4 and 6 February 1943 Z 31 and *Theodor Riedel* accompanied the minelayer *Brummer* to the Kildin roadstead for the only mining operation along the Murmansk coast during 1943. She participated in the Spitzbergen landings in early September 1943. While running into Barentsburg she received eight hits on the main deck from shore batteries, one man being killed and another wounded.

At the beginning of November Z 31 was deployed to southern Norway for patrols and minelaying in the Skagerrak between the 23rd of the month and 4–7 December, operating on the latter mission with *Hans Lody*. In December Korvettenkapitän Karl Paul was appointed commander.

On completion of these tasks Z 31 entered the yards at Wesermünde for a refit and did not return to operations until August the following year, when she transported 100 shipyard workers with materials and equipment from Germany to Altafjord, where they were required for repairs to *Tirpitz*. Z 31 was then employed as an AA battery for the battleship, and during an air raid on 29 August sustained casualties and damage to her superstructure from cannon-fire.

From October to December Z 31 did escort duty and conducted patrols to cover the evacuation of the Polar Front from Tanafjord and laid mines in Honnigsvaag. On 1 December she escorted the storm-damaged troop transport *Adolf Binder*, under tow by Z 34, into Hammerfest, and on the 27th of the month she participated in a flotilla mining operation in Persangerfjord.

On 3 January 1945, working with Z 33, she took aboard mines at Hammerfest for an operation in Reppfjord and later in the month laid barriers in Laafjord and the Mageröy and Brei Sounds with Z 34 and Z 38. On the 25th Z 31 set out with Z 34 and Z 38 from Tromsö for the Baltic, but the force was intercepted off Sognefjord on the 28th by British naval units which included the light cruisers *Diadem* and *Mauritius*. Z 31 received seven hits, the twin turret forward being destroyed and casualties numbering 55 dead and 24 wounded. She disengaged and ran into Bergen, where the worst damage was patched over and the wreckage of the turret removed. At Horten a single 10.5cm gun was fitted on the forecastle as a temporary measure (although, in the event, she retained it until the capitulation).

On 15 March 1945, after more repairs at Oslo, Z 31 arrived at Gotenhafen, where she shelled Soviet land forces from 22 March. The following day she towed the hulk of the battleship *Gneisenau* across the harbour approaches, where it was scuttled as a blockship. Over the next three days Z 31 continued in the bombardment of Soviet positions from the Gulf of Danzig.

On 27 March a shell exploded in a 15cm barrel, killing four men and wounding eighteen; sabotage was suspected when the 'accident' recurred aboard Z 34 in April

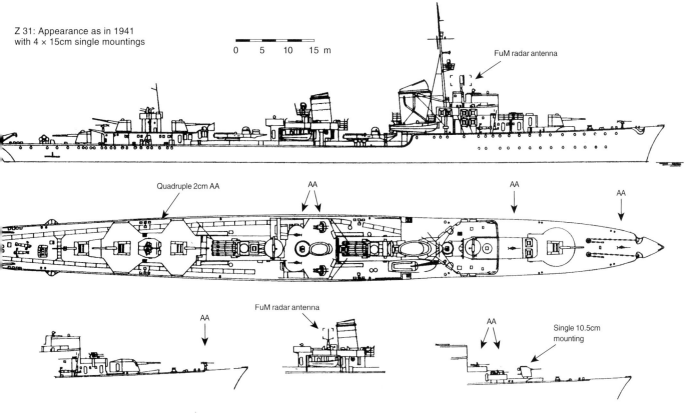

Z 31: Appearance as in 1941
with 4 × 15cm single mountings

0 5 10 15 m

FuM radar antenna

Quadruple 2cm AA

AA

AA

AA

FuM radar antenna

AA

Single 10.5cm
mounting

Z 31: Appearance as in 1944, with twin 15cm turret

Z 31: Appearance as in 1945

and a particular make of shell was identified and banned. From 28 March Z 31 was on escort duty and acted as an anti-aircraft ship for *Kampfgruppe Thiele*.

On 5 April, operating off Gotenhafen/Neufahrwasser, Z 31 assisted in the evacuation of Oxterhöfter Kämpe with Z 38 and the torpedo boats T 33 and T 36, and on the 8th this group escorted *Prinz Eugen* and *Lützow* to the west. During an air attack Z 31 was hit by two bombs and required repairs at Swinemünde, which were carried out on the 10th. While the destroyer was making for Kiel on 27 April, a further Soviet air attack inflicted splinter damage and wounded three crewmen. She arrived at Brunsbüttel on 30 April and was decommissioned on 8th May.

After the war Z 31 was sailed by a mixed British-German crew to Wilhelmshaven. She arrived in Great Britain in August 1945 for experiments, but in January 1946 she arrived at Cherbourg, passing into the French Navy on 2 February 1946 and entering commission as *Marceau* on 1 April that year. She was decommissioned in 1948, underwent an extensive conversion and did not re-enter service until 18 October 1952. On 1 February 1954 she was laid up as a hulk (Q 103) and on 2 January 1958 was deleted from the register. That autumn she was sold for scrap. The purchaser moored her at Brest, where for some years she was used as a pier for swimmers. She was finally broken up in the early 1960s.

Z 32

Career

Z 32 was a Type 1936A (Mob) ship and commissioned on 15th September 1942 by Fregattenkapitän Ritter George von Berger, her only commander. Operational on 3 March 1943, she sailed with 6. Zerstörerflottille from Kiel for France for escort work (*Himalaya*) on 22 July and into the eastern Atlantic with Z 23 to meet *Pietro Orsedo* on 2 August. The duty also involved giving cover to inbound and outbound U-boats. On 28 December, during the Battle of Biscay—an engagement with the British cruisers *Glasgow* and *Enterprise*— Z 32 fired off six torpedoes but without success.

On 30 January 1944 during exercises conducted by 8. Z-Flottille off Bordeaux, Z 32 and Z 37 collided. The former sustained a short circuit in her degaussing system and fire broke out on the forecastle after ready-use anti-aircraft ammunition had been catapulted forward by the force of the impact. After the flames had been extinguished, Z 32 anchored off Royan on 31 January. She was operational again on 2 May but spent a further month repairing after going aground in the Gironde on 5 May.

On 6 June Z 32 set out for Brest with Z 24, ZH 1 and the torpedo boat T 24; during an air attack on the way she was hit by two rockets. On 8 June, en route to Cherbourg to load mines to lay off Brest (an operation known to Allied intelligence), the German ships were met by a larger force of Allied destroyers. The flotilla dispersed and Z 32 made for St-Malo. After a while Korvettenkapitän Berger reversed course and a second encounter occurred with the enemy destroyers. This time Z 32 was so badly damaged that she had to be run aground on rocks off the Île de Bas to save the crew, who got away in boats and rafts under heavy enemy fire. The survivors were picked up later by German patrol craft.

Z 33

Career

Z 33, a Type 1936A (Mob) ship commissioned on 6 February 1943, was first commanded by Kapitän zur See Erich Holtorf. After concluding her trials and working up on 22 July 1943, she sailed for northern Norway with Z 27 to join the Kampfgruppe. In the Spitzbergen raid in early September she received 33 hits from the initially accurate coastal batteries, sustaining damage to her bridge and hull and suffering three dead and 25 wounded. On 25 December she sailed as part of the five-destroyer escort for the battleship *Scharnhorst* on her voyage of no return beyond the North Cape.

Fregattenkapitän Rudolf Menge was appointed commander in June 1944. During an air attack on *Tirpitz* on 17 July that year, Z 33 was damaged by cannon-fire, five days' repairs being necessary. From October to December she carried out various escort and protection duties to cover the evacuation of the Polar Front from Tanafjord and laid mines in Persangerfjord and Reppfjord with Z 31. Minor damage sustained during these operations was repaired at Narvik.

On 5 February 1945 she was the last German destroyer in northern Norway. She set off for Germany that day, but grounded in Brufjord on the 7th. The port shaft and propeller were dislodged, both engines failed and the outer plating was gashed. She was taken in tow towards Trondheim under persistent air attack and received further damage from bombing and cannon-fire. She put into Trondheim on 11 February. First Officer Kapitänleutnant Heinrich Peter-Pirckham served as acting captain for the rest of the destroyer's career.

Z 33 left Trondheim for Swinemünde under her own power on 26 March, arriving there on 2 April. Because of the acute fuel shortage, it was being considered necessary at Swinemünde to lay up various units, including Z 33, and she had unshipped all her AA weapons before it was decided to send her westwards. The immobilised heavy cruiser *Lützow*, lying alongside, was cannibalised to replace the missing armament. Landed naval personnel on standby in Naval Rifle Battalion 1031 were hastily mustered, and on 27 April Z 33 sailed for Cuxhaven via Kiel and Brunsbüttel to be decommissioned.

In June 1945, flying the White Ensign, Z 33 was sailed with a mixed crew to Wilhelmshaven, where, after an overhaul, she was awarded to the Soviet Union as reparation in December 1945 and handed over in a convoy sailing for Libau on 2 January 1946. She entered service with the Baltic Red Banner Fleet as *Provornyy*, was relegated to training duties on 30 November 1954 and became an accommodation ship on 22 April 1955. Devastated by a fire in 1960, she sank at her moorings and was raised and scrapped in 1962.

Z 34

Career

A Type 1936A (Mob) ship commissioned on 5 June 1943 by Korvettenkapitän Karl Hetz, her only commander, Z 34 became operational on 1 November that year. She sailed to northern Norway and was one of the five destroyers escorting the doomed battleship *Scharnhorst* into the Arctic Ocean on Christmas Day 1943.

During 1944 Z 34 acted as a defence ship for *Tirpitz*. She sustained casualties and structural damage from cannon-fire during air raids on 17 July and 29 August and helped extinguish a serious fire aboard the tanker *C. A. Larsen* from the same cause. Between October and December Z 34 escorted troop transports during Operation 'Nordlicht', the evacuation of the Polar Front.

On 1 December she towed the storm-damaged troopship *Adolf Binder* into Hammerfest and continued with the escort to Tromsö on the 11th, where she went into the yards for a refit. On 25 January 1945, in company with Z 31 and Z 38, she laid a mine barrier in Laafjord and Mageröy and Brei Sounds, and three days later, accompanied by the other two destroyers, set out from Tromsö for the Baltic. Intercepted off Sognefjord by a superior British naval force including the cruisers *Diadem* and *Mauritius* on 28 January, Z 34 made three unsuccessful torpedo attacks and was hit by a shell on the waterline. She made Kiel, from where she arrived at Gotenhafen on 3 February with 200 coastal artillerymen. During the remainder of the month she ran escort duties between Gotenhafen and Libau and with the *Kampfgruppe* supported the Army with her guns off Tolkemit.

On 6/7 March Z 34 escorted *Lützow* and *Admiral Scheer* from Gotenhafen to Swinemünde, took part in the bombardment of Dievenov on 9–10 March and sailed to Kolberg on the 11th, where she embarked 1,000 refugees and wounded for Swinemünde. On 15 March, after conducting shore bombardment, she took aboard 250 wounded and 1,600 refugees. She remained off Kolberg until the 18th, when the last defenders were taken out aboard Z 34, Z 43 and T 33, returning next day for the remnants for Swinemünde.

On 21st March she escorted *Lützow* to Gotenhafen from where *Lützow*, *Prinz Eugen* and destroyers engaged Soviet land forces up until 1 April. Z 34 was slightly damaged in an air attack on the 29th. On 31 March she became the first German naval unit to fire on aircraft with rockets.

In the first days of April she escorted the liners *Deutschland* and *Pretoria*, with 17,000 refugees, aboard to Copenhagen. She drydocked at Swinemünde on 4 April but was operational again from the 10th and supported the Army from seaward at Grossendorf. This operation was followed by patrol duties in the roadstead at Hela which included a duel with the Soviet coastal battery at Oxhöft. A 15cm gun was ruined when a shell exploded in the barrel.

Returning to Hela after running escort for *Pretoria* and three freighters on 15 April, Z 34 was torpedoed by a Soviet MTB operating from Neufahrwasser and lay listing to starboard and immobile without engine power or current. She was attacked next day from the air and an anti-aircraft rocket exploded on deck, killing eight and wounding sixteen. She was towed by T 36 and the minesweeper M 204 into Swinemünde, where, such were the priorities, additional AA guns, taken from *Lützow*, were installed at once.

On 4 May, loaded with refugees and Wehrmacht personnel (including the Admiral Commanding Western Baltic) she made her final operational voyage, from Swinemünde to Copenhagen, and decommissioned at Kiel on 10 May.

She was awarded to the United States in the general distribution of German warships, but her condition was such that she was rejected and on 26 March 1946 she was sunk in the Skagerrak.

Z 35

Career

Z 35 was a Type 1936B (Mob) Type ship, commissioned on 22 September 1943 by Korvettenkapitän Niels Bätge, her only commander. Operational from February 1944, she sailed for Reval (Talinn) in Estonia on the 13th of that month and from there carried out a major minelaying operation in the Gulf of Finland on 13, 19, 23, and 25 April with Z 25, Z 39, T 30 and the minelayers *Brummer*, *Roland* and *Linz*. Between 30 July and 19 August she operated with the other three Baltic destroyers as Kampfgruppe II, escorting *Prinz Eugen* and bombarding Soviet positions on Oesel, at Kurland and at Tukkum. On 20 August she brushed the seabed and had to return to Gotenhafen to change a damaged propeller.

Between 10 and 24 October, with Kampfgruppe Thiele and in company with alternately *Prinz Eugen* or *Lützow*, Z 35 and the other three destroyers attacked 28 land targets in defence of Memel, Libau and Karkelbeck. On 15 October she and Z 36 stood by the cruisers *Prinz Eugen* and *Leipzig*, locked together after their collision in the Gotenhafen roads. On 22 October, in company with *Lützow*, Z 28 and three torpedo boats, she bombarded Soviet positions around Memel and the Sworbe peninsula. On the 23rd the barrel and breech of No 3 main gun flew overboard after a shell exploded in the barrel (one man was wounded). During further operations against land targets the following day, Z 35 received splinter damage as a result of a Soviet air attack.

On 9 December 1944, as flag vessel of Kapitän zur See Kothe, 6. Zerstörerflottille, Z 35 sailed with Z 36, Z 43 and two torpedo boats for a mining operation code-named 'Nil' off the the Estonian coast. On 12 December the force ran into the German Nashorn minefield in thick fog and Z 35 and Z 36 blew up and sank with all hands.

Z 36

Career

Korvettenkapitän Freiherr Lothar von Hausen was the only man to command Z 36, a Type 1936B (Mob) destroyer commissioned on 19 February 1944. The ship became operational in mid-1944, and on 28 June that year she took part in Operation 'Tanne West' in the Aaland Sea with *Lützow*, Z 35, Z 25 and Z 28. Off Turku between 30 July and 1 August, and in company with the same destroyer group, she bombarded selected Soviet positions ashore under Army direction. On 2 August 1944 she undertook escort duties between Libau and Dünamünde and on 20 August fired on land targets with Kampfgruppe II off Tukkum. On 16 September, along with Z 28, she escorted the refugee

ship *Monte Rosa* from Baltisch Port to Gotenhafen and between 10 and 15 October operated against Soviet positions at Memel, Libau and Karkelbeck. On the 16th she stood by *Prinz Eugen* and *Leipzig* with Z 35 outside Gotenhafen after the cruisers' collision in the approach channel.

On 8th November Z 36 conveyed Generaladmiral Kummetz from Libau to Gotenhafen and on 9 December she sailed with Z 35, Z 43 and two torpedo boats for the mining operation code-named 'Nil' off the coast of Estonia. Three days later a navigational error ran the force into the 'Nashorn' minefield in thick fog and Z 35 and Z 36 exploded and sank, taking their entire crews with them.

Z 37

Career

Z 37 was a Type 1936A (Mob) ship commissioned on 16 July 1942. Her first commander was Korvettenkapitän Georg Langheld. The long delay between launching and commissioning was occasioned by shortage of raw

materials, more essential shipyard work and the transfer of skilled shipyard workers from Germania Werft to Norway. She eventually became operational in December 1942; however, whilst she was proceeding from Kiel to Swinemünde to begin her working-up she collided

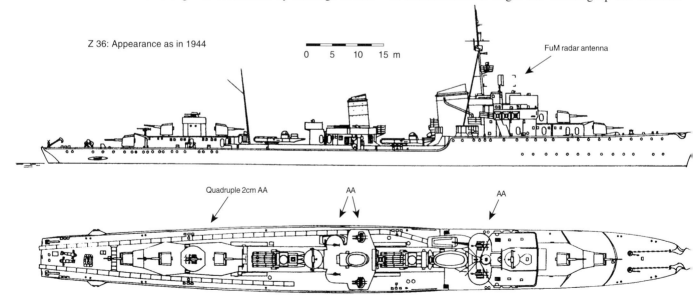

Z 36: Appearance as in 1944

0 5 10 15 m

FuM radar antenna

Quadruple 2cm AA   AA   AA

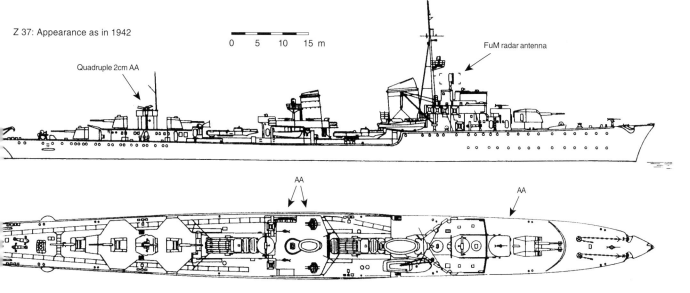

Quadruple 2cm AA

0 5 10 15 m

FuM radar antenna

AA

AA

with a freighter and was forced to return to the repair yard.

On 24–26 January 1943, she was en route to Norway with *Scharnhorst*, *Prinz Eugen*, *Paul Jacobi* and *Erich Steinbrinck* on Operation 'Domino', but once this was abandoned she was redeployed to France, sailing from Kiel on 3 March with Z 32. On 6 March she damaged her starboard propeller after running aground at Le Havre. Repairs were completed by the 18th.

Later in March and in April she escorted the blockade-runner *Himalaya* and U-boats in the Bay of Biscay, in December took part in the large escort into Bordeaux with the homecoming *Osorno* and on 28 December fired four torpedoes during the three-hour Battle of Biscay.

In January 1944 Fregattenkapitän Heinrich Gerlach was appointed Z 37's commander. On 29 January, whilst exercising off Bordeaux with Z 23 and Z 32, the destroyer collided with Z 32. A torpedo warhead exploded, causing a serious fire which led to the 3.7cm ready-use ammunition exploding. She began to take water through gashes in the outer plating and was towed by Z 23 into Bordeaux listing heavily to starboard. It was decided that repairs would be too extensive, and the 15cm guns were landed for coast defence duties in the Gironde estuary.

Z 37 was decommissioned on 24 August 1944. Her machinery was disabled by the crew, who then re-mustered ashore as the Narvik Naval Battalion. She was scrapped by the French in 1949.

Z 38

Career

Z 38 was a Type 1936A (Mob) ship and was commissioned on 20 March 1943. Korvettenkapitän Gerfried Brutzer was her first commander.

As with Z 37, this Germania Werft-built destroyer suffered a long delay before entering service. In August 1943 she served the lowly function of practice torpedo retrieval vessel for the training cruisers *Nürnberg* and *Emden*. On 24 September she came up from Sassnitz to Trelleborg to join the escort for *Lützow*, inbound from northern Norway. On 22 October she left Swinemünde for the Kampfgruppe at Kaafjord and formed part of the escort for *Scharnhorst* on her last voyage commencing on 25 December.

Until October 1944 she served as defence ship for the battleship *Tirpitz*, Korvettenkapitän Freiherr Wilhelm Nikolaus von Lyncker being appointed her second commander in September 1944.

Following the destruction of *Tirpitz*, Z 38 covered the evacuation of the Polar Front from Vardö and Honnigsvaag. While leaving Tromsö for a minelaying mission in Persangerfjord, she grounded aft in shallows and, after transferring her mines to Z 33, she had to return to Bogen Bay for repairs to her propellers.

After another minelaying operation in Laafjord and the Mageröy and Brei Sounds on 25 January 1945, Z 38 left Tromsö for the Baltic in company with Z 31 and Z 34. Off Sognefjord on the 28th the small force was

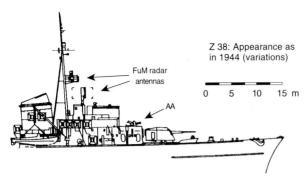

Z 38: Appearance as in 1944 (variations)

FuM radar antennas

AA

0 5 10 15 m

intercepted by a British squadron which included the light cruisers *Diadem* and *Mauritius*. During the ensuing action fire broke out in a funnel. When a boiler tube split, Z 38 broke off the engagement, making for Kiel with Z 34. There she took on board 200 coastal artillerymen for Gotenhafen.

Between 16 and 20 February 1945, in company with Z 34, T 5 and T 6, she escorted the liner *Hamburg* to Sassnitz, returning on the 22nd with the liner *Deutschland*. Over the period 23–28 February Z 38 bombarded Soviet positions on the Samland coast; on one occasion she and T 28 found themselves icebound in the channel between Königsberg and Fischhausen and had to be freed by tugs.

From 4 to 6 March Z 38 bombarded Soviet forward positions and armour before embarking refugees at Pillau for Gotenhafen. From there she set out on the 7th for Copenhagen with Z 35 and T 28, protecting the refugee liner *Pretoria*. After her return to Gotenhafen on 13 March she took part in the bombardment of Grossendorf, and she remained under Army direction until the end of the month. A crewman was killed on 29 March when a 15cm shell exploded in a gun barrel.

On 4 April the upper deck was damaged by shrapnel during an air raid. The next day Z 38 became involved in the fighting off Oxhöfter Kämpe. On 9 April, after escorting *Lützow* and *Prinz Eugen* from the Bay of Danzig to Swinemünde—where she had a propeller changed—the fuel shortage was so acute that part of the complement was disembarked for combat training ashore. On 28 April Z 38 moved out to the roadstead and took part in the continuing fighting for Dievenov and the Oder estuary, which occupied the destroyer until 4 May. One man was killed by the blast from a near-miss during an air attack. On 4 May, when the training ship *Hektor* (the former raider *Orion*) was devastated in an air raid, her crew and others were rescued by Z 38, T 33 and smaller craft and the derelict then being destroyed by shellfire. On 3 May Z 38 and Z 39 had rendered assistance to the old battleship *Schlesien* which had been mined off Swinemünde, and on the 4th Z 38 also embarked refugees and Wehrmacht personnel and sailed for Copenhagen, returning on the 7th to repeat the exercise. She arrived at Kiel on the 9th, putting into Flensburg Förde to deliver the War Diary to the commander at his home address, then returned to Kiel next day to decommission.

She was transferred to Wilhelmshaven with an Anglo-German crew, and after a brief overhaul she sailed for Portsmouth on 6 July 1945 for use as an trials vessel. The German technical hands remained aboard until 22 September 1946. Renamed *Nonsuch* in Royal Navy service, Z 38 was used to test underwater explosives in one-ton batches. At the first trial an 8m high plume of water erupted, the keel broke and within two seconds boiler room II flooded, the other two filling by way of the bulkhead. Obviously, no destroyer could survive experiments of this nature for long.

Z 39

Career

A Type 1936A (Mob) destroyer commissioned on 21 August 1943, Z 39 was commanded by Korvettenkapitän throughout her existence. A very lengthy delay preceded commissioning, and Z 39 was not operational until 7 January 1944, when she worked in the Skagerrak and Kattegat. In March she was transferred to Reval on the Gulf of Finland and on the 10th of the month took part in a minelaying operation with Z 25 and Z 35. While making for Baltisch Port in Estonia on 23 June, Z 39 was damaged by bombs outside the port and had to be escorted to Libau by Z28. From there she made

Kiel on 29 June via Swinemünde for repair. On 24 July, at Kiel, she was hit by a bomb which exploded below the quarterdeck and as a result had to be towed back to Swinemünde.

On 28 February 1945 Z 39 was sufficiently seaworthy to make the journey to Copenhagen to work up, but the fuel situation was so severe there that she returned to Sassnitz. On 25 March the shipyard work at Swinemünde was completed, and on 1 April Z 39 returned to operations. Between the 5th and 7th of the month she acted as escort in the Bay of Danzig for transports and Kampfgruppe Thiele, and on 8–9 April gave the German

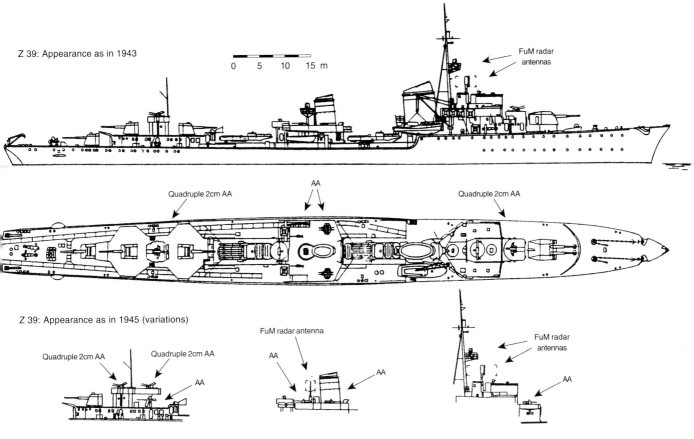

Z 39: Appearance as in 1943

0 5 10 15 m

FuM radar antennas

Quadruple 2cm AA

AA

Quadruple 2cm AA

Z 39: Appearance as in 1945 (variations)

Quadruple 2cm AA

Quadruple 2cm AA

AA

FuM radar antenna

AA

AA

FuM radar antennas

AA

Army gunnery support. On 10 April she escorted the damaged Z 43 to Warnemünde and Swinemünde, sustaining light damage during an air raid.

On 2 May she bombarded Soviet units from the Oder estuary, next day covering the bridge across the River Peene at Wolgast with the old battleship *Schlesien*. When the latter was mined and seriously damaged at Greifswalder Oie, Z 39 towed her to Swinemünde and grounded her in such a position that her after turret had a field of fire over the approach roads to the city. The bombardment was maintained until 4 May, when Z 38, Z 39, the torpedo boat T 33, the tender *Jagd* and five steamers proceeded to Copenhagen with 35,000 refugees and Wehrmacht wounded. Z 39 made one final trip to Hela to collect refugees between 7 and 9 May and decommissioned at Kiel on the 10th.

After the cessation of hostilities Z 39 was sailed by an Anglo-German crew to Wilhelmshaven, from there proceeding to Plymouth on 6 July 1945 for delivery to the US Navy. She left Britain on 30 July, arriving on 7 August at Boston Navy Yard, where she was subjected to extensive trials. On 14 September 1945 the remnants of the German crew were demobilised and Z 39 entered commission in the US Navy as DD 939.

By the end of 1947 she had outlived her usefulness to the Americans and was handed over to the French Navy. After arriving at Casablanca under tow in January 1948 she was taken to Toulon, designated Q 128 and cannibalised for spares for *Kléber* (ex Z 6), *Hoche* (ex Z 25) and *Marceau* (ex Z 31). Nothing came of a scheme to restore her to operational condition, and in 1953 she was deleted and broken up.

Z 43

Career

Z 43 was a Type 1936B (Mob) vessel and commissioned on 31 May 1944. Fregattenkapitän Carl Heinrich Lampe was her only commander. Operational from October 1944, she was assigned to 6. Zerstörerflottille in the

eastern Baltic. Between 22 and 24 November she worked with Z 25, *Admiral Scheer* and 2. T-Flottille, supporting the German withdrawal from Oesel. On 9 December she sailed with Z 35 (flag, 6. Z-Flottille), Z 36

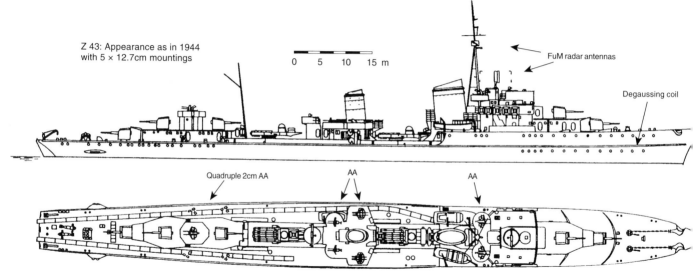

Z 43: Appearance as in 1944
with 5 × 12.7cm mountings

0 5 10 15 m

FuM radar antennas

Degaussing coil

Quadruple 2cm AA

AA

AA

and two torpedo boats for the mining operation 'Nil' off the Estonian coast, but three days later the force ran into the German Nashorn minefield in thick fog. Z 35 and Z 36 blew up and sank with all hands; no rescue could be attempted, the operation was abandoned and Z 43 returned to Gotenhafen.

Between 18 and 25 January and 29 January and 9 February 1945 Z 43 carried out escort duties between Gotenhafen and Libau and on 23 February bombarded Soviet positions along the Samland coast. After delivering the liner *Hamburg* into Sassnitz with Z 25 on 27 February, she served as a flak ship until escorting *Lützow* and *Admiral Scheer* from Danzig Bay to Swinemünde on 7th March, operating off Kolberg for the next week, as an air defence ship for transports.

Between 17 and 19 March Z 43 supported the German Army with her guns and escorted refugee ships: over the period from 23 March to 7 April, in company with two torpedo boats, she provided AA protection for *Lützow* at Gotenhafen and Kampfgruppe Thiele in the Gulf of Danzig and also fired her main guns on Soviet positions inland. On 9 April she was hit by a bomb which failed to explode, but the following day she was mined and was towed to Neptun Werft, Rostock, for emergency repairs, after which she took up position in the roadstead at Warnemünde once again to bombard Soviet inland targets.

Z 43 returned to Kiel on 2 May and was scuttled in Geltinger Bay near Flensburg the next day.

ZG 3 *Hermes*

Career

This destroyer was a British-built confiscation commissioned on 21 March 1942 with *Fregattenkapitän* Rolf Johannesson as commander. The vessel was built by Yarrow, Glasgow, for the Greek Navy, launched as *Vasilefs Georgios* on 3 March 1938 and first commissioned on 15 February 1939. She bore a strong resemblance to the British 'G', 'H' and 'I' class ships, of which 24 were built for the Royal Navy.

ZG 3 had a displacement of 1,414 tons standard and 2,088 tons full load, a length of 101.2m overall and 98.5m waterline, a beam of 10.4m and a draught of 2.334/3.23m. Propulsion comprised two Parsons turbine sets in two rooms, providing 34,000shp for 32 knots. A bunkerage of 465 tonnes gave a range of 4,800nm at 19 knots.

Three Yarrow three-drum watertube boilers in three rooms, operating pressure 16atm, supplied the steam and the ship had one rudder and two propellers. The armament differed from the British standard and was of German origin—four 12.7cm, four 3.7cm, four 2cm and eight quadruple torpedo tubes.

Vasilefs Georgis had been bombed and sunk by Stukas in drydock at Salamis on 20 April 1941 but was later raised and repaired. She entered service as ZG 3 on 21 March 1942, and received the name *Hermes* on 22nd August that year. She was operational from June 1942 and was the only German destroyer in the Mediterranean, carrying out escort duties in the Aegean and to North Africa supplying Rommel. On 5 August 1942 she escorted the damaged U 97 to port, repeating the duty a fortnight later for U 83. On 16 November 1942, with the assistance of the anti-submarine trawler UJ 2102, she sank the British submarine *Triton*.

From 2 April 1943, under new commander Fregatten-kapitän Curt Rechel, *Hermes* was based in Italy, from where she carried out mining operations, including the laying of a field in the Straits of Messina in which the British submarine *Splendid* was mined and sunk on 21 April. She ran a shuttle service between Italy and Tunis as the German North Africa front collapsed, but on 30 April she was bombed and badly damaged. The shafts seized and, unmanoeuvrable, she was towed into La Gouette, Tunisia, but there was no possibility of repair. On 7 May 1943 she was scuttled as a blockship in the harbour approaches.

ZH 1

Career

ZH 1 was another foreign acquisition for the Kriegs-marine. She was one of the four destroyers of the Royal Dutch Navy's *Tjerk Hiddes* class which had been built partly to a British (Yarrow) design. She was launched on 12 October 1939 as *Gerard Callenburgh* at Rotter-damsche Droogdok and was still completing when the Netherlands capitulated to German forces in May 1940. The ship was scuttled by her crew on 10 May. Two of her three sister ships were scrapped on the stocks and the hull of the third was towed off to Britain.

Gerard Callenburgh was raised on 14 July 1940 and towed to Blohm & Voss, Hamburg, for repair on 11 October 1040. From there she was returned to Rotterdam for completion and fitting out, commissioning as ZH 1 on 11 October 1942 with Korvettenkapitän Claus Barc-kow as her only commander. She displaced 1,604 tons standard and 2,228 tons full load, her length was 106.7m overall and 105.2m waterline, with a beam of 10.6m and a draught of 2.82m standard and 3.52m deep load. Propulsion was provided by two sets of Parsons turbines delivering 45,000–49,500shp (three Yarrow watertube boilers with superheaters, operating press-ure 28atm), and she had two shafts and a single rudder. Maximum speed was 37.5 knots and range 2,700nm at 19 knots, bunker capacity being 560 tonnes. Her original armament comprised five 12cm/L45 arranged in two twin turrets and one single gunhouse, four 4cm Bofors, four 12.7mm AA and eight torpedo tubes in four sets, but in German hands the Bofors were replaced by the same number of 3.7cm and the 12.7mm by 2cm.

The ship worked up in the Baltic, with a visit to Hamburg for completion on 18 January 1943. While continuing with training in the Baltic she collided with the Danish freighter *Douro* on 11 April, but damage was light and swiftly repaired at Blohm & Voss during June. However, air raids on the dockyard damaged her further, and ZH 1 was forced to wait out at anchor, substantially delaying the time spent under repair, and it was not until October 1943 that she finally became operational.

She left Kiel for the Gironde on 31 October 1943 in company with Z 27, being attached to 8. Zerstörer-flottille on 5 November. While escorting the *Osorno* into Bordeaux in December, she had to be towed into port by T 25 after shutting down her turbines because of salination problems. She was operational again from March 1944.

ZH 1 was on hand for escort duties in the Bay of Biscay, and on D-Day she proceeded with Z 32, Z 24 and T 24 to Brest. On 8 June she was making for Cherbourg to load mines when the four German vessels, having been subjected to unrelenting air attack, were intercepted by a superior force of Allied destroyers. ZH 1 was badly damaged in the engagement that followed, and suffered 39 dead, including her com-mander. On 9 June she was scuttled with explosive charges in position 48°52'N 4°28'W.

Photo Gallery: The *Zerstörer*

Left, upper: Z 1 *Leberecht Maass* is commissioned at Deutsche Werke, Kiel, on 14 January 1937.

Left, lower: Z 1 as completed with rounded bridge, and flying the pennant of the FdT at the masthead.

Top: *Leberecht Maass* after her 1938 refit to modify the bows, with additional sheer and rake for improved sea-keeping.

Above: *Georg Thiele* after her first refit, with angular bridge and spray deflector forward.

Right: Z 2 *Georg Thiele* at Memel, 23 March 1939.

Above: Another photograph of *Georg Thiele* at Memel on 23 March 1939, affording a view of the two after 12.7cm guns, the 2cm AA on the deckhouse (guns covered) and the port propeller guard. Minesweepers can be seen in the background.

Left, upper: *Thiele* on 13 April 1940, after having been run on to the rocks in Rombakenfjord.

Left, lower: *Georg Thiele*'s forecastle projects from the water in Rombakenfjord. She remains in this position today.

Right, upper: Z 3 *Max Schultz* as originally completed, with rounded bridge.

Right, lower: Z 3 in April 1939, photographed from the bridge of another destroyer in Spanish waters during Fleet manoeuvres.

Above: Z 3 *Max Schultz* with new bridge and modified bows.
Below: Z 4 *Richard Beitzen* as completed, with rounded bridge.
The ship is seen working up, 7 June 1937.

Above: Z 4 after refit, with rectangular bridgework and modified bows.
Below: *Richard Beitzen* at the Naval Review of 22 August 1938.

Far left: *Richard Beitzen* dressed overall for Hitler's birthday, 20 April 1938. Below the 'tub' is a loudspeaker with ventilation piping to the left, and in the distance is the rear of a twin 3.7cm mounting.

Left, upper: Z 4 on 17 June 1939 after returning home from the Mediterranean, having been rammed by the fleet escort F 7.

Left, lower: Z 4's forecastle in the severe winter of 1940, coated with ice.

Below left: *Beitzen* off Brittany in the autumn of 1940.

Above: Z 4 in refit at Kiel, autumn 1941: a view from aft.

Below: Z 4, in camouflage, during Operation 'Cerberus'—the 'Channel Dash' of February 1942.

Left, upper: Z 5 *Paul Jacobi* during her formal commissioning into the Kriegsmarine at Bremen on 29m June 1937.

Left, lower: *Paul Jacobi* at Wilhelmshaven in the summer of 1937. Astern of her is the old cruiser *Medusa*, relegated to the status of accommodation ship.

Right: Z 5 negotiating a lock of the Kiel Canal in 1938, before the war a frequent procedure—sometimes every other day—for destroyers in transit from the Baltic to the North Sea and vice-versa during manoeuvres and training. This photograph provides a view of the forward torpedo tubes and the bridge structure forward of the forefunnel. Below, on the funnel mantle, is the compact boiler ventilator housing. Very evident here are the long pipes attached to the funnel: some are exhaust gas and ventilation pipes, others are for blowing the boiler after opening or shutting down the safety valves. The derricks either side are for lowering or raising the ship's boats.

Below: A pre-war study of Z 5.

Left, upper: Z 5 *Paul Jacobi* at Trondheim in the spring of 1940. Notice the camouflaged after 12.7cm gunhouses and the flak crew at readiness.

Left, lower: *Jacobi* takes on supplies, Trondheim, spring 1940.

Above: Heavy units occasionally made forays from Trondheim. *Jacobi* is seen here with the heavy cruiser *Admiral Hipper* off the starboard quarter. The forward 12.7cm guns are cleared for action.

Right, upper: A dazzle-camouflaged Z 5, photographed in 1943.

Right, lower: *Paul Jacobi* in 1945 at Wilhelmshaven. The destroyer now has the so-called 'goalpost' foremast (to enable the radar 'mattress' to be rotated) and also an 'Atlantic' bow.

Left, top: Z 6 *Theodor Riedel* as completed, with rounded bridge.

Left, centre: Z 6 *Theodor Riedel* on 22 August 1938 during the Naval Review. She has been refitted with a 'box'-shaped bridge, and her bows have been given what amounts to no more than a cosmetic alteration designed to improve sea-keeping. At the foretop is the Hungarian national flag in honour of VIP Admiral Horthy.

Left, bottom: Z 6 sheers to port during high-speed formation manouevres with 2. Zerstörerflottille in 1938. Even in a light swell and glassy sea, she was a wet ship.

Above: Running in formation in line abeam, the black smoke pouring from the forefunnel indicates that Z 6 has too little air for the correct combustion balance in her boilers.

Below: German destroyers execute a turn to port while steaming in line abreast and refuelling (as appears to be the case—notice the hose connection between the two leading ships). *Theodor Riedel* is nearest the camera.

Far left, top: Z 6 *Theodor Riedel* wearing camouflage, in Norwegian waters during 1941.

Far left, centre: Z 6 *Theodor Riedel* in Norwegian waters in 1942, camouflage-painted and fitted with tripod mast and radar antenna.

Far left, bottom: *Riedel* in November 1942. with an additional 2cm AA mounting forward of the forecastle breakwater.

Left: Z 6 in Norway in 1943, her camouflage paintwork now showing a different pattern. Many units varied their camouflage according to circumstance.

Below: In February 1946 some of the destroyers originally allocated to Britain were handed over to the French Navy. This photograph shows (from right) Z 6 *Theodor Riedel*, Z 5 *Paul Jacobi*, Z 25 and Z 31 at Cherbourg.

Top: Z 7 *Hermann Schoemann* as originally completed, with rounded bridge.

Above: *Hermann Schoemann* during trials over the measured mile at Neukrug.

Left: Hitler in Z 7's wheelhouse to witness torpedo practice in Eckernförde Bay, 22 July 1938. Other members in the party included Göring and Keitel.

Right: Summer visitors aboard Z 7 *Hermann Schoemann*: Keitel (left foreground) and Hitler with Korvettenkapitän Schulte-Mönting after inspecting the ship's company. Following her return to Kiel, Z 7 took Göring to Brunsbüttel to re-join his private yacht *Carin II*.
Below: *Hermann Schoemann* during the Naval Review of 22 August 1938 to mark the launching of the heavy cruiser *Prinz Eugen*.

Far left, upper: On 1 May 1942 the destroyers Z 7 *Hermann Schoemann*, Z 24 and Z 25 sailed from Kirkenes to attack convoy QP.11, the escort for which was numerically far superior to the German force. A cruiser of the escort, *Edinburgh*, had been disabled by a torpedo from U 456, but when approached by the German destroyers early on 2 May she managed to score heavily on Z 7. The photograph shows the destroyer in a sinking condition, with a list to port.

Far left, lower: Z 8 *Bruno Heinemann* at the August 1938 Naval Review.

Above: Z 8 alongside the commissioning quay at Deschimag, Bremen, on 8 January 1938. This destroyer was, as an experiment, fitted with four obsolete 15cm guns, (No 4 gun being in view here). They were later unshipped in favour of four 12.7cm weapons.

Left: Z 8 *Bruno Heinemann* in the icy Jade estuary off Wilhelmshaven during the winter of 1939, at the outset of an offensive minelaying operation. Each mine is seated on a trolley and placed on a rail track mounted on the upper deck.

Left, upper: Z 8 *Bruno Heinemann* (left) and Z 14 *Friedrich Ihn* at La Pallice in the spring of 1941. At this time there was little danger of air attack. The crews wear tropical kit while working, and an awning has even been erected to keep the deck cool. Both destroyers have the tripod mast, and Z 8 also has a radar antenna.

Left, lower: Z 8 moored off the French Naval Academy at

Brest in 1941 and wearing temporary hull camouflage.
Above: *Bruno Heinemann* in full camouflage, Biscay, 1941.
Below: Z 9 *Wolfgang Zenker* took part in the first naval battle of the war, against Polish units early on 3 September 1939. However, after failing to break out from Narvik on 10 April 1940, she fought to the last in Rombakenfjord and was then scuttled.

Left, upper: Z 10 *Hans Lody* is commissioned at Germania Werft, Kiel, 17 September 1938. A U-boat is in the background.
Left, lower: Z 10 (right) and Z 20 *Karl Galster* in the Holtenau Lock of the Kiel Canal. Notice the differing forms of the hulls forward, particularly the greater flare of the 'Atlantic bow' of Z 20 (which ship has also been fitted with a tripod foremast).
Above: *Hans Lody* stops a merchantman (the hull of which is seen far right) for contraband investigation in the Skagerrak or Kattegat, autumn 1939.
Below: Z 10 leaves the Holtenau Lock to transit the Kiel Canal, 28 July 1940. Notice, on the quarterdeck, the depth charges and two small handling cranes, the latter for deploying and streaming the paravanes or 'otters' (which are clearly visible).

Above: Z 10 *Hans Lody*, port side amidships, in the summer of 1941. The boilers forward are apparently getting up steam. Notice the pipework at the rear of the forward funnel (compare with Z 5 *Paul Jacobi*).

Left: In grounding incidents, the propellers were usually damaged: Z 10 in drydock, on 3 July 1942 with her starboard blades shaven.
Below left: *Hans Lody* in camouflage at Kiel, March 1943.
Above: Z 10 in the summer of 1945 at the Bonte Quay, Wilhelmshaven; astern are Z 15 *Erich Steinbrinck* and Z 33. Notice the 'goalpost' foremast, which some destroyers

received to help cope with the huge radar mattress.
Below: *Hans Lody* in January 1946 under tow to Portsmouth, where she was commissioned by the Royal Navy as R 38 for experimental purposes.

Left, upper: Z 11 *Bernd von Arnim* is commissioned at Kiel, 6 December 1938.

Left, lower: *Bernd von Arnim* in ice during the severe winter of 1939/40. During the Norwegian operation she fought an action on three successive days: on 8 April in the North Sea against the British destroyer *Glowworm*, scoring several hits; on the 9th in Narvikfjord, when she torpedoed and sank the coast defence ship *Norge*; and on the 10th in Ofotfjord, when, with Z 2 *Georg Thiele*, she engaged and disabled the British destroyer *Hardy*.

Right, top: Z 12 *Erich Giese* commissions at Kiel, 4 March 1939.

Right, centre: Z 12 working up on 12 April 1939.

Right, bottom: *Erich Giese* sinking at the approach to inner harbour, Narvik, 13 April 1940

Left, upper: Z 13 *Erich Koellner* in 1939.
Left, lower: Z 13 and another destroyer docked at the Westwerft, Wilhelmshaven, winter 1939.
Right, top: A model of the fjord-fissured landscape of Narvik, looking from the east above Ofotfjord towards the sea. In the foreground is a part of Rombakenfjord; to the right, the spit of land lies opposite the town of Narvik behind the large promontory. The model was built in 1941–42 by young sailors of *2. Marine-Unteroffizier-vorschule* (2nd Naval Preparatory School) at Hohenschwangau and stood until the end of the war in the Winter Garden (a barracks annexe) together with the ship's bell and naval ensign from Z 13. These and other honours were packed in a chest just before the capitulation and buried near the school. The exact location is not known.
Right, centre: Crewmen from *Erich Koellner* at work near the ship's two propellers, clearing away ice and snow during a spell in drydock
Right, bottom: This photograph, taken from a British warship, shows Z 13 positioned in Djupvik Bay on 13 April 1940 as advance gun battery—it had apparently not been thought appropriate to arm her with torpedoes as well—to delay the entry of the expected British naval force. Here she is under fire from the battleship *Warspite* during her eleven-minute battering. The width of the fjord at this point is 10km.

Left, upper: Z 14 *Friedrich Ihn* in drydock during completion work. This photograph shows the keel wedge added to the ship's flat bottom to stream the flow downwards. It was hoped that this would have the effect of lengthening the resistance-reducing trough abaft the stern (a measure equivalent to lengthening the hull). The resistant stern-heavy trim was indeed reduced, and, depending on the load, this resulted in an increase of up to half a knot in speed, but ultimately the measure was not all that successful.

Left, lower: A prewar view of Z 14 at sea.

Above: *Friedrich Ihn* in camouflage, running escort for the battleship *Gneisenau*, Biscay, 1941.

Below: Z 14 at the Hoplaelven Pier in Norway. The censor touched out the radar antenna.

153

Lock Gate III, 6 February 1946: Z 20 *Karl Galster* and Z 14
Friedrich Ihn leave Wilhelmshaven for delivery to the Soviet
Union. Both vessels entered service with the Red Navy, first as
destroyers and later as accommodation ships.

Left: Z 15 *Erich Steinbrinck* under repair at Trondheim after a collision with a Norwegian freighter on 26 November 1943.
Bottom: Z 15 at Cuxhaven, in May 1945. At this time she had only one serviceable engine. Note the 'goalpost' foremast.
Below: After transfer to Wilhelmshaven, Z 15 was repaired for delivery to the Soviet Union. She is seen here flanked by Z 33 (to starboard) and an unidentified destroyer.
Right: *Steinbrinck* at Wilhelmshaven, summer 1945; behind her is *Paul Jacobi*. The 'goalpost' and the 2 × 6m antenna are prominent, with, at top, the FuMB Sumatra aerial. Note the two 3.7cm twin mountings on the bridge platforms.

Left, upper: The Steubenhöft at Cuxhaven on 6 April 1940, shortly before troops embarked for the invasion of Norway. Z 16 is seen here with other destroyers.

Left, lower: Z 17 *Diether von Roeder* in April 1939. She was the fastest of all the named German destroyers over the measured mile, achieving 41.45 knots at Neukrug in the Baltic the previous November.

Above: *Diether von Roeder* at Narvik on 10 April 1940 after the first clash with British destroyers. Notice the shell hits in the hull below the forefunnel and No 2 gun.

Below: Z 17, unable to fire her guns or make way, moored stern-to at the Postpier at Narvik with her bows facing towards the sea. The ship had been prepared as a floating bomb for the entry of the British naval force into the inner fjord. As a British destroyer cautiously approached her on 13 April 1940, a Gebirgsjäger machine-gunner in the rocks above the town lost his nerve and opened fire. The British destroyer reversed out at high speed and the chance was lost.

Above: Z 18 *Hans Lüdemann* prewar. The Type 1936 destroyers are easily identified by the searchlight platform on the mainmast set higher than the forefunnel cap

Below: Z 18 with fires raging astern, aground in Rombaken-fjord on 13 April 1940. Two boats from the British destroyers *Hero* and *Icarus* went alongside and the vessel was searched, but nothing of value was found, after which a torpedo from *Hero* reduced the German ship to a wreck.

Right, upper: The wreck of *Hans Lüdemann* in 1941.

Right, lower: The Narvik Seaman's Home where survivors from *Lüdemann* and other destroyers were lodged between 15 and 28 April 1940. After the Allied landing at Narvik, these crewmen were forced to withdraw into the hills.

160

Left, upper: Z 19 *Hermann Künne* lowering the ship's pinnace: a photograph taken in April 1939.
Left, lower: *Hermann Künne* ablaze after being scuttled in Herjangsfjord, 13 April 1940.
Above: The wreck of Z 19 *Hermann Künne* in 1941.
Below: Z 20 *Karl Galster* in ice in the outer Jade, 18 or 19 February 1940.

Left, upper: Z 20 *Karl Galster* alongside at Brest, 1941, affording a good view of the bridge. The guns and fire control equipment are covered by tarpaulins.

Left, lower: A dashing representation of the destroyer engagement off Plymouth on 18–19 November 1940. This painting, which hung in the entrance hall to the Reichs Chancellery in Berlin, reputedly shows Z 20.

Above: *Karl Galster*, with radar antenna, in spring 1944.

Below: *Galster* at Wilhelmshaven in the summer of 1945

Left, upper: The commissioning ceremony for Z 21 *Wilhelm Heidkamp* at Bremen, 10 June 1939.

Left, lower: *Heidkamp* running trials between June and September 1939, with main guns elevated. As flag vessel of the Führer der Zerstörer (CinC Destroyers), she led the destroyer force into Narvik, sinking, on the way, the Norwegian coast defence ship *Eidsvold*.

Above: *Wilhelm Heidkamp* torpedoed and partially submerged at Narvik on 10 April 1940 following the explosion of her after magazine. She lost her stern section, which accommodated the FdZ, Kommodore Friedrich Bonte, and his staff, plus 83 of the destroyer's complement.

Right: Z 22 *Anton Schmitt*'s commissioning ceremony at Bremen on 24 September 1939. She was the last of the named German destroyers to enter service.

Left, top: *Anton Schmitt* was the last of the Type 1936s and entered service after the outbreak of war. Pleasing to the eye with their sleek form and raked bow—although still suffering from topweight—the Type 1936 ships, unlike the earlier 1934 versions, did not rely on minimum bunkerage for stability. Z 22 was hit by two torpedoes and sunk while queuing to refuel at Narvik on 10 April 1940.

Above: Z 23 outbound in 1942 in Norwegian waters, loaded with mines and effecting a mailbag transfer with another destroyer. Notice the square liferafts atop the gunhouses.

Left: Z 23, seen here in the winter of 1942 alongside the Hoplealven Pier, was the first German destroyer to be fitted with a twin turret on the forecastle.

169

Left: Three photographs of Z 23 in the Bay of Biscay in 1943 labouring in a strong swell, showing how difficult it was for German destroyers to remain fully combat-ready or bring their weapons to bear in inclement conditions.

Right, upper: Z 23 anchored in the Gironde estuary in 1944 after a mission which has left its mark on the hull.

Right, lower: It was not always possible for destroyers to return to home yards for repair—besides which, they were urgently needed where they were—and refits were severely curtailed. One way of getting things done was to use U-boat bunkers, as here at La Pallice. The photograph shows the forecastle of Z 23, the stern being inside the bunker. This measure required the deck structures abaft the bridge to be dismantled. The forward section was of course exposed to air attack. The photograph was taken between 1 and 16 August 1944, and Z 23 did not survive her refit unscathed: during an air raid on 10 August she was bombed beyond useful repair, towed into the harbour basin and decommissioned. Z 24 was repaired successfully in the La Pallice U-boat bunker between January and May 1944.

Left, upper: Z 24 wearing a dazzle paint scheme, photographed in the Bay of Biscay in 1941.

Left, lower: Z 24, now fitted with a 15cm twin turret on the forecastle deck.

Right: Superficial damage to Z 24 after being strafed by a low-flying fighter in the Bay of Biscay, 10 April 1943.

Below: The career of Z 24 came to a violent end on 24 August 1944. Whilst she was lying in the roadstead at Le Verdon with the torpedo boat T 24, Beaufighters of Nos 236 and 404 Squadrons RAF carried out an attack lasting 45 seconds, sinking T 24 (lower vessel). Z 24 received serious damage but managed to reach port, only to capsize the next day. One crewman was lost. The two units had sailed to attack the Allied invasion fleet.

Above: Z 25 in the Bremerhaven roads.
Below: Z 25 anchored near Bornholm on 26 May 1941 and, judging by the grid markings on the hull forward, acting as a torpedo target ship.
Right, upper: A view from starboard of Z25's bridge. Notice the laterally stowed floats.
Right, lower: Z 25 on 2 May 1943 in Arctic waters. Despite the season, the icing is severe.

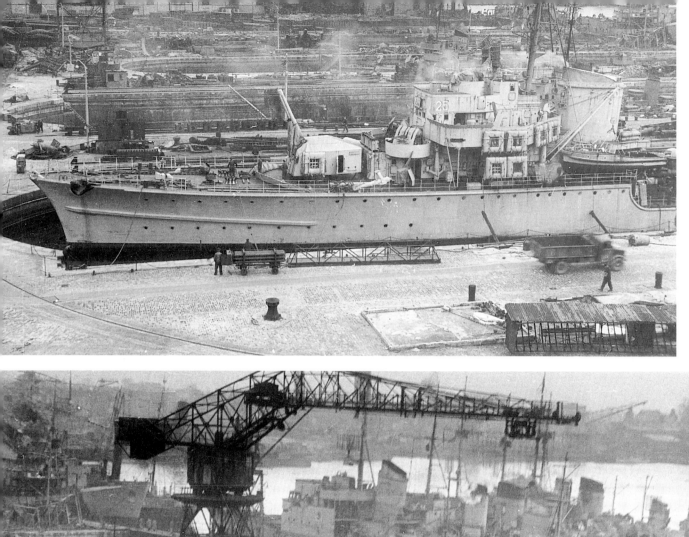

Above left: Z 25 in Drydock I, Wilhelmshaven, in December 1945, shortly before being taken over by Allied crews; this and the following photograph are usually incorrectly described as having been taken in the summer. Notice the spray deflector between the anchor cluse and No 1 gun turret. In the background, in Dock V, can be seen the light cruiser *Nürnberg*, and in Dock II two former torpedo boats of the Imperial Navy—T 151 *Komet*, used as a remote control vessel for the target ship *Hessen*, and T 153 *Eduard von Jungmann*, a radar training boat—can be made out.

Left: Another view of Z 25 in dock. Across the dock entrance are a number of torpedo boats in a cluster and across the basin is the wreck of the light cruiser *Köln*.

Above: Z 26 at sea in camouflage.

Left, upper: In an ill-fated operation against convoy PQ.13, the destroyers Z 24, Z 25 and Z 26 sailed from Kirkenes on 18 March 1942 and in poor visibility next morning encountered the light cruiser *Trinidad*, which quickly found Z 26's range. The photograph shows the first hit on the destroyer.

Left, lower: Z 26 escaped in a squall, and there now followed a period of hide-and-seek in which torpedoes were exchanged, *Trinidad* being hit by her own torpedo. Z 26 was brought to a standstill when torpedoed by the British destroyer *Eclipse*. Z 24 and Z 25 scored heavily on *Eclipse* but allowed her to escape and remained to save the survivors of Z 26 before the latter went down. Death came quickly in the Arctic waters.

Right: The death plunge of Z 26. German destroyers and U-boats rescued 96 of her crew, but 240 were lost.

Below: Z 27 fitting out at Deschimag, Bremen, 1941.

Left, upper: Z 27 in the customary dazzle scheme for Norwegian waters, with a *Kampfgruppe* including the heavy cruisers *Admiral Hipper*, *Admiral Scheer* and *Lützow*.
Left, lower: Z 28 commissioning, 9 August 1941.

Above: Z 28 in September 1941, showing the enlarged deckhouse aft.
Below: Z 28 alongside the heavy cruiser *Admiral Scheer* at an anchorage near Trondheim, summer 1942.

Above: Z 28 in Norwegian waters, deceptively camouflaged
with a false, painted bow wave.
Below: Z 29 passing through a snowscape.

Above: Z 29 in disruptive camouflage, at anchor in Norway.
Below: Z 29 on 6 June 1945, alongside the quay in the Kaiserhafen at Wesermünde. The destroyer was by this time in such poor condition as to be beyond repair, and the Allies sank her with a cargo of unwanted munitions in the Skagerrak.

Above: Z 30 in her original form, with a flying bridge above the two banks of torpedo tubes either side of the after funnel. These were later unshipped.

Below: Z 30 in camouflage finish and alongside a makeshift pier in Norway.

Right, upper: Z 31 at anchor in Altafjord, with the backdrop of the snow-covered mountains—an apparently peaceful picture. The destroyer has a 15cm single gunhouse on the forecastle; this would later be replaced by a twin turret.

Right, lower: Activity in the narrow waters of a fjord as Z 31 passes some torpedo boats, one of which is T 20. At the outbreak of war the tactical numbers painted on the hull were removed and the vessels' tactical numbers or abbreviations— for example, 'ES' for 'Erich Steinbrinck', or, as in this case, '20' (just above the shoulder of the sailor on the quay nearest the vessel)—were painted on the bridge coaming where they could be concealed when required by sliding boards. It is unusual to see such a designation in a shore photograph: the identification was only supposed to be exhibited at sea—and removed in contact with the enemy—or when entering or leaving port.

Left, top: In January 1945 several destroyers returning from northern Norway to Germany was intercepted near Sognefjord by a superior enemy force which included the light cruisers HMS *Diadem* and HMS *Mauritius*. The destroyers disengaged at speed and made for Bergen, but Z 31 received seven hits and suffered 55 dead and 24 wounded. The photograph shows hits to the forward section of the destroyer and the ruins of the main twin turret.

Left, centre: Shell damage on the starboard side directly below the 15cm turret forward.

Left, bottom: The 15cm twin turret seen from directly behind. After emergency repairs at Bergen, Z 31 made Horten in Oslofjord for a temporary refit which included the addition of a 10.5cm single gunhouse to replace the wrecked twin turret.

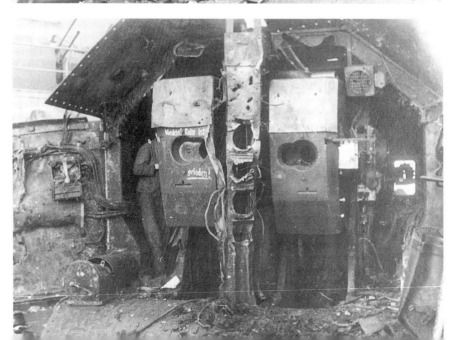

Left: Z 31's wrecked twin turret from the port side (the turret is trained astern).

Below: Two photographs of Z 31 taken in the summer of 1945 at Wilhelmshaven, The destroyer is leaving the *Westwerft* (West Yard) for the 'Frozen Fleet' anchorage, ready for delivery to the Allies. Notice that she has retained the 10.5cm single gun on the forecastle.

Above: A camouflaged Z 32 at anchor in the Gironde in 1943

Left: On 9 June 1944, en route for Brest, Z 32, ZH 1, Z 24 and T 24 were engaged by British destroyers off Wissant. The flotilla dispersed, but Z 32 regained contact with the enemy and was badly damaged. She was run aground near the Île de Bas and subjected to further attacks from the air by RAF Coastal Command. The photograph shows the burning wreck of Z 32. Twenty-six of her crew were lost.

Right, upper: The wreck of Z 32 on the rocks.

Right, lower: Many destroyer captains adhered rigidly to the official disruptive camouflage scheme. Z 33's commander was one.

188

189

Left, upper: After the war, all German destroyers and torpedo boats scheduled for distribution amongst the Allies were shepherded into a group in the eastern chamber of No IV lock at Wilhelmshaven, December 1945. At far left is Z 33; beyond the tug are torpedo boats.

Left, lower: Z 33 about to clear No III Lock, Wilhelmshaven, on 15 January 1946 prior to her voyage to the Soviet Union. In the adjacent lock chamber can be seen the funnel of the U-boat tender *Otto Wünsche*, which had also been promised to the Russians and meanwhile had the task of escorting the vessels to the rendezvous point and returning to port with the German crews.

Right and below: Two views of Z 33 leaving Wilhelmshaven.

Left, upper: Z 34 in Norwegian waters.

Left, lower: A stern view of Z 34.

Right, top: Z 35 in the Baltic, 1944. Initially based at Reval in Estonia, this vessel was one of the four destroyers giving valuable offshore gunnery support to German land forces in Estonia and Latvia during the 1944 rearguard actions and withdrawal. While minelaying in thick fog as flag vessel of 8. Z-Flottille on 12 December 1944 in the Gulf of Finland, she ran into the adjacent Nashorn minefieldand was lost with all hands.

Right, centre: A photograph of Z 36 taken against the sun in the Baltic, 1944. Operational from June 1944, Z 36 served with Kampfgruppe II, using her guns to cover the German withdrawals from Estonia and Latvia. During the ill-fated 'Nil' minelaying operation of 12 December 1944, she suffered the same fate as Z 35 and went down with all hands.

Right, bottom: Z 37 under construction, seen from forward. The turret foundations and bridge superstructure are already in place.

Left, top: Z 37 under tow to the fitting-out basin at Germania
Werft, Kiel, after her launching on 24 February 1941.
Left, centre: Z 37 nearing completion at Kiel, summer 1942.
Left, bottom: A starboard broadside view of Z 37 after her
commissioning.
Above: Z 37 on exercises with Z 32 (laying smoke) in the Bay
of Biscay in 1943.
Right: On 29 January 1944 Z 32 and Z 37 collided in the Bay
of Biscay. A torpedo head aboard the latter destroyer detonated,
causing a fire which ignited 3.7cm ready ammunition. Z 37 was
towed into drydock at Bordeaux by Z 23, and she remained
there until the capitulation of German forces in the area. She
was decommissioned in August 1944, her guns were unshipped
for use as shore batteries and her machinery was rendered
unusable. This photograph shows Z 37 in November 1944. She
was eventually scrapped by the French in 1949.

196

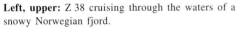

Left, upper: Z 38 cruising through the waters of a snowy Norwegian fjord.

Left, lower: Z 38 was allocated to Great Britain and used for various trials, including underwater explosions. The photograph shows one of the latter at the instant of detonation.

Top: Z 39 after her commissioning at Kiel.

Above: Z 39 in camouflage paintwork in Finnish waters, where she operated during the first half of 1944.

Right: Z 39 under netting alongside the quay at Baltisch Port, Estonia, in 1944. On 23 June she was bombed by a Soviet aircraft offshore, and she remained *hors de combat* until 1 April 1945.

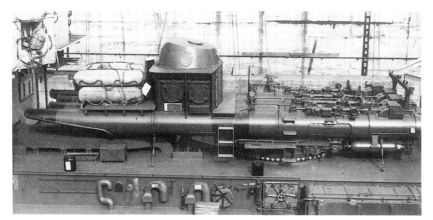

Left, upper: Z 39's after torpedo tubes. The control position has an armoured dome.

Left, lower: The external radar equipment of Z 39 as on 11 August 1945: 1. FuMO 24/25; 2. FuMB 4 Sumatra (fixed on the platform); 3. infra-red or detector (?); 4. FuMB 26 Tunis antenna; 5. FuMB Bali; 6. FuMB 81 Berlin-S.

Right, upper: Z 39 was sailed to the United States in 1945 and used for tests. In this photograph she is seen in drydock at the Boston Navy Yard. Notice the cut-down barrel of the superfiring 15cm gun.

Right, lower: Z 43 was the last destroyer of the series to enter commission. She is seen here during trials off Bornholm in the summer of 1944. The design of the degaussing coil seen along the hull at upper deck level varied from ship to ship. Z 43 was the only destroyer of three to survive the ill-fated 'Nil' minelaying operation. After the hectic four months of escort duties and shore bombardment sorties experienced by most German units subsequently, she was scuttled off Flensburg on 3 May 1945.

198

Photo Gallery: Requisitioned Destroyers

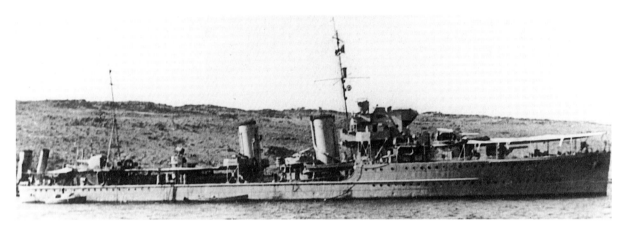

Opposite, top: A deceptively peaceful scene: ZG 3 *Hermes* lies at anchor in Suda Bay, Crete, 1 August 1942, her awnings set despite the threat of aerial attack. The two funnels visible at the extreme left of the photograph are those of the British heavy cruiser *York*, which was run aground on 26 March 1941 after receiving damage from an Italian explosive motor boat during the fighting for Greece. After being bombed by German aircraft she was finally given up on 22 May 1941, although she was not scrapped until 1952.

Opposite, bottom left: A view aft along the forecastle of ZG 3 *Hermes*, showing the bridge structure. No 1 and No 2 guns traversed to port.

Opposite, bottom right: *Hermes* running trials in the spring of 1942—at high speed, as the broad wake and the black smoke from the after funnel show. The view is from forward, looking aft along the port side. The AA platform is not yet occupied.

Above: ZG 3 with dazzle paintwork, summer 1942.

Below: ZH 1 during her work-up period, here on moorings in the outer roads at Kiel.

Photo Gallery: *Zerstörer* Life

Left, upper: Destroyers of 2. Zerstörerflottille at the Gazelle-Brücke, Wilhelmshaven, towards the end of 1939. The quay was later renamed Bonte Kai in memory of the Führer der Zerstörer who fell at Narvik.

Left, lower: A view of the destroyers of 2. Zerstörerflottille taken at the same location but on a different occasion that same winter. The vessel with the searchlight on the foremast is Z 20 *Karl Galster*.

Above: On 18 February 1940 the battleships *Scharnhorst* and *Gneisenau* and the heavy cruiser *Admiral Hipper*, escorted by three destroyers, made an anti-shipping foray as far as the Shetlands in response to the *Altmark* affair two days earlier. This was known as Operation 'Nordmark'. It achieved nothing, and all units were back in home waters by the 20th. Following *Hipper* in this photograph are Z 1 *Leberecht Maass* (flag), with Z 20 *Karl Galster* and Z 21 *Wilhelm Heidkamp* astern.

Right: There were few occasions during the war when a large group of destroyers sailed in formation. This is 8. Z-Flottille as seen from Z 28, with Z 24, Z 27, Z 29 and Z 30 astern.

Above: A destroyer's bridge at sea. At top centre is the direction-finding equipment; other navigational elements are draped with canvas. Evidently no enemy contact is expected, although alertness is being maintained. The seamen are command-relay ratings or runners; in front of them, in conversation, are two warrant officers (with shoulder straps—the WO to the right is a senior coxswain) and a senior midshipman (facing camera).

Left: In actual operational conditions it looked more like this: a view of the after command position, starboard side. The 3.7cm AA crew is closed up. This photograph was taken during Operation 'Cerberus' in February 1942.

Right: In anything of a swell a destroyer rolled like this. As this vessel heels to port, the deck lookout (wearing lifejacket) has the task of staying aboard and also preventing the ready-use ammunition from going over the side.

Below: This sort of photograph could be taken in a quieter period aboard ship. This is either an officers' or senior NCOs' wardroom—both grades are present—where etiquette is observed in the form of the white mess jacket.

Left, upper: 'Kriegswache Ruhe!' (Watch stand down!). The guns remain manned, but an opportunity to take the sun cannot be missed. On some operations crews often had to spend very many hours at their battle stations—whatever the weather.

Left, lower: A destroyer at sea: a view from aft, starboard side, looking forward. The AA is manned; the command relay ratings are wearing headphones.

Right, upper: A view from astern, to starboard. An engagement with the enemy may be expected, for the crew on deck are wearing lifejackets and steel helmets.

Right, lower: One of the twin 3.7cm anti-aircraft guns.

Left: Looking forward along the port side of a *Zerstörer*.
Below left: The second main weapon of the destroyer was the torpedo. Here an 'eel' is being manoeuvred manually into a torpedo tube.
Below right: A 2cm single. The net is a cartridge trap: raw materials were scarce and had to be conserved.
Right, upper: The calibre of main guns aboard the Kriegsmarine's destroyers were either 12.7cm or 15cm. Here the two forward single gunhouses have been trained to starboard during loading drill.
Right, lower: Gunnery exercises and actual firing practice were carried out in all types of weather. In this photograph, the ship's guardrail has been removed. The forecastle deck, generously coated with ice, demands great care from the gun crew.

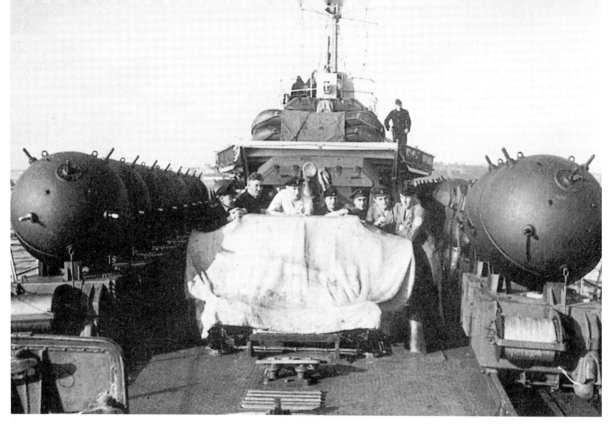

Left, top: A view of a destroyer's fantail, showing two lines of mines mounted on wheeled trolleys before a laying operation.

Left, lower: Torpedo firing. In the torpedo control stand are the fire control NCO and a command-relay rating. The tubes have been trained athwartships for firing.

Right, top: The characteristic 'spoon' shape of German torpedo tubes. Notice that the inner two tubes were set back a little to avoid any interference with the outer tubes when a fan of four was fired.

Right, centre and bottom: 'Sperr-waffe' is a term meaning any shipboard equipment to do with mines. Here, anti-mine paravanes—known as *Otter* (otters)—are about to be streamed. This minesweeping activity was for the destroyer's own protection only, although the technique involved was similar to that employed by mine-sweepers. The drums are depth charges in their containers.

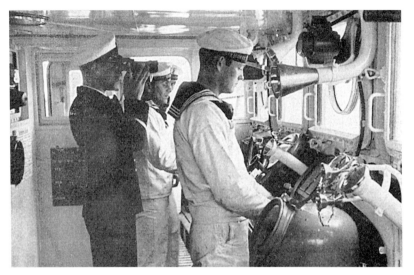

Left, top: A destroyer's wheelhouse; the white rig suggests that this is peacetime, in summertime or in a warm clime. To the left of the watch officer are command-relay ratings. To his right, the helmsman has a voicetube at mouth height; in the cupola before him is a gyro compass and at hip height, right and left, other voicetubes, the rudder position indicator, etc.

Left, centre: Another view of a wheelhouse. The helmsman, a rating highly experienced in steering by electrical button and lever, was expected in rough seas or other emergencies to act on his own initiative without waiting for the commander's or watch officer's order. He came into his own in critical situations. The instruments are arranged differently from those in the photograph above: the man's hands rest on the 'tiller'; in front of him is the rudder position indicator and nearby the gyro compass equipment; and at left is the machine telegraph, etc. At breast height is a voicetube.

Left, bottom: A glimpse into the radio room aboard a German destroyer.

Right, top: A destroyer's switching room. Notice the numerous monitoring instruments and the relatively cramped conditions. As all machinery was steam driven, leather wear was compulsory in order to protect the men against scalds.

Right, centre: The turbine control aboard a destroyer. The narrowness was oppressive: there were too many people—engineer of the watch, command-relay ratings etc.—and too little room. In the foreground is an NCO at the main valve wheel. He had to keep a watchful eye at all times on every gauge in front of him—a job demanding the highest concentration.

Right, bottom: The very narrow boiler room, in which comprehensive knowledge, technical understanding and expertise went hand in hand with a feeling for the machinery. There was an art to watching all the gauges amongst the maze of pipes.

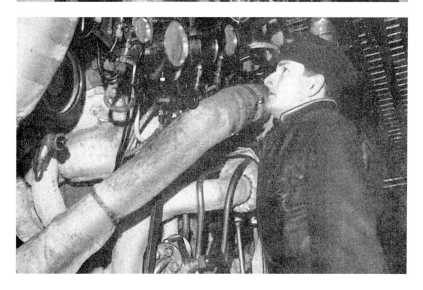

Left: Close in to a destroyer's forefunnel with six steam/ventilation pipes attached aft.

Below and bottom of page: The stern of a destroyer in dock at Wilhelmshaven in the summer of 1945. Notice the redesigned form in comparison to the Types 1934 and 1936 Types. The bottom photograph gives a good view of the mine rails on the upper deck and the two small hand cranes for the paravanes. The after 15cm gun has no splinter shield (it has probably been removed for overhaul), and the superfiring gun has been landed for repair.

Camouflage Schemes

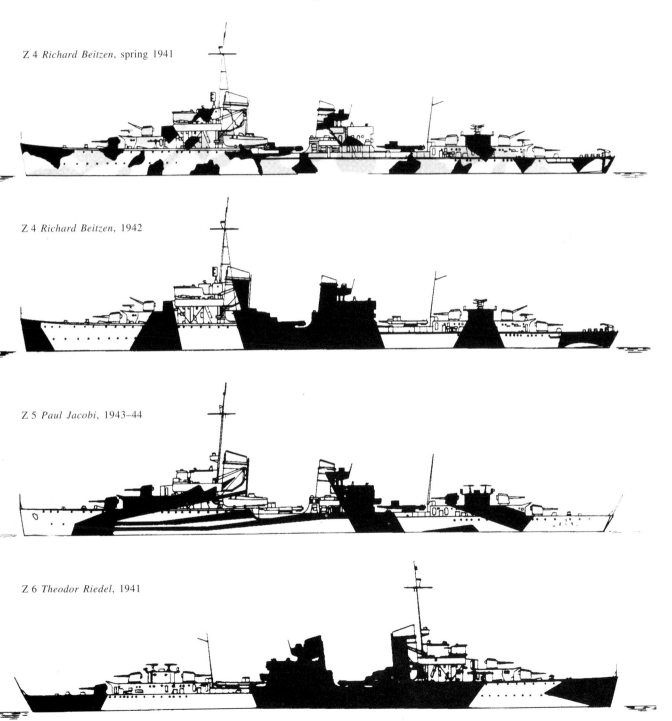

Z 4 *Richard Beitzen*, spring 1941

Z 4 *Richard Beitzen*, 1942

Z 5 *Paul Jacobi*, 1943–44

Z 6 *Theodor Riedel*, 1941

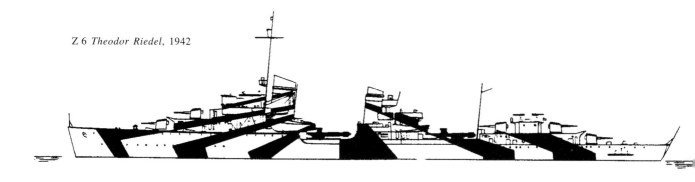

Z 6 *Theodor Riedel*, 1942

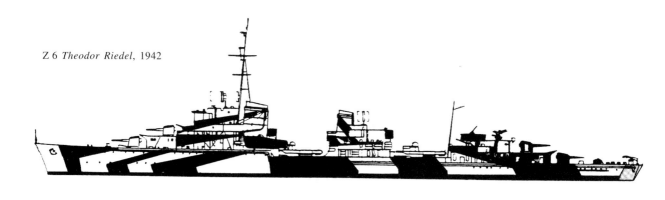

Z 6 *Theodor Riedel*, 1942

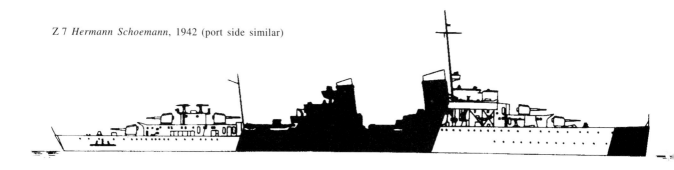

Z 7 *Hermann Schoemann*, 1942 (port side similar)

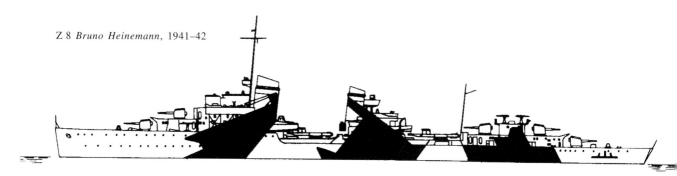

Z 8 *Bruno Heinemann*, 1941–42

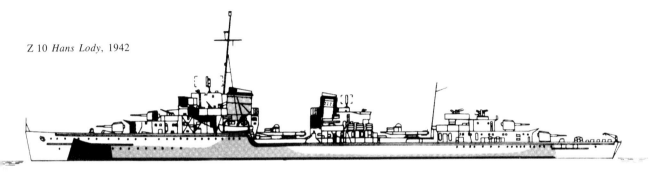

Z 10 *Hans Lody*, 1942

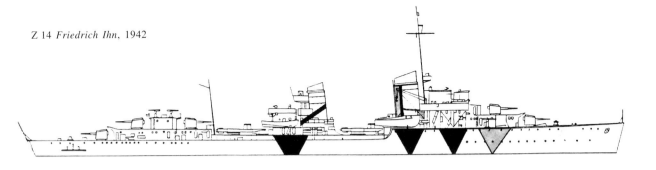

Z 14 *Friedrich Ihn*, 1942

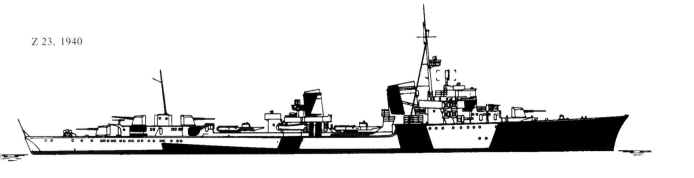

Z 23, 1940

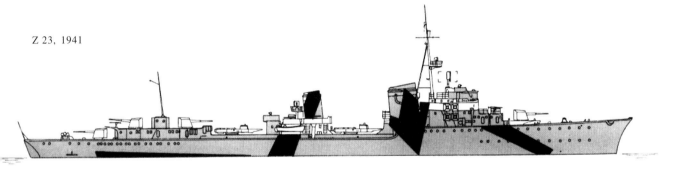

Z 23, 1941

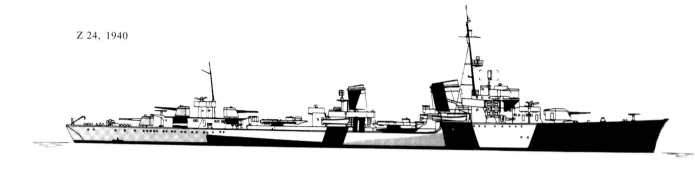

Z 24, 1940

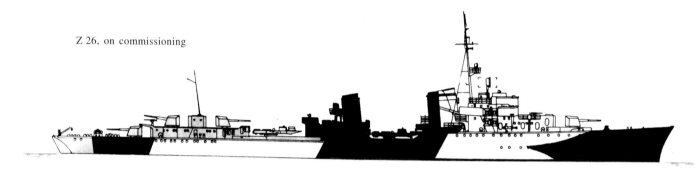

Z 26, on commissioning

Z 29, 1942

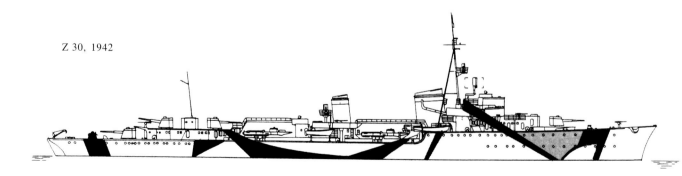

Z 30, 1942

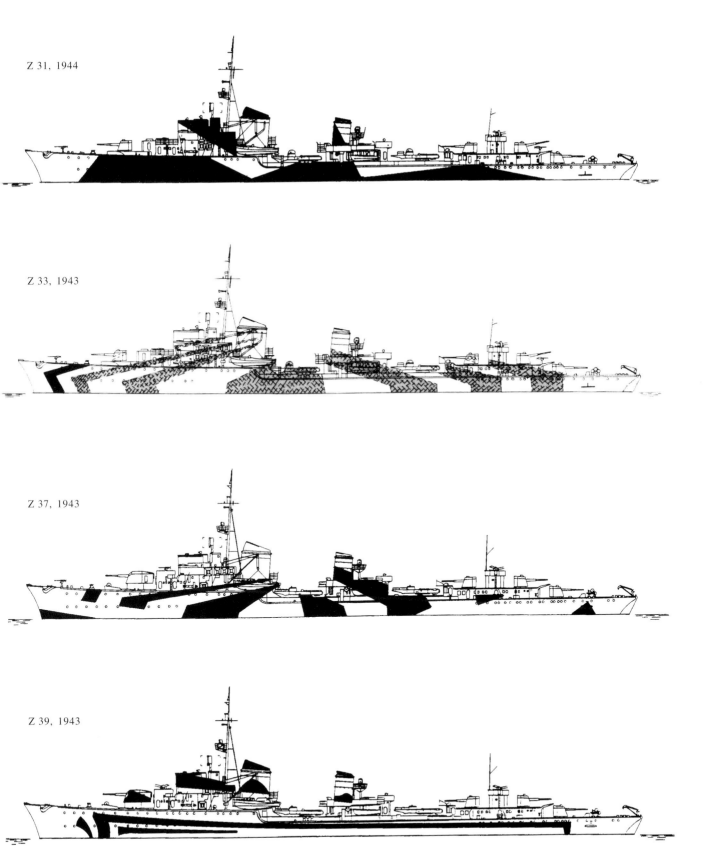

Z 31, 1944

Z 33, 1943

Z 37, 1943

Z 39, 1943

219

Conclusions

An impetuous expansion of the Kriegsmarine followed on the heels of the ratification of the Anglo-German Naval Treaty in June 1935. In 1938 the 'Z Plan' was worked out: it approved by Hitler on 27 January 1939 and came into force on 28 April that year following the Führer's renunciation of the Naval Treaty. In principle, the Z Plan envisaged the construction and commissioning by 1945 of:

Ten capital ships (*Bismarck*, *Tirpitz*, *Scharnhorst* and *Gneisenau*, plus six diesel driven 50,000-tonne battleships) armed with 40.6cm guns;

Nine 20,000-tonne *Panzerschiffe* and three 29,000-tonne battlecruisers of mixed steam/diesel drive capable of 34 knots and armed with 38cm guns;

The three existing, nominally 10,000-tonne *Panzerschiffe* (pocket battleships)—*Deutschland*, *Admiral Scheer* and *Admiral Graf Spee*;

Four 20,000-tonne aircraft carriers;

The five heavy cruisers—*Admiral Hipper*, *Prinz Eugen*, *Blücher*, *Seydlitz* and *Lützow*;

Sixteen 8,000-tonne light cruisers;

The existing 6,000-tonne light cruisers—*Emden*, *Königsberg*, *Karlsruhe*, *Köln*, *Leipzig* and *Nürnberg*;

22 5,000-tonne small scouting cruisers (*Spähkreuzer*);

68 destroyers;

90 torpedo boats;

27 U-cruisers;

62 Type IX U-boats;

100 Type VII U-boats;

60 Type II U-boats; and

300 other units, including minelayers, S-boats, minesweepers, submarine-chasers and escort vessels, together with a corresponding number of auxiliaries.

Theis was a Utopian programme which, even had it been fulfilled, would still not have made Germany into a sea power in the true sense of the term. The nation lacked overseas bases and the wherewithal to support

and defend such a system: in short, the 'Z Plan' had no logistic component, and, if it came to the crunch, the Fleet would have suffered the same fate as that of the Kaiser—blockaded, useless.

With the outbreak of war on 1 September 1939, the plan was consigned to the waste-paper basket.* The hasty naval rearmament exposed Germany's weakness. German industry, its shipyards, heavy industry, the weapons manufacturers and supply firms were simply not in a position to meet the demands of this enormous programme. They lacked the necessary capacity, materials and workforce, and in the event this caused bottlenecks and delays.

The problems affected destroyer construction. The first of these units into service soon revealed their design flaws in heavy-weather trials. Their construction was weak and their use limited. Outwardly they looked quite impressive, but that was all. In heavy seas their behaviour was evil, which major refits did little to alleviate. The difficulties were never fully overcome, even with the later types. Another design failure lay below the waterline, particularly at the stern, where wooden patchwork proved no answer. The standard 12.7cm weapon in five single gunhouses was good. No benefit was gained from the later idea—for whatever

---

* But what were the logistic components of the 1938 wargame which convinced *Admiral* Schniewind it would work? If Spain, which allowed German warships to refuel in breach of her neutrality, had permitted German forces to capture Gibraltar from the land side, this would have enabled the German Navy to bottle up the Mediterranean and given it a true Atlantic base. The other clue is supplied by the *Admiral Graf Spee* mystery. No convincing reason has ever been offered why Langsdorff put into the trap of Montevideo, Uruguay, instead of the naval base at Bahía Blanca in friendly Argentina. As the author himself pointed out in his earlier volume *Pocket Battleships of the Deutschland Class*, Langsdorff was told that flight to Japan was out of the question for fear of compromising a then neutral Tokyo. It may be that both Japan and the Peronist regime of Argentina had earlier given secret conditional undertakings to supply full bases to Germany in certain contingencies. Argentina may also have been interested in assisting a German invasion of the Falkland Islands, which would have given Germany control over merchant traffic coming round both Capes. These possibilities, with Gibraltar, would surely have put the situation in a new light.—Tr.)

reason it was realised—to upgrade the calibre to 15cm and fit a twin turret on the forecastle deck. These modifications, together with an enhanced anti-aircraft battery and the heavy radar 'mattresses' aloft, contributed to the problems of stability. As a consequence, speed restrictions had to be introduced and operations tailored to weather conditions. That German destroyers always put to sea without regard to safety instructions and in full recognition of the dangers, whatever the wind and weather, remains a credit to the officers and men.

The standard armament also included two quadruple banks of torpedo—to maintain the picturesque old tradition in which destroyer flotillas ran through the battle line to deliver a massed torpedo attack. That there was no longer a battle line, and that the last occasion when it had been tried (in May 1916 at Jutland) it had not been a great success, were ignored. For commerce warfare in near-coastal waters or for other tasks, one set of tubes would have been sufficient and gained a saving in weight.

The choice of high-pressure hot steam for the machinery was correct, bearing in mind the original idea that the destroyers were designed for use in the Baltic or southern end of the North Sea and would not be sent further afield. The engines were too sophisticated, the step to high-pressure hot-steam too precipitate. The boiler rooms were too narrow and the steam-driven auxiliaries, though all were essential, too many in number. Because of the narrowness of the workspaces, they tended to be inaccessible.

The idea of having diesels work the auxiliary machinery had been found unacceptable for some reason, so that in the event of a hit in the boiler room the auxiliaries were also likely to be unserviceable if the current failed. As they had to be kept running at all times, the quantity of steam required to keep one or two boilers permanently fired for this purpose was enormous. The use of high-pressure hot steam placed heavy demands on the structural materials, which were often not adequate to the demands of the frequent changes in loading. The challenge of the numerous breakdowns in the machinery was never met. Aboard Royal Navy destroyers, machinery breakdown was rare. One can only wonder why their example of wet steam with superheating was not followed.

Personnel were good throughout. Less good and advantageous was the endless procession of sometimes comprehensive personnel changes. In peacetime,

a straightforward routine of regular switching between ship and shore service for the purpose of training was acceptable; it was less profitable in wartime, even though necessary. The standing time aboard ship was too short, and the constant chopping and changing meant an endless succession of new training schedules from scratch—shipboard drills, operational training, getting the crew welded together as a team, then battle training. Eventually it began to string out and became sporadic. Here the ship's officers had to rely completely on the veterans, while hoping for 'initiative' from the new men (which, on the whole, they got). The same applied in the engine rooms. The boilers, with their automatic regulators, needed a highly qualified staff, and the Chief relied on the willingness of the engine-room hands, whose pride it was to throw themselves wholeheartedly into the task of serving 'their' ship.

German destroyers were fully deployed from the outbreak of war onwards, interrupted by breakdowns, mainly in the engine room. The Norwegian campaign involved, at a calculated risk, virtually any ship or boat capable of movement in the water. Ten of the twenty German destroyers had Narvik as their goal, where they were to land mountain troops. On the way there a hurricane raged, and after the troops had been disembarked there was a pause to repair storm damage. At this stage their luck changed for the worse. Of the two expected tankers, only one arrived, the *Kattegat* having been intercepted and sunk by the Norwegian Navy. The surviving oiler, the *Jan Wellem*, had insufficient fuel and inadequate pump capacity. When a numerically superior British naval force arrived, the fate of the German destroyers at Narvik was sealed. The objective of the occupation of Norway was to pre-empt a British invasion. The casualties, which included one heavy and two light cruisers and ten destroyers, were disastrous, though at that time not indefensible. However, the losses made heavy inroads into Kriegsmarine numbers and could not be made good.

The 'After Narvik' routine of destroyer warfare saw the surviving ten units and the new ships entering commission in action continually, not only in the Baltic, North Sea and Kattegat but now also in the sea areas off the French Atlantic coast, in the Bay of Biscay and in the waters around Norway. Here they tended to be prone to collisions and groundings. The harbours and river estuaries on the French Atlantic coast and the Norwegian fjords and coastal skerries were quite different from German waters. There were plenty of charts, but many were inaccurate and at the time there was no question of carrying out new surveys. The local pilotage authority, understandably, tended to be uncooperative and, where possible, was not used. Operations took place by day in beaming sunshine, but also at night, when coastal beacons and navigational lights were extinguished. Then destroyers were expected to keep to narrowly defined, swept channels, often in close sailing order, and frequently at high speed when passing through areas where unseen dangers were expected. Weather conditions can change very swiftly, not only in narrow coastal tracts such as the German estuaries of the Elbe, Weser, Jade and Ems but also in Norwegian waters. Within minutes one can suddenly be enveloped in thick fog. And that requires great alertness. It is no surprise, therefore, in the sudden advent of fog for example, that a small flotilla running at high speed might suddenly find itself in difficulties. Perhaps one destroyer would throw her rudder hard over to avoid a shadow in the fog (if not too late), or there would be a collision; or a commander might be forced to accept a collision as an alternative to running aground or on the rocks. Added to all these perils there were the unforeseeable shipboard breakdowns—engine trouble, rudder failure and so on. These things happen at sea; groundings, collisions and suchlike occur amongst all fighting and mercantile navies in peace and war. In January 1994, in a fjord near Bergen, the Norwegian frigate *Oslo* ran aground and sank after engine failure. Collisions and groundings are therefore not the special preserve of wartime German destroyers and arise from a multitude of situations.

Index of Ships

Page references in **bold type** refer to illustrations; those in *italic type* refer to ships' main entries.

A

Achates, HMS, 71
Admiral Graf Spee, 220
Admiral Hipper, 50, 54–5, 66–7, 69, 70, 71, 72, 220
Admiral Scheer, 67, 69, 70, 71, 76, 220
Alaska class (US), 17
Alsterufer, 73
Altmark, 65
Amazon, HMS, 70
Anton Schmitt (Z 22), 24, 45, 50, *102*, **167–8**; and 'Weserübung', 53, 56, 63; loss of, 58, 59, 60, 63
Atlantis, 66

B

Bateau, 69
Beagle, HMS, 70
Bedouin, HMS, 65
Bernd von Arnim (Z 11), 24, 45, 46, *91*, **148**; and 'Weserübung', 53–4, 57, 58, 59; loss of, 63
Beverley, HMS, 70
Bismarck, 67, 220
Blücher, 220
Blyskawica, 47
BO-78, 71
Bramble, HMS, 71
Bremse, 18, 68
Brummer, 19, 75
Bruno Heinemann (Z 8), 24, **33**, 34, 45, 46, 48, 49, 50, 65, 66, 67, 68, *87–8*, **140–3**, **216**; and 'Weserübung', 53, 54, 55; loss of, 69
Bulldog, HMS, 70
Burza, 47

C

Ceuta, 76
Charkov, 49
Clyde, HMS, 66
Cobra, 66, 67
Cossack, HMS, 65

D

Deutschland, 18, 35, 46, 220
Deutschland class, 13
Diadem, HMS, 76
Diether von Roeder (Z 17), 24, 45, 46, 47, *98*, **158–9**; and 'Weserübung', 53, 56, 58, 59, 60
Donbass, 71

E

Eclipse, HMS, 70
Edinburgh, HMS, 70
Eidsvold, 56–7
Emden, 12, 17, 75, 220
Empire Ranger, 69
Enterprise, 73
Erich Giese (Z 12), 24, 45, 46, 47–8, *91–2*, **149**; and 'Weserübung', 53, 56, 58, 59, 60, 61; loss of, 63, 64, 65
Erich Koellner (Z 13), 24, 45, 46, 50, 51, *92*, **150–1**; and 'Weserübung', 53, 55–6, 58, 59, 60; loss of, 61–2
Erich Steinbrinck (Z 15), 16, 20, 24, 34, 40, 45, 46, 48, 49, 50, 65, 66, 67, 71, 72, *94–6*, **156–7**; and 'Weserübung', 53; and 'Juno', 66; and 'Nora', 66; and 'Seelöwe', 67; and 'Wunderland', 70

F

Falke, 9, 69
Fletcher class (US), 17
Foresight, HMS, 70
Forester, HMS, 70
Foxhound, HMS, 65
Friedrich Eckholdt (Z 16), 24, 45, 46, 47, 48, 50, 51, 53, 54, 55, 65, 68, 71, *96–7*, **158**; and 'Seelöwe', 67; and 'Wunderland', 70; and 'Regenbogen', 71–2
Friedrich Ihn (Z 14), 20, 24, 34, 40, 45, 46, 47, 48, 49. 50, 65, 67, 72, 75, 76, *92–4*, **143**, **152–5**, **217**; and 'Weserübung', 53; and 'Seelöwe', 67; and 'Cerberus', 69; and 'Rösselsprung', 70
Furious, HMS, 55
Fury, HMS, 69

G

Georg Thiele (Z 2), 20, 24, **25**, 32, 45, 46, *78–9*, **123–4**; and 'Weserübung', 53, 57, 58, 59; loss of, 63
Glasgow, HMS, 73
Glorious, HMS, 66
Glowworm, HMS, 53–4
Gneisenau, 53, 66–7, 68–9, 220
Greif, 9
Grille, 47
Grom, 47
Gryf, 46

H

Hans Lody (Z 10), 11, 20, 24, 34, 40, 45, 46, 48, 65, 66, 67, 68, 70, 72, 76, *89–90*, **144–7**, **217**; and 'Weserübung', 53; and 'Juno', 66; and 'Seelöwe', 67
Hans Lüdemann (Z 18), 24, 45, 46, 47–8, 54, *98–9*, **160–1**; and 'Weserübung', 53, 56, 58, 59, 60, 61
Hansa, 76
Hardy, HMS, 58
Havock, HMS, 57, 58
Hazard, HMS, 68
Hermann Künne (Z 19), 24, 45, 46, 47, 48, 49, *99*, **162–3**; and 'Weserübung', 53, 56, 58, 59, 60, 61; loss of, 63
Hermann Schoemann (Z 7), 24, 45, 46, 47–8, 49, 50, 65, 66, 68, 70, *86–7*, **138–40**, **216**; and 'Weserübung', 53; and 'Juno', 66; and 'Cerberus', 69
Hermes (ZG 3), 68, *120*, **200–1**; loss of, 72
Hessen, 19
Himalaya, 72
Hostile, HMS, 58
Hotspur, HMS, 58
Huascaran,. 69
Hunter, HMS, 58

I

Icarus, HMS, 65
Iltis, 9, 67, 69
Intrepid, HMS, 52
Isar, 76
Ivanhoe, HMS, 52
Izora, 69

J

Jackal, HMS, 67
Jaguar, 9, 48, 67, 69
Jan Wellem, 57, 58, 61
Javelin, HMS, 67
Jersey, HMS, 48, 67
Juniper, HMS, 66
Jupiter, HMS, 67
Juno, HMS, 48

K

Kaiser, 66
Karl Galster (Z 20), 20, 24, 33, 34, 40, 44, 45, 46, 47–8, 50, 65, 70, 72, 75, 76, *99–101*, **154–5**, **163–5**, **203**; and 'Weserübung', 53, 66, 67, 68; and 'Juno', 66; and 'Seelöwe', 67
Karlsruhe, 14, 220
Kashmir, HMS, 67
Kattegat, 57
Kent, HMS, 68
Köln, 14, 17, 46, 47, 48–50, 68, 72, 220

Kondor, 9, 66, 69
Königsberg, 14, 220

L
Leberecht Maass (Z 1), 24, 32, 45, 46, 50, *77–8*, **122–3**, **203**; loss of, 50–3
Levante, 66
Leipzig, 17, 18, 46, 47, 48–9, 67, 75, 220
Leopard, 9, 66
Linz, 75, 76
Luchs, 9, 67
Lützow (Hipper class heavy cruiser), 220
Lützow (ex Deutschland), 35, 68, 70, 71, 75

M
M 453, 76
Marne, HMS, 70
Martin, HMS, 70
Mauritius, HMS, 76
Max Schultz (Z 3), 24, 32, 45, 46, *79–80*, **125–6**; loss of, 50–3
Meridian, 68
Mikoyan, 71
Möwe, 9, 66

Nautik, 76
Nordkapp, 57
Nordmark, 67
Norge, 56–7
Nürnberg, 18, 47, 48–9, 66, 67, 68, 220

O
Obdurate, HMS, 71
Obedient, HMS, 71
Oil Pioneer, 66
Onslaught, HMS, 70
Onslow, HMS, 71
Orama, 66
Orion, 67
Orwell, HMS, 71
Oslo, 222
Osorno, 72

P
Paloma, 76
Passat, 68
Paul Jacobi (Z 5), 24, **33**, 34,
40, 45, 46, 47, 65, 67, 72, *82–4*, **130–3**, **137**, **157**, **215**; and 'Weserübung', 53–4; and 'Seelöwe', 67; and 'Cerberus', 69
Peitro Orsedo, 72
Pompeii, 76
Preussen, 66
Prinz Eugen, 46, 67, 68–9, 72, 75, 76, 220

R
Rauenfels, 57
Renown, HMS, 53
Revenge, HMS, 54
Richard Beitzen (Z 4), 20, 24, 32, **33**, 40, 45, 46, 48, 49, 50, 65, 66, 67, 68, 70, 71, 72, 75, *80–2*, **126–9**, **215**; and 'Weserübung', 53; and 'Seelöwe', 67; and 'Cerberus', 69; and 'Wunderland', 70; and 'Regenbogen', 71–2
Roland, 66, 67, 75

S
Salmon, HMS, 49
Scharnhorst, 53, 65, 66, 67, 68–9, 220
Seeadler, 9, 48, 67, 69
Seydlitz, 220
Sheffield, HMS, 72
Skagerrak, 57
SKR-12, 68
Spähkreuzer, 23, 220
Speedy, HMS, 68
Sperrbrecher 13, 67
Suffolk, HMS, 57

T
T 2, 69
T 4, 69
T 5, 67, 69
T 11, 69
T 12, 69
T 13, 69
T 15, 69
T 16, 69
T 17, 69
T 22, 73
T 23, 73
T 24, 73, 75
T 25, 73
T 26, 73

T 27, 73
Tannenberg, 67
Theodor Riedel (Z 6), 11, 24, 34, 40, 45, 46, 47–8, 50, 51, 65, 70, 72, 75, 76, *84–6*, **134–7**, **215–16**; and 'Weserübung', 53, 54, 55; and 'Seelöwe', 67; and 'Seelöwe', 67; and 'Regenbogen', 71–2
Thor, 67
Tiger, 9
Tirpitz, 20, 68, 69, 70, 72, 75, 220
Trident, HMS, 69
Trinidad, HMS, 69–70

U
U 25, 57
U 48, 57
U 51, 57
U 85, 71
U 88. 70
U 456, 70
U 505, 73
U 618, 73
Uckermark, 18–19
UJ 1702, 75
Ulm, 70
Ursula, HMS, 50

V
V 303, 76

W
Warspite, HMS, 61
Weserburg, 76
Wicher, 46
Wilhelm Heidkamp (Z 21), 24, 45, 46, 47–8, 50, *101–2*, **166–7**,   ; and 'Weserübung', 53, 56; loss of, 58, 59, 60, 63
Wolf, 9
Wolfgang Zenker (Z 9), 24, 45, 46, 50, *88–9*, **143**; and 'Weserübung', 53, 56, 58, 59, 60; loss of, 63

Z
Z 23, 24, 65, 67, 68, 72, 74, *102–3*, **168–71**, **217**; and Battle of Biscay, 72–3; loss of, 75

Z 24, 24, 40, 65, 67, 68, 69–70, 71, 72, 74, 75, *104–5*, **172–3**, **203**; and 'Rösselsprung', 70; and Battle of Biscay, 72–3; loss of, 75
Z 25, 24, 34, 40, 65, 67, 68, 69–70, 72, 75, 76, *105–7*, **137**, **174–7**; and 'Cerberus', 69
Z 26, 24, 67, 68, *107*, **177–9**, **218**; loss of, 69
Z 27, 24, 67, 68, 70, 71, 72, *108*, **179–80**, **203**; and 'Rösselsprung', 70; and Battle of Biscay and loss of, 72–3
Z 28, 24, 34, 67, 71, 72, 75–6, *108–10*, **180–2**, **203**; and 'Rösselsprung', 70
Z 29, 24, 32, 34, 68, 70, 71, 72, 75, *110–11*, **182–3**, **203**, **218**; and 'Cerberus', 69; and 'Rösselsprung', 70; and 'Regenbogen', 71–2
Z 30, 24, 34, 68, 69, 71, 72, 75, *111–12*, **184**, **203**, **218**; and 'Rösselsprung', 70; and 'Regenbogen', 71–2
Z 31, 24, 34, 40, 68, 72, 75, 76, *112–13*, **137**, **185–7**, **219**; and 'Regenbogen', 71–2
Z 32, 24, 72, 74, *113–14*, **188–9**; and Battle of Biscay, 72–3; loss of, 75
Z 33, 24, 40, 72, 75, 76, **76**, *114*, **156**, **189–91**, **219**
Z 34, 24, 40, 72, 75, 76, *114–15*, **192**
Z 35, 24, 31, 40, 75–6, *115–16*, **193**
Z 36, 24, 40, 75, 76, *116*, **193**
Z 37, 24, 40, 72, 74–5, *116–17*, **193–5**, **219**; and Battle of Biscay, 72–3
Z 38, 24, 40, 72, 75, 76, *117–18*, **196**
Z 39, 24, 40, 75, 76, *118–19*, **197–9**, **219**
Z 43, 24, 40, 76, *119–20*, **199**
Z 44, 14, 24
Z 45, 14, 24
Z 51, 14, 22
ZH 1, 72, 74, *121*, **201**; loss of, 75

224